Cruising Guide to British Columbia Vol. 1

GULF ISLANDS

and Vancouver Island from Sooke to Courtenay

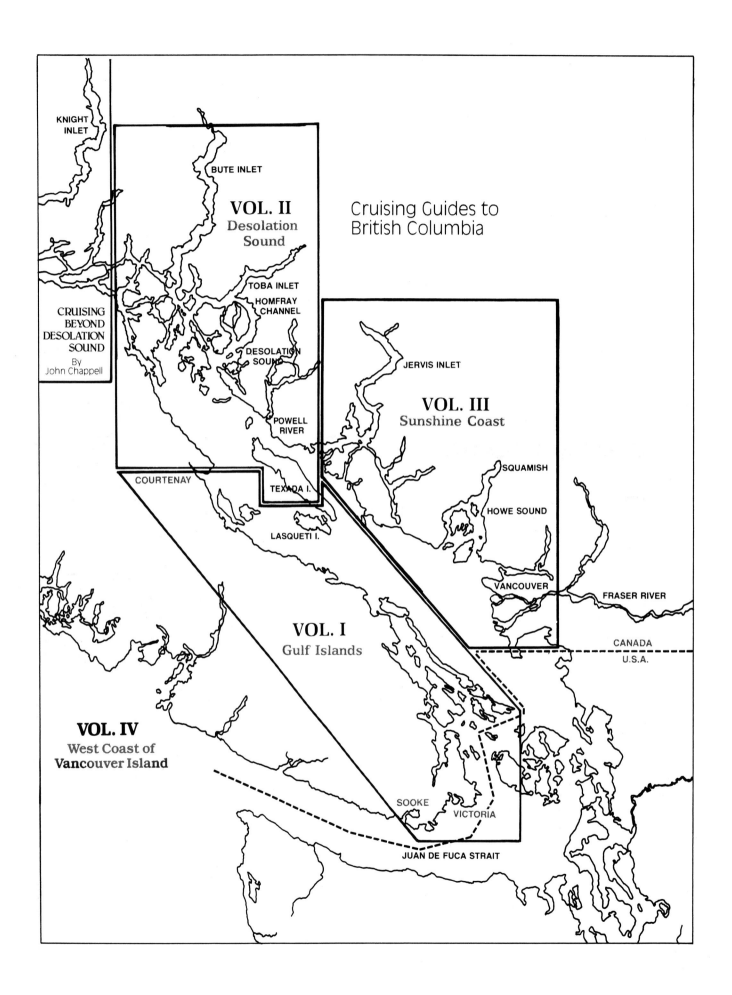

KNIGHT INLET

BUTE INLET

VOL. II
Desolation
Sound

Cruising Guides to
British Columbia

TOBA INLET

HOMFRAY
CHANNEL

CRUISING
BEYOND
DESOLATION
SOUND
By
John Chappell

DESOLATION
SOUND

JERVIS INLET

VOL. III
Sunshine Coast

POWELL
RIVER

SQUAMISH

COURTENAY

HOWE SOUND

TEXADA I.

LASQUETI I.

VANCOUVER

FRASER RIVER

CANADA
U.S.A.

VOL. I
Gulf Islands

VOL. IV
West Coast of
Vancouver Island

SOOKE

VICTORIA

JUAN DE FUCA STRAIT

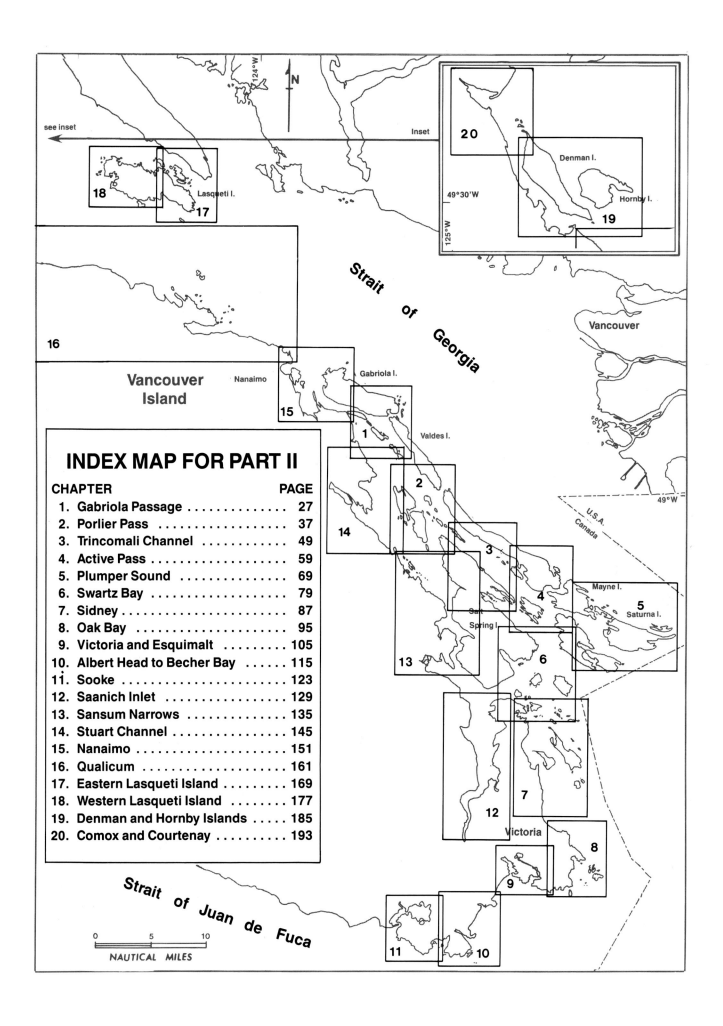

INDEX MAP FOR PART II

124°W

N

see inset

Inset

20

Denman I.

49°30'W

125°W

Hornby I.

19

Strait of Georgia

Vancouver

18

Lasqueti I.

17

16

Vancouver
Island

Nanaimo

Gabriola I.

15

1

Valdes I.

2

49°W

14

U.S.A.
Canada

3

Mayne I.

5
Saturna I.

4

Salt
Spring I.

6

13

12

7

Victoria

8

9

11

10

Strait of Juan de Fuca

0   5   10

NAUTICAL MILES

Cruising Guide to British Columbia Vol. 1

GULF ISLANDS

and Vancouver Island from Sooke to Courtenay

by Bill Wolferstan

Whitecap Books
Vancouver/Toronto

Dedicated to Clementien and to my parents

I am a part of all that I have met;
Yet all experience is an arch wherethro'
Gleams that untravell'd world, whose margin
fades...
There lies the port; the vessel puffs her sail:
Come, my friends,
'Tis not too late to seek a newer world...

"Ulysses"
Alfred Lord Tennyson
1809-1892

FOREWORD

Many years ago, in a paddy field in Burma, I was talking to another soldier about what we were going to do after the war. I told him that my wife and I were going to a place in the Gulf Islands that we had got, but had never seen. "How wonderful," he said. "I have always heard that once you have seen the Gulf Islands, your heart is forever there." Bill Wolferstan has written a book for those who wish to cruise in the Gulf Islands, and I feel that with it he has ensured that more people will lose their hearts to those lovely waters.

This is not a book of navigational directions, and will not keep a sailor off the rocks if he chooses to ignore the charts and Admiralty instructions, but it tells him where to go, where there are sheltered anchorages, something of their history and what is there now. It is a book written for those who plan to spend a holiday afloat. It promises pleasant days amongst tree-clad islands. It tells of small deserted anchorages where the only sound may be the splash of a diving loon or the squawk of a heron and the gentle ripple of water along the beach. For those who have already experienced their peace it will bring back memories to be enjoyed and sometimes perhaps they will wonder, why they ever went away.

Brigadier Miles Smeeton
Cochrane, Alberta

PREFACE

This book has stood the test of time. When first published in 1976, it immediately became a regional best-seller. A guide to one of the most fabulous cruising areas in the world, it also contained information on history, famous (and infamous) personalities, and interesting tidbits of local knowledge. That distinctive combination has been retained in this new and completely revised version of the guide, which offers the latest and most up-to-date information on the area and a substantial number of new photographs.

In the original hardcover edition, the decision to include a large number of full-colour photographs was made despite a three-fold increase in cost. It was felt that the many full-colour aerial and sea-level photographs were not only the most useful way to identify shoal areas and shoreline growth, but gave the book an added dimension — it was a unique and complete guide to the Gulf Islands and a beautiful coffee-table book as well.

With this new soft-cover edition we have managed to bring down the price substantially, while maintaining, and improving on, the full-colour presentation, and the accuracy and comprehensiveness of the text. Readers familiar with the old guide book will recognize that this is virtually a totally new book. Bill Wolferstan has revisited every anchorage and marina over the past few years, resulting in a text that reflects the many changes, especially to cruising facilities, that have taken place in the last decade. Much new information has been culled from recent publications — particularly local histories and books of coastal lore which are of interest to boaters. Not least, all of the chart numbers have been revised to current standards.

Despite these changes, the Gulf Islands, by their nature, change slowly. They are still one of the world's great year 'round cruising grounds. They still harbour an amazing variety of wildlife, and boast an assortment of environments, from isolated coves to busy convivial wharves. Those who cruise these islands still return year after year to experience the special enchantment of the Islands of the Gulf, and they still need good guides to enhance their enjoyment.

So it is with pride that we introduce this new and completely revised softcover edition of the original *Cruising Guide to the Gulf Islands*.

Michael E. Burch
Publisher
Whitecap Books

July 1987

INTRODUCTION

This Cruising Guide is divided into two parts. The first part gives an introductory look at several aspects of cruising the Gulf Islands including weather and tides, natural features, marina facilities, anchorages, parks and recreational activities. The second part describes and illustrates 20 individual areas from the point of view of a small boat explorer or cruising yachtsman. These chapters were originally published in *Pacific Yachting* magazine from 1972 to 1975 but have been substantially revised for this new tenth anniversary edition of the original book.

This guide is not intended to be a definitive pilot listing every rock, reef and navigational hazard; although it does pay particular attention to the safety or exposure of various anchorages and landing places, and to particular rocks and hazards which have proved troublesome to cruising yachtsmen or other small boat explorers. It is intended more as a descriptive handbook of the many attractions of the Gulf Islands and a guide to the enjoyment of the recreational opportunities in this area.

The reader in need of the detailed pilotage information not contained in this guide should consult *The British Columbia Small Craft Guide* published by the Canadian Hydrographic Service and the pertinent Canadian Hydrographic Charts (see endpaper index). Some portions of the original *Pacific Yachting* articles have been reprinted in the *Small Craft Guide* with the permission of the author.

Every cove and harbour described in this book has been visited by the author. While every effort has been made to ensure that navigational, historical and marina data is accurate, users of the guide may come across some errors, omissions or changes. Cruising yachtsmen are invited to improve future editions by contributing historical material, anecdotes, updates, corrections and opinions. We welcome all suggestions.

Several books were invaluable as references in completing this guide. Many of these are listed in the bibliography but the most important were: *Coastal Cruising*, by Will Dawson (for basic seamanship and coastal hazards); the *Small Craft Guide* (for navigation and pilotage); and *British Columbia Coast Names*, by Captain John T. Walbran (for history of the coast).

Information from coastal books and brochures published since 1976 have been incorporated in this new edition and specially noted in an expanded bibliography.

ACKNOWLEDGEMENTS

The author wishes to thank the many people, friends and acquaintances who have assisted him over the last 15 years in the continuing improvement of this guide. In particular, for this revised edition: John Arber, Michael Burch, Paul Burkhart, Peter Chettleburgh, Elaine Jones, Bruce Jones, Stafford Reid, Barbara Tomlin; the staffs of *Pacific Yachting*, the British Columbia Provincial Archives, the Victoria Public Library, the Canadian Hydrographic Service; and the hundreds of other coastal explorers and inhabitants who have knowingly or unknowingly shared their knowledge and love for this coast with me.

CONTENTS

PART ONE

Introduction to the
GULF ISLANDS
and Vancouver Island
from Sooke to Courtenay

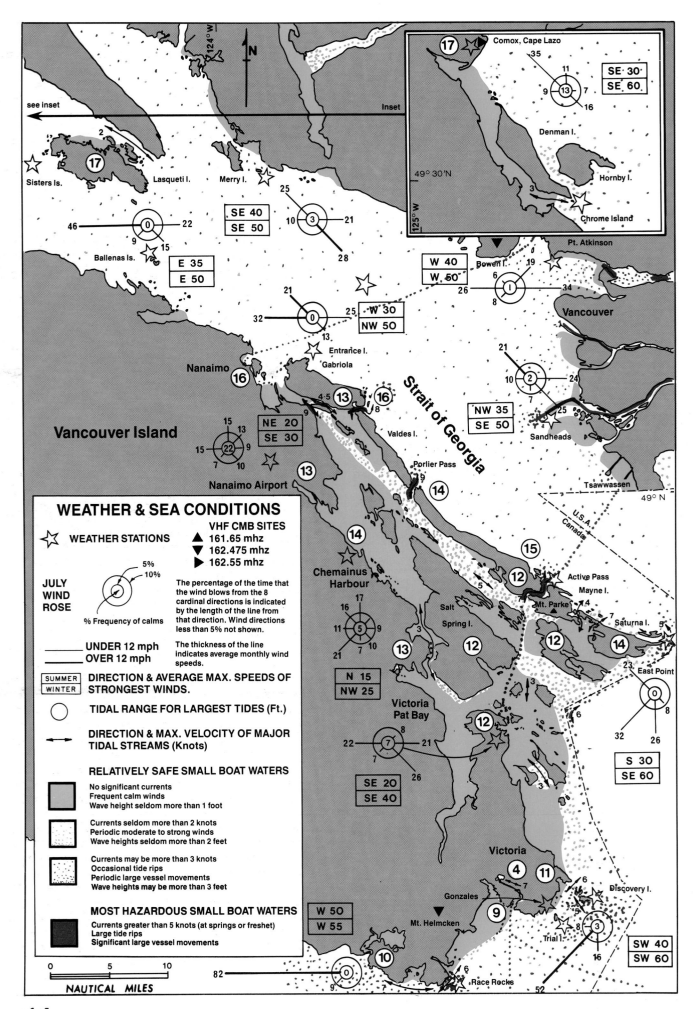

WEATHER & SEA CONDITIONS

⭐ WEATHER STATIONS

VHF CMB SITES
▲ 161.65 mhz
▼ 162.475 mhz
▶ 162.55 mhz

JULY WIND ROSE

5%
10%

% Frequency of calms

The percentage of the time that the wind blows from the 8 cardinal directions is indicated by the length of the line from that direction. Wind directions less than 5% not shown.

———— UNDER 12 mph
▬▬▬▬ OVER 12 mph

The thickness of the line indicates average monthly wind speeds.

| SUMMER |
| WINTER |

DIRECTION & AVERAGE MAX. SPEEDS OF STRONGEST WINDS.

◯ TIDAL RANGE FOR LARGEST TIDES (Ft.)

◄——► DIRECTION & MAX. VELOCITY OF MAJOR TIDAL STREAMS (Knots)

RELATIVELY SAFE SMALL BOAT WATERS

No significant currents
Frequent calm winds
Wave height seldom more than 1 foot

Currents seldom more than 2 knots
Periodic moderate to strong winds
Wave heights seldom more than 2 feet

Currents may be more than 3 knots
Occasional tide rips
Periodic large vessel movements
Wave heights may be more than 3 feet

MOST HAZARDOUS SMALL BOAT WATERS

Currents greater than 5 knots (at springs or freshet)
Large tide rips
Significant large vessel movements

0   5   10
NAUTICAL MILES

Sisters Is.
Lasqueti I.
Merry I.
Ballenas Is.
Nanaimo
Vancouver Island
Nanaimo Airport
Entrance I.
Gabriola
Valdes I.
Strait of Georgia
Porlier Pass
Chemainus Harbour
Salt Spring I.
Victoria Pat Bay
Victoria
Gonzales
Mt. Helmcken
Race Rocks
Trial I.
Discovery I.
East Point
Saturna I.
Mt. Parke
Active Pass
Mayne I.
Sandheads
Tsawwassen
Vancouver
Pt. Atkinson
Bowen I.
U.S.A. / Canada
49° N

Comox, Cape Lazo
Denman I.
Hornby I.
Chrome Island
49° 30'N
125° W
124° W

SE 40 / SE 50
E 35 / E 50
W 40 / W 50
W 30 / NW 50
NE 20 / SE 30
NW 35 / SE 50
SE 30 / SE 60
N 15 / NW 25
SE 20 / SE 40
W 50 / W 55
S 30 / SE 60
SW 40 / SW 60

N

see inset
Inset

14

WEATHER and SEA

The map opposite indicates the approximate wind and water conditions one is likely to meet while cruising the Gulf Islands region.

Weather forecasts and observations of wind, sea and visibility conditions at the various light or weather stations (☆) on the map opposite are broadcast by Canadian Coast Guard Stations (see *Radio Aids to Navigation*), commercial radio stations and from VHF-FM continuous marine broadcast sites. Warnings are broadcast as soon as possible after they have been issued by Environment Canada.

Up-to-date marine weather information is also available in Vancouver by telephone 270-7411, Nanaimo — 245-4032, Comox - 339-3613, and in Victoria at 656-2714 or 656-7515.

The Gulf Islands, in the lee of Vancouver Island, have a cool Mediterranean-type climate with an average rainfall of less than 760 mm (30 inches) per year, the bulk of this falling between November and March. Frequent summer drought conditions result in dangerous fire hazards for the predominantly open grass and arbutus, garry oak and fir woodlands of the islands.

Cruising is ideal between May and mid-October when mean temperatures are over 10 degrees C (50 degrees F). Mean daily temperatures in July are around 16 degrees C (60 degrees F) and maximum temperatures seldom exceed 32 degrees C (90 degrees F) because of the cooling effects of sea breezes. In winter, the inhibiting factors are occasional strong winds, colder temperatures and rain, but quite frequently, stable periods and clear skies bring good cruising weather and less crowded anchorages than in the summer.

WINDS

In the Gulf Islands and areas between Nanaimo and Comox, winds in the summer generally blow from the northwest quadrant, bringing good weather with sunny skies, or from the southeast indicating change, possible storm and rain. At the southern tip of Vancouver Island, summer winds blow strongly mainly from the southwest, indicating good weather with little rain.

Diurnal winds caused by the heating of the land during the day will often be onshore and will counteract the prevailing wind pattern during the afternoon, but offshore winds caused by cooling of the land mass at night may intensify the northwest wind pattern near certain places, such as Nanaimo and Qualicum.

In late summer, evening calms are prevalent north of Saltspring Island and morning calms prevalent south of Haro Strait; this is the best time of year for motorboating and canoeing. There is also a greater chance of morning fogs, especially in the southern Gulf Islands.

Winter winds are generally much stronger and often from the southeast, especially north of Nanaimo. Northeast winds are common along the southern Vancouver Island coast down to Victoria, and although the weather is colder and more variable, sunny conditions are frequent.

Winds in the spring are quite fresh and there are fewer calms than during the summer months. This time of year is often best for crews in cruising sailboats as long as they are prepared for the stronger winds.

Though summer winds are generally light in the Gulf Islands, they often build to over 15 knots about mid-day in Juan de Fuca Strait and off the Victoria waterfront (above).

A wind rose for the month of July for the major weather stations is shown on the map. The length of the line from one of the eight cardinal directions indicates the approximate percentage of the time that the wind will be blowing from that direction. The central five percent circle encloses a figure which indicates the percentage frequency of calms. This figure may be misleading, for extremely light winds (under 3 m.p.h.) which are not classified as calms, prevail for much of the time during the summer months.

The direction and average maximum speeds of the strongest winds during the summer and winter months are shown in a double box beside each of the major weather stations. While the strongest winds generally blow from the direction of greatest fetch, it should be noted that strong winds from other directions may be experienced as well. These figures are averages only and although a useful guide as to what one may expect, they should be treated with caution. A more extensive description of the winds for each particular area is included at the beginning of each chapter.

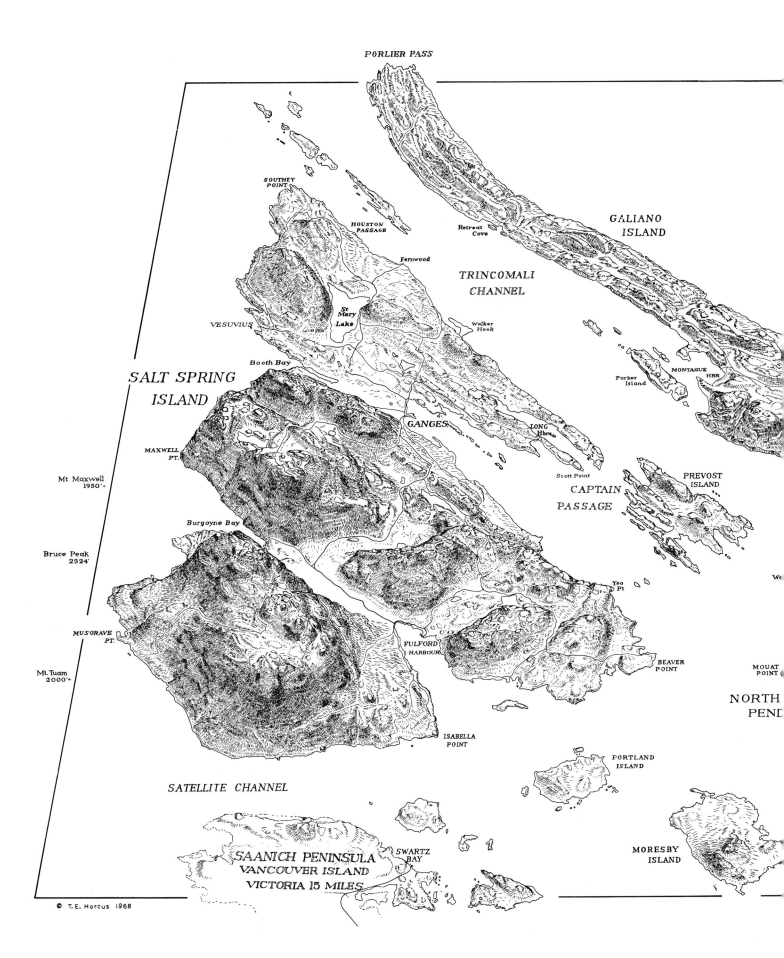

PORLIER PASS

GALIANO
ISLAND

SOUTHEY
POINT

HOUSTON
PASSAGE

Retreat
Cove

Fernwood

TRINCOMALI
CHANNEL

St
Mary
Lake

VESUVIUS

Walker
Hook

Booth Bay

SALT SPRING
ISLAND

MONTAGUE HBR

Parker
Island

GANGES

LONG
Hbr

MAXWELL
PT.

Mt Maxwell
1950'+

Scott Point

PREVOST
ISLAND

CAPTAIN

PASSAGE

Bruce Peak
2324'

Burgoyne Bay

Wc

Yeo
Pt

MUSGRAVE
PT.

Mt. Tuam
2000'+

FULFORD
HARBOUR

BEAVER
POINT

MOUAT
POINT

NORTH
PENI

ISABELLA
POINT

PORTLAND
ISLAND

SATELLITE CHANNEL

MORESBY
ISLAND

SWARTZ
BAY

SAANICH PENINSULA
VANCOUVER ISLAND
VICTORIA 15 MILES

© T.E. Harcus 1968

16

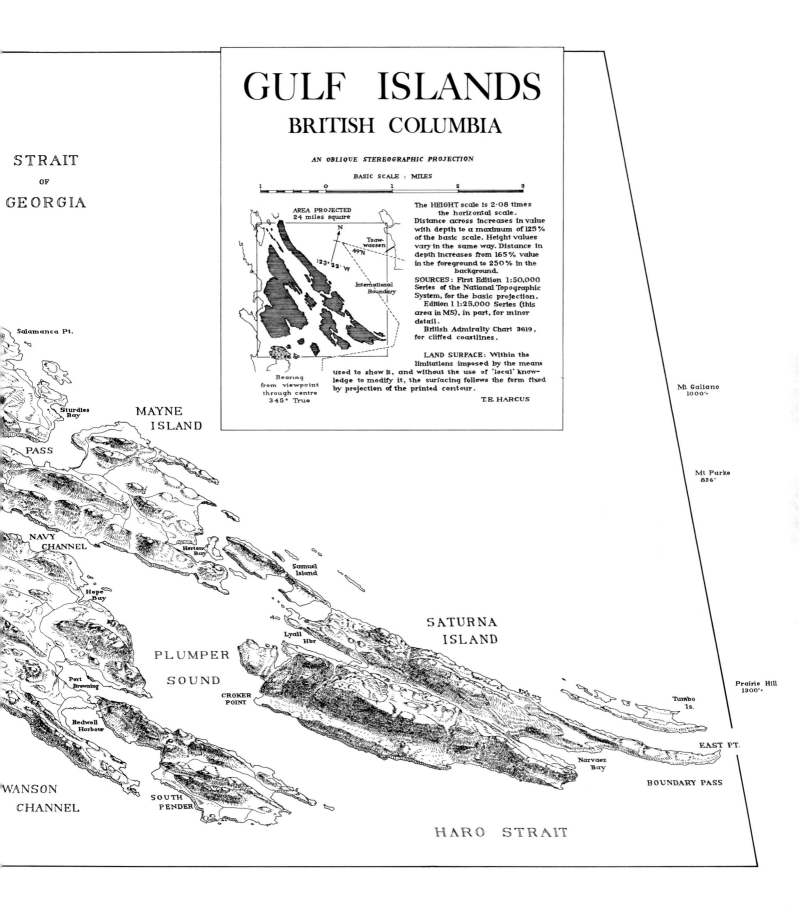

GULF ISLANDS
BRITISH COLUMBIA

AN OBLIQUE STEREOGRAPHIC PROJECTION

BASIC SCALE : MILES

AREA PROJECTED
24 miles square

N

Tsaw-
wassen
49°N

123°22'W

International
Boundary

Bearing
from viewpoint
through centre
345° True

The HEIGHT scale is 2·08 times
the horizontal scale.
Distance across increases in value
with depth to a maximum of 125%
of the basic scale. Height values
vary in the same way. Distance in
depth increases from 165% value
in the foreground to 250% in the
background.
SOURCES: First Edition 1:50,000
Series of the National Topographic
System, for the basic projection.
Edition 1 1:25,000 Series (this
area in MS), in part, for minor
detail.
British Admiralty Chart 3619,
for cliffed coastlines.

LAND SURFACE: Within the
limitations imposed by the means
used to show it, and without the use of 'local' knowledge to modify it, the surfacing follows the form fixed
by projection of the printed contour.

T.E. HARCUS

STRAIT
OF
GEORGIA

Salamanca Pt.

Sturdies
Bay

PASS

MAYNE
ISLAND

NAVY
CHANNEL

Herton
Bay

Samuel
Island

Hope
Bay

PLUMPER

SOUND

Lyall
Hbr

SATURNA
ISLAND

Port
Browning

CROKER
POINT

Bedwell
Harbour

WANSON

CHANNEL

SOUTH
PENDER

Narvaez
Bay

HARO   STRAIT

Mt Galiano
1000'+

Mt Parke
836'

Prairie Hill
1300'+

Tumbo
Is.

EAST PT.

BOUNDARY PASS

SEAS

Because of the limited fetch, or distance over open water in the Strait of Georgia, the height of waves generated by strong winds seldom exceeds four feet. With a fetch of almost 120 miles, northwest winds can develop the largest waves in the southern Strait. The largest seas generated by southeasterly storms are to be found in the vicinity of Lasqueti, Denman and Hornby islands. Very short, steep seas which are dangerous to small craft can be found wherever a strong wind meets an opposing tidal stream.

TIDES

The level of the water in the Strait of Georgia fluctuates daily because of the gravitational interaction of moon and sun on the earth's layer of water. When the moon is full or new the tides fluctuate at their greatest range — anywhere from eight or nine feet at Victoria to 17 feet at Comox. These are called spring tides, though they happen throughout the year, approximately twice a month over a period of several days. During the moon's first and last quarters the tides are referred to as neaps or normal tides and the range is generally a little more than half of what is experienced at spring tides.

The tides generally affect cruising yachtsmen in two ways. First, the flow of water into (flood) and out of (ebb) the Strait of Georgia produces currents which generally run at rates of 1 to 2 knots but can reach maximum speeds of 10 knots in the passes between the islands. These passes can be dangerous for small craft when the tidal streams are running at a high rate, not only because of the speed of the flow, but also because of cross-currents, overfalls, rips, steep seas, whirlpools, eddies and standing waves which may be encountered. Consequently the passes should be navigated as close as possible to slack water (generally, high or low water). Knowledge of the direction of tidal current flow is very useful when planning one's cruise, particularly for small boats with maximum speeds under 4 or 5 knots such as canoes, small sailboats, or powerboats whose owners want to conserve fuel. For instance, if the tide happens to be ebbing during the morning, it helps to be heading south, while if one wants to go north it sometimes pays to wait until afternoon for the flood.

Secondly, the state of the tide often determines how close to shore, or in what cove or bay, a small craft can anchor. The majority of anchorages in the Gulf Islands have sufficient water depth at all stages of the tide.

An interesting feature of tides in the Strait of Georgia is that higher high water in summer generally occurs at night, with lower low water occurring in the early morning or during the day. This factor will also affect where one chooses to anchor, but beware of low water in the early morning.

The strength and direction of the tidal streams through the Gulf Islands are given in the *Current Atlas: Juan de Fuca Strait to Strait of Georgia* (1983); and the heights and times of high and low water and maximum tidal stream rates and times for all the major passes are given in the *Canadian Tide & Current Tables, Volume 5*, which is published annually by the Canadian Hydrographic Service.

GEOLOGY and TOPOGRAPHY

The geology of the Gulf Islands and adjacent Vancouver Island coast is fascinating and the topography varied. An understanding of the various rock types will aid in finding the best beaches, the best hills for climbing, the deepest (or shallowest) anchorages and the type of bottom preferred for anchoring.

All of the Gulf Islands, with the exception of southern Saltspring, Lasqueti, northern Denman, Sidney and James are composed of sedimentary rock — mainly sandstone, conglomerate and shales. The sandstone is often interbedded with the conglomerate and has a sandpapery texture which is frequently eroded at the shoreline into a typical honeycomb or pockmarked texture. Some of the indentations are only big enough for nesting cormorants (as at East Point, Saturna Island) while others are big enough for several people to crawl into, as at Malaspina Point on Gabriola Island or along the Galiano shoreline.

Conglomerate, or "puddingstone", is a mixture of

Picturesque Tent Island cove is characteristic of some of the attractive topography that makes the Gulf Islands so popular with cruising yachtsmen.

various rounded pebbles and boulders all cemented together in a matrix of finer material. Some conglomerate boulders can be very large, as at Sangster Island. The conglomerate is generally harder than the sandstone and is less easily eroded.

These beds of shale, sandstone and conglomerate rock have been extensively folded and faulted and are generally aligned in a NW-SE direction parallel to the

Vancouver Island coastline. The folding and subsequent erosion has resulted in a series of ridges and valleys. The ridges are formed from the harder sandstone and conglomerate rock and are cuesta-like in appearance, with the steep side facing southwest and usually sparsely vegetated, and the gentle slope facing northeast and usually thickly forested. These ridges generally form the points and headlands at the extremities of the islands, and reefs and shallow patches often extend underwater for some distance beyond the points. A good example is Enterprise Reef which extends half a mile northwest of Crane Point on Mayne Island. Beaches in these areas are generally small (pocket beaches) and composed of pebbles or shell fragments, with the sea bottoms of rock, sometimes overlain with a thin layer of mud. The ridges are separated by long narrow valleys which constitutes the best farmland on the islands, and are generally underlain by the softer shales. Where these valleys run down to the sea we find sheltered bays with good holding ground for anchors in mud derived from the shale. Long Harbour on Saltspring and Horton Bay on Mayne are good examples.

Southern Saltspring, Lasqueti and most of the southern tip of Vancouver Island are composed of very hard volcanic or igneous rocks, some of which have been metamorphosed or altered by heat and pressure. These areas are generally much higher or more rugged with deeper shorelines and fewer anchorages.

Sidney Island, James Island and the northern tip of Denman Island are almost entirely composed of drift deposits. These are very loose sands and gravels which were left by the glaciers when they retreated over 10,000 years ago. The coastlines of these areas are constantly changing because of fairly rapid erosion and deposition. These areas contain the best sand beaches and good holding ground for anchors, but anchorage can be treacherous in some areas where large boulders have been left behind in the foreshore area. The shoreline of Cordova Bay, Royal Roads, Parry Bay, Qualicum Bay to Parksville and Comox are also composed of these drift deposits.

NATURAL FEATURES

There are many areas in the Gulf Islands where one can sit (on shore or on your boat) and watch the fascinating world of birds or marine life. Some of these areas are protected as wildlife sanctuaries (such as Esquimalt Lagoon), ecological reserves (Rose Islets) or nature parks (Ballingall Islets); but many are not. With this in mind it is important not to disturb those birds and species of marine life whose existence is dependent upon a high degree of isolation, especially during the breeding season (May to July).

The British Columbia Provincial Museum has published an excellent handbook (No. 21) entitled *Guide to Marine Life of British Columbia* by Clifford Carl, which includes short descriptions and illustrations of many forms of marine life found in the Gulf Islands. Mammals to look for include the killer whale, the harbour porpoise, the Dall porpoise (which delights in playing about the bows of a moving ship, and is seen only occasionally in the Gulf Islands), the humpback whale, pike whale, harbour seal, sea lion, river otter (which sometimes will climb aboard a deserted boat or float), mink and racoon.

Birds include loons, grebes and cormorants (of which there are three species common to British Columbia — the double-crested, brandt's and pelagic); brant geese, mallards, scoters and other ducks; bald eagles, osprey and hawks; pigeon guillemots and a variety of other shorebirds; and waders of which the great blue heron is the largest. A variety of fishes, shellfish and the sea monster — Cadborosaurus are described in the handbook as well.

SPORTSFISHING

The best fishing areas are generally found where tidal upwellings and strong tidal streams provide food for feeding salmon. There are a number of excellent guidebooks, some of which are listed in the bibliography. Excerpts from the BC Outdoors *Salt Water Fishing Guide* have been included in the introductory section of each chapter in Part II of this guide. It is interesting to note the close correlation between seabird areas and good fishing areas. The Federal Department of Fisheries and Oceans occasionally closes certain areas of the Gulf Islands to sportsfishing in an effort to prevent over-depletion of the resource. These spot closures are for varying periods and are advertised in local newspapers.

This cruising guide is not intended to encourage harvesting of oysters and clams, since the Gulf Islands have been seriously depleted of shellfish by over-harvesting and pollution. There are many areas closed to harvesting because of pollution. These generally include any area within 400 feet of a private or government wharf and almost all harbours, major anchorages, or shorelines fringed with residential development.

If you are digging for clams, take only as many as you really need. All mud or sand should be replaced in the hole so as not to smother smaller animals under the pile, and to re-establish the area for recolonization.

ARCHAEOLOGICAL SITES

No one knows who actually carved or pecked these ancient figures into the boulders and rock faces along the B.C. coast. It is surmised that they were left by the ancestors of the Indians many hundreds of years ago. Their meaning and exact age remain a mystery, but it is likely that they were connected with the spirit world and possibly with attempts by the Indians' ancestors to personify their own identity.

By visiting these sites and contemplating the figures one can begin to feel some sense of their value, which will hopefully lead to a respect for the sites, the traditions they represent, and the descendants of the people who originally fashioned them.

Other Indian remains, including burial grounds, caves, shell-heaps, middens, cairns and habitation and petroglyph sites are protected under the Archaeological and Historic Sites Protection Act. This Act makes it an offence to destroy, dig, move, remove artifacts from, or otherwise deface any of the above-noted sites.

SETTLEMENTS

The map gives a rough indication of the density of shoreline settlement in the Gulf Islands. Most of the Gulf Islands are sparsely populated with Saltspring having the most people of all the islands — over 7000. The total permanent population of all the islands is probably less than 15,000 but this almost doubles in the summer time. Hospitals and R.C.M.P. detachments are located at Ganges, Saltspring Island and at most of the major Vancouver Island communities.

MARINAS

Over 50 marinas are found along the Vancouver Island coastline between Sooke and Courtenay. At present, there are 15 or so marinas in the Gulf Islands. The smaller marinas have a great deal of difficulty making ends meet and yachtsmen should patronize these without using them solely as landings or places to dispose of garbage. Some of the marinas include boat repair yards and these are indicated on the map.

FERRY ROUTES

The major ferry routes linking the mainland to Vancouver Island run between Tsawwassen and Swartz Bay, and Horseshoe Bay and Nanaimo. The ferries leave their terminals every hour on the hour 7 a.m. to 10 p.m. during the summer months and produce a considerable wash into anchorages which face the ferry route. In addition to these larger ferries a number of smaller ferries operate between Vancouver Island and the mainland to the major Gulf Islands. These ferries are ideal for access to the islands for canoeists and kayakers since you can carry a canoe onto the ferry for a foot passenger's fare. Many of the terminals are located close to public floats or marinas, and it is sometimes possible to leave your boat for the week and return to weekend sail a particular area. Sailboat skippers must not, by law, insist on the right of way in constricted passes or adjacent to terminals and yachtsmen should never moor directly alongside the ferry slips.

20

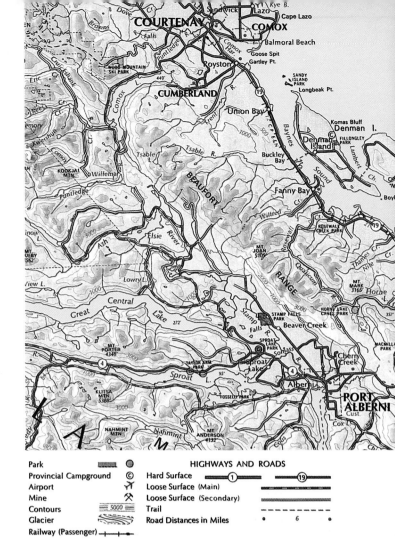

Park	▨ ◯	HIGHWAYS AND ROADS	
Provincial Campground	Ⓒ	Hard Surface	
Airport	✈	Loose Surface (Main)	
Mine	⚒	Loose Surface (Secondary)	
Contours	≡ 5000 ≡	Trail	
Glacier		Road Distances in Miles	• 6 •
Railway (Passenger)	┼─┼─		

Note: Elevation to 500 feet is shown coloured green, with higher elevations in shaded brown relief.

Drawn and produced by and obtainable from Map Production Division, Surveys and Mapping Branch, Ministry of Environment, Parliament Buildings, Victoria, B.C., 1967. Revised 1979.

PRIVATE PROPERTY

Most of the shoreline in the Gulf Islands and along the adjacent Vancouver Island coast is private property. Yachtsmen should respect the privacy of shoreline residents and always request permission to explore ashore. If you introduce yourself and explain your intent, with a promise to be careful and considerate, most residents will grant access. Their biggest worry is fire, along with vandalism and litter. By being especially careful you will help ensure that the cruising yachtsman remains a welcome visitor to the islands.

CROWN FORESHORE

There is no such thing in Canada as a private beach. All foreshore (land between high and low water) is Crown land. It is administered by the provincial government to ensure public access. In some cases, foreshore leases are given for building private jettys or piers, for oyster farms, for log booming and storage and for marina or port operations. These leases do not permit the owner to restrict public access across the leased area unless the public may endanger the purpose of the lease.

Montague Harbour, the most popular anchorage in the Gulf Islands, can accommodate hundreds of small craft.

PUBLIC FLOATS / ANCHORAGES

Since the early part of this century the federal government has provided wharf facilities to meet basic transportation requirements for small communities along the coast. The majority of these public wharves have floats attached and are easily recognized by their bright red railings. Since these early facilities were built, additional floats have been added to wharves in the more populated areas, especially where there is a large fishing fleet. Most of the floats in the Gulf Islands have under 200 feet of berthing space — only enough for six or eight small craft of average length — 25 feet overall. In the summer when many of the fishing boats are away on the West Coast, these floats are available for temporary moorage. At many of the floats there is a nominal moorage fee.

At some locations, these floats are very crowded and boats secure alongside one another. In these cases it is common courtesy not to monopolize float space for more time than is really needed.

The major anchorages are generally found in the harbours containing public floats. If an anchorage is crowded, yachtsmen can reduce their swinging room by taking a line ashore or by securing alongside a friend's boat. If the water is deep enough close to the shore, it is sometimes possible to secure your boat within stepping distance of land. This practice is advisable only with a rising tide and flat calm conditions.

Each chapter in Part II of this guide includes a map of the area outlining the best anchorages which are generally suitable for use in all weather. In addition, possible temporary anchorages are indicated by asterisks (*) on the map. These temporary or contitional anchorages may be suitable for overnight anchorage and be fairly well protected from most winds and seas. Some are only usable when tide conditions permit (they may dry at lower water) or when there is a flat calm with stable, high pressure conditions prevailing. For every temporary anchorage indicated on the map there are probably four or five others, just as suitable, in the vicinity. Nevertheless, these temporary anchorages should be used with caution, especially if weather conditions are unstable.

PARKS and RESERVES

British Columbia's marine parks are intended to provide essential facilities for the enjoyment of the boating public, keeping in mind the need to maintain the natural surroundings of the area. Many have safe anchorages and mooring buoys, some have landing floats, some have campgrounds and some have picnic grounds. Wherever possible, fresh water is also available, though it is sometimes difficult to obtain on some

Marine parks such as this popular facility at Montague Harbour are regular destinations for kayakers and other small craft operators who use the public campgrounds as a base for further explorations.

of the islands. Since most marine parks are located some distance from shops, stores and fuelling stations it is recommended to stock up before your arrival. Sanitary facilities and provision for collection and disposal of refuse are located at all developed parks.

Complete information on B.C.'s marine parks is available in Peter Chettleburgh's *An Explorer's Guide: Marine Parks of British Columbia* (1985).

In addition to the marine parks which are mainly confined to the Gulf Islands, there are a number of shorefront parks on Vancouver Island and in the Gulf Islands which could be used by cruising yachtsmen or other coastal explorers. These, however, are mainly oriented to visitors arriving by road.

The majority of regional parks are found in the Capital Regional District around Victoria. Provincial Park Reserves are undeveloped but protected from other uses. In addition to those shown on the map, all unsurveyed islands and islets in the Strait of Georgia have been reserved for the use, recreation and enjoyment of the public. There are several nature reserves, wildlife sanctuaries, ecological reserves and special areas for protection of unique flora, fauna, avi-fauna or marine life. Ecological reserves are not intended for recreational use but mainly for scientific research and education. At present, ecological reserves are not closed to the public and casual non-consumptive, non-motorized use, such as hiking, photography, birdwatching and mountain climbing is permitted.

Perhaps in the future some of the more fragile reserves may have to be closed to the public, but the need has not yet arisen.

FIRST EXPLORERS

The first European explorer to visit the Strait of Georgia may have been Juan de Fuca who discovered the strait which now bears his name in 1592. He sailed up this strait for more than twenty days, found many islands and also a broad sea, which could have been the Strait of Georgia. In 1790 Manuel Quimper explored as far as Haro Strait and was followed in 1791 by Jose Maria Narvaez and Francisco Eliza who travelled north as far as Cape Lazo, just east of Comox. The work of these Spanish explorers was completed the next year by Galiano and Valdes who visited many of the Gulf Islands while circumnavigating Vancouver Island. In the course of their voyage they encountered Captain George Vancouver who was engaged in exploring the mainland side of the Strait of Georgia.

Captain John Walbran in *B.C. Coast Names* gives an interesting account of the naming of the Strait of Georgia. It was originally named "Gulf of Georgia" by Vancouver in 1792 . . .

". . .In honour of His Majesty King George III. The previous year Lieutenant Eliza, of the Spanish navy, had named it "Gran Canal de Nuestra Senora del Rosario la Marinera." The name of gulf was changed to strait by Captain Richards, 1865, after he had been appointed Hydrographer, but, notwithstanding the alteration, it is to-day always locally spoken of as "the Gulf." The name of King George was a significant and potent one among the Indians of this coast in the days of the fur traders because, owing to his long reign, he was so frequently mentioned by British subjects and others that in the native mind his name became synonymous with power and authority, so much so, that all Britishers were called "King George Men," and their ships "King George Ships," in contradistinction to those of other nationalities with whom the natives came in contact. Other traders were styled "Boston Men," because they nearly all then belonged to American vessels which were fitted out and hailed from Boston, New England." (Walbran)

CANOEING and KAYAKING

The Gulf Islands are ideal for exploration by small craft, especially in later summer and early fall and during other periods of calm, stable weather. Many of the shallower bays and coves, tidal pools, lagoons, rivers, creeks and streams which are inaccessible to deeper draught craft are open to canoes. Small boats such as canoes should not venture more than a mile or two from shore because wind and sea conditions can change quickly, raising breaking waves which are hazardous to open boats. The outer coasts of the Gulf Islands are fascinating to explore because of their relative isolation but since good landings may be a fair distance apart, they should only be attempted by those experienced in handling small open boats in rough conditions.

HIKING TRAILS

Roads, tracks, trails and open meadows are integral parts of the Gulf Island countryside. The possibilities for hiking up mountainsides or hills to see magnificent views, beachcombing along coastlines and strolling along narrow winding roads beside pastoral farmlands are countless. Excellent topographic maps of the Gulf Islands are available at a scale of 1:15,840 (4 inches to 1 mile) with a contour interval of 25 feet. These show all the sandy beaches, roads and major trails as well as buildings and wooded areas. They are essential for anyone seriously interested in exploring the Gulf Islands and can be obtained from the B.C. Provincial Government Map and Air Photo Sales Office, Room 111, 553 Superior Street, Victoria, B.C.

WARM WATER SWIMMING

Swimming in the Gulf Islands and around the southern tip of Vancouver Island is usually a chilling experience with water temperatures in summer averaging 7 to 10 degrees C (45 to 50 degrees F). In a few places (such as wide sandy beaches which transfer their heat to a rising tide, or locations at the end of long narrow bays with little tidal exchange) waters reach temperatures of 18 to 21 degrees C (65 to 70 degrees F).

WRECKS and DIVING AREAS

In the Gulf Islands area the remains of many wrecks are to be found on shores, beaches, shallow areas and reefs. A few of these wrecks are permanently visible; some can only be seen at low water, but the great majority of wrecks have settled in deeper water, and the only feasible way to explore them is with scuba apparatus. Divers interested in exploring wrecks should refer to Fred Rogers' book, *Shipwrecks of British Columbia*.

MUSEUMS/HISTORICAL SITES

There are many historical sites and small community museums which give valuable insight into the background of early inhabitants and local natural features. Many of these are described in Part II of the guide. The people who operate these museums tend to be remarkable characters themselves, full of anecdotes about the Gulf Islands. The yachtsman who only ventures ashore for fuel and groceries is missing a great deal if he doesn't take advantage of the opportunity to meet the people who live on these fascinating islands.

PART TWO

Cruising Guide to the
GULF ISLANDS
and Vancouver Island
from Sooke to Courtenay

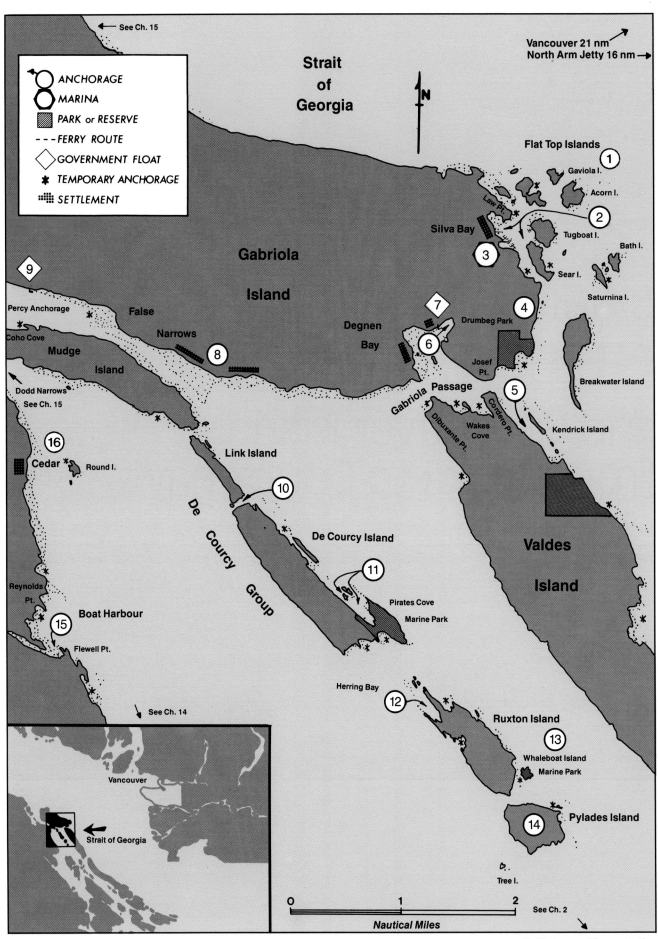

Strait of Georgia

← See Ch. 15

Vancouver 21 nm →
North Arm Jetty 16 nm →

N

Flat Top Islands

① Gaviola I.

Acorn I.

② Tugboat I.

Law Pt.

③ Silva Bay

Sear I. Bath I.

Saturnina I.

④

Gabriola

Island

⑨

Percy Anchorage

False

Coho Cove

Mudge

Narrows

⑧

Degnen Bay

⑦

Drumbeg Park

⑥

Josef Pt.

Breakwater Island

Island

Dodd Narrows
See Ch. 15

⑤

Gabriola Passage

Dibuxante Pt.

Wakes Cove

Cordero Pt.

Kendrick Island

⑯

Cedar

Round I.

Link Island

⑩

De Courcy Island

De Courcy Group

⑪

Pirates Cove
Marine Park

Valdes

Island

Reynolds Pt.

⑮ **Boat Harbour**

Flewell Pt.

↓ See Ch. 14

Herring Bay

⑫

Ruxton Island

⑬

Whaleboat Island
Marine Park

⑭ **Pylades Island**

Tree I.

Legend

⊗ ANCHORAGE
⊘ MARINA
▨ PARK or RESERVE
--- FERRY ROUTE
◇ GOVERNMENT FLOAT
✳ TEMPORARY ANCHORAGE
▦ SETTLEMENT

Vancouver

Strait of Georgia

0   1   2
Nautical Miles

See Ch. 2

Not to be used for navigation

26

CHAPTER ONE

Gabriola Passage

Valdes, Gabriola and the De Courcy Islands

... the larger Gulf Islands seen by ... the Gulf by the shortest possible route from Vancouver. Valdes is a long, narrow continuation of the ridge-like range of outer islands, and Gabriola is the northernmost of the "traditional" Gulf Islands. Gabriola and Valdes together act as a buffer, protecting the inner islands from weather in the Strait of Georgia. The eastern tip of Gabriola was first named "Gaviota" or "Gaviola" (seagull) by Jose Maria Narvaez in 1791.

Winds

Wind conditions on the Gulf Islands' side of the Strait of Georgia are usually quite different from conditions on the mainland side, especially in summer, when the effects of diurnal heating are more evident. Daytime winds in July at Entrance Island (five miles to the northwest of Silva Bay) are generally from the east (30% frequency, increasing to 45% in the afternoon) or from the northwest (45% frequency, decreasing to 25% in the afternoon). Night winds are usually from the west, with over 50% frequency. The strongest winds (over 30 mph) in summer come from the northwest, and in the autumn from the east and southeast.

Fishing

There is excellent blueback fishing in April to May with larger Coho coming through in July and continuing through September. Chinook are fair most of the season. Troll outside (east of) Thrasher Rock and Gabriola Reefs, keeping outside of a line between Thrasher and the buoy off Gabriola Passage. It is excellent water for drift fishing, working the underwater reefs where water runs 7-10 fathoms. There is good trolling between Thrasher Rock and the Flat Tops and good mooching and drift fishing inside Thrasher and Gabriola Reefs.

1 Flat Top Islands

Approaching the Flat Top Islands from the east, one can easily be confused by the lack of distinguishing landmarks. Thrasher Rock Light, one mile east of Bath Island, marks the northward extension of the dangerous Gabriola reefs and should be left to port. The rock is named after a wooden sailing ship loaded with coal from Nanaimo which stranded here in 1880. Scuba divers may still find bits of coal and wreckage in 30 feet of water northeast of the rock (Pratt-Johnson).

The Flat Top Islands are all privately owned, but sparsely inhabited. If you don't mind being confined to your boat or to the narrow beaches (crown foreshore below the high tide line is public), these delightful, smaller Gulf Islands offer some pleasant temporary anchorages and beaches for small craft landing, subject to wind and tide conditions. Tree species vary from one island to another according to the relative exposure. If you do venture ashore, *be careful*. Acorn Island shows the result of past carelessness in its

CHARTS
3310 — Sheet 4 — PORLIER PASS to
　　　　DEPARTURE BAY (1:40,000)
3443 — THETIS ISLAND to NANAIMO
　　　　(1:40,000)
3475 — Plan of DODD NARROWS to FLAT TOP
　　　　ISLANDS (1:18,000)

gaunt, silver snags, remnants of a fire that swept the island several years ago. The exposed nature of this island with frequent high winds and salt spray has impeded forest regeneration.

2   Silva Bay

Silva Bay is one of the few completely protected anchorages on the outer coast of the Gulf Islands. Entrance to Silva Bay or to Gabriola Passage is usually made between Acorn and Bath islands, but can also be made on either side of Vance Island, or south of Breakwater Island, or between Sear Island and Gabriola. If the central entrance into Silva Bay is used, keep well to the north of the beacon between Vance and Tugboat islands to avoid the reef (known locally as Shipyard Rock) extending north from Tugboat Island. When

Protected by the outlying Flat Top Islands, Silva Bay is one of the few completely sheltered anchorages on the outer coast of the Gulf Islands.

rounding the beacon, avoid the temptation to head straight for the Silva Bay floats, but steer for Law Point until you are halfway there. Otherwise you will join the thousands who have grazed this rock or the hundreds who have spent the night sitting on top of it (Boshier, *Pacific Yachting*, April 1985). The floats on the inside of Tugboat Island are reserved for members and guests of the Royal Vancouver Yacht Club. Abundant space for anchoring in depths averaging two to four fathoms is available throughout the bay, or in shallower depths between Lily Island and Law Point, or in a cove on Gabriola west of Sear Island. Silva Bay is named after a pioneering Portugese family whose descendants still live in the area.

28

When entering Silva Bay keep well to the north of the reef (Shipyard Rock) which extends out from Tugboat Island.

3   Silva Bay Facilities

Silva Bay serves as a major marine centre with a variety of facilities for anyone exploring the coast. Silva Bay Resort (247-9267) provides moorage, fuel, boat rentals, laundry, showers, lodging, restaurant, gift and craft shops, and a marine pub offering nightly entertainment during the summer. Silva Bay Marina and Shipyard (247-9317) has a 200-ton railway and 12-ton travelift and facilities for complete hull and engine repairs and parts for sail, power or commercial fishing vessels. The Ship Chandlery, which is operated by the Shipyard, offers a variety of marine hardware, books, charts and groceries. The Silva Bay Boatel and Store (247-9351) provides moorage, groceries, hardware, laundromat and self-contained suites.

4   Drumbeg Park

Fifty-acre Drumbeg Provincial Park was established in 1971. Small boats can anchor temporarily in the bays or be hauled out on the beach. The park offers opportunities for swimming, fishing, picnicking, beach hiking and scuba diving offshore.

Valdes Island

Valdes Island is almost totally uninhabited and is the largest of all the Gulf Islands without a ferry service. Over one-third of the island is Indian reserve. The outer shore of Valdes is exposed and lined with many drying rocks and reefs. While these dangers discourage many large boats from exploring closely, smaller boats can find limited protection in a few tiny coves where it may be possible to anchor temporarily or pull a boat ashore. The area is laced with deserted logging roads which provide access to the interior.

5   Kendrick Island

A good place to wait for the tide to change or to anchor for the night if need be, is behind the long, narrow reef surmounted by three islets — the last and longest being named Kendrick. A very narrow and shallow passage is possible between the southernmost islet and Valdes Island. Kendrick Island serves as an outstation for the West Vancouver Yacht Club; there are floats, mooring buoys and many boat names painted on the sandstone shore.

Degnen Bay, on the north side of Gabriola Passage is a favorite spot for yachtsmen wishing to escape the crowds in Silva Bay or Pirates Cove.

A good place to wait out a tide change in Gabriola Passage is behind Kendrick Islet at the eastern entrance to the passage.

Gabriola Passage

Gabriola Passage, between Gabriola and Valdes Islands, is the smallest of the three major passes leading into the Gulf Islands from the Strait of Georgia, but the most popular access for recreational boats all the same. During a peak summer weekend over 1,000 boats may use this pass, most of them converging on the pass near slack water. Tidal currents run up to eight knots at spring tides and slack water sometimes does not exist at all — the current changing direction before you even know it has happened. Three of the points projecting into the pass were named by the Royal Navy in honour of Josef Cordero, a map maker and draughtsman (Spanish — *dibuxante*) who served with Galiano and Valdes when they explored these waters in 1792. Several coves indent the northern end of Valdes Island. Wakes Cove is the safest anchorage out of the current, but is moderately exposed to occa-

sional northwesterly winds blowing across the pass from Degnen Bay and to the wash from vessels powering through Gabriola Passage.

6 Degnen Bay

This is a favourite anchorage for those wishing to escape crowded conditions in Silva Bay. The northeastern arm provides abundant shelter, and although there are no commercial facilities, there is a public wharf (#7) with over 400 feet of float space for about 15 or more boats (more can be accommodated by rafting one to another). Near the head of Degnen Bay, on a slab of sandstone rock only a few feet above low tide, is a unique "killer whale" petroglyph. This carving led Mary and Ted Bentley, the authors of a recent book — *Gabriola: Petroglyph Island* — to photograph, record and work for the preservation of over 50 other petroglyphs on this island. Silva Bay is about a mile and a half walk down the road and Drumbeg Park is located a mile to the southeast. Entrance to Degnen Bay should be made close to the Josef Point shoreline as many rocks surround the island in the centre of the bay. A launching ramp is located in the western end of the bay.

8 False Narrows

False Narrows is a beautiful area with green fields running down to the water on both the Mudge and Gabriola sides. Those wishing to navigate the narrows should study Chart 3475 carefully and follow the Mudge shoreline fairly closely until the leading beacons are in line and then cross over to the Gabriola shore to avoid the sandstone reef extending two-thirds of the way across the narrows from Mudge Island. The beach here appears in places to be cobbled with bricks, remnants of a brick factory which operated from 1895 to 1952. The second pair of beacons should be lined up over your shoulder and followed back to the Mudge shore to exit into Percy Anchorage. Currents in the narrows reach four and a half knots at spring tides.

Lush fields lie adjacent to the water on both sides of False Narrows between Mudge and Gabriola Islands.

9 Percy Anchorage

This is a good anchorage with a shell bottom, but it is open to westerly winds, which are frequent in this area. A small public float known locally as "the green wharf at Brickyard Hill" is a convenient place to recuperate or to await a favourable tide in Dodd or False narrows. Coho Cove Yacht Club on Mudge Island has a private dock offering temporary moorage (maximum 72 hours) for guests of local residents.

10 Link Island

The passage between Mudge and Link dries about nine feet and is scattered with boulders making it unsafe for small craft either for passage or anchorage. There is a peaceful nook between Link and De Courcy islands which provides limited anchorage and is protected from all directions except the northeast. A shoal area with three feet of water at chart datum is located in the centre of this anchorage. From here it is possible to walk through the woods to the western shoreline of De Courcy Island, where one may find some remnants of Brother Twelve's island colony.

Brother Twelve

De Courcy Island was one of the last retreats of Brother Twelve — a notorious mystic and confidence man who had originally set up his Aquarian Founda-

Percy Anchorage (top in photo) on Gabriola Island is a good spot to wait out the tide in Dodd or False Narrows. Coho Cove Yacht Club on Mudge Island is in the foreground.

31

The channel into Pirates Cove should be negotiated with caution to avoid the reef which actually extends north of the beacon at the end of Pirates Point.

tion near Cedar on Vancouver Island in the 1920s. His exploits are recounted in a fascinating book by H.E. Wilson, *Canada's False Prophet.* Just before the downfall of his foundation, Brother Twelve had three forts with machine gun emplacements built around De Courcy Island to keep away the curious. These forts have all been completely demolished, but some of the barracks-like bunkhouses and farm buildings still remain. Fishermen and Indians who visited Pirates Cove in the 1930s were sometimes greeted with rifle fire. Other visitors sometimes found their wives talked into joining the colony by the mesmerizing magnetism of Brother Twelve. Husbands were discarded unless they had money to contribute to the foundation. The colony was unique; all males were confined to the north end of the island while the females shared the southern half with Brother Twelve. This set-up seemed to work quite well until one of Brother Twelve's favourite wives, a Madame Zee, started using a bull whip to drive the other wives off the island.

On a cliff above Dibuxante Point, Valdes Island he is reported to have built his last "House of Mystery" — a temple with concrete vaults in the floor where he stored millions of dollars in gold contributed by his followers. When the police finally closed in, Brother Twelve had disappeared and the gold with him, leav-

The unique dodecagonal floats in Pirates Cove are designed to allow dinghy landings only, discouraging large yachts.

ing his distraught followers alone on the De Courcy Islands.

11   Pirates Cove Marine Park

The popular anchorage of Pirates Cove, formerly known as The Haven or Gospel Cove in Brother Twelve's time, is now a 76-acre provincial marine

Pirates Cove.

park. The channel leading into Pirates Cove should be negotiated with care. The beacon at the entrance does not mark the end of the reef extending north from Pirates Point, as the reef actually extends another 100 yards beyond the beacon. White marks on a tree and rock ashore should be aligned before turning into the entrance channel. A large shoal area which is about four feet below chart datum is located in the central part of the channel near the entrance to the cove. At low tide, boats should keep east of the red buoy if there is a chance of grounding on the shoal. Before placement of the buoy, groundings were a common occurrence, since most boats heading north leave just before low water to catch the slack in Gabriola or Dodds narrows. The western shore north of the private dock is private. There are two unique "Fairhurst" dodecagonal public floats for dinghys, one on each side of the cove. There is a water pump, walk-in campsites, picnic areas and toilets in the park. Visitors should bear in mind that maintenance of marine parks is extremely difficult when there is no road access and should co-operate by taking their garbage away with them (even if containers are provided). A reef which dries at low tide extends over 100 yards to

When Pirates Cove is too crowded skippers sometimes hold over in the more exposed anchorage at the south end of DeCourcy Island.

the northwest from the eastern side of the cove and is located about 100 yards south of the first dinghy float. This reef can become troublesome if a strong northwesterly wind is blowing through the cove and anchors are dragging. In crowded conditions alternative anchorage is possible just north of the small islands at the entrance or in two small bays at the south end of De Courcy in Ruxton Pass. These bays are exceptionally beautiful with fine white shell beaches and overhanging arbutus limbs. Sandstone caverns indent the point separating the bays.

12   Ruxton Island

Ruxton Island has been subdivided into over 200 lots (as has De Courcy), but fortunately few have been built upon and the island is still largely undeveloped. An overgrown road encircles the island passing several water pumps at strategic locations. While there are several bays suitable for fair weather anchorage,

At one time the peninsula at the head of Boat Harbour was used as a shipping point for coal from the Nanaimo coal fields.

White shell beaches like this one on the reef in Herring Bay, Ruxton Island, are found throughout the Gulf Islands.

the best is Herring Bay at the northwest end of the island. This bay is partially protected by drying reefs, but strong northerly winds can make the anchorage unsafe. Several small craft were reported to be wrecked in this bay after the infamous 1975 Easter storm. A small cove on the west coast of the island is filled with mooring buoys and open to winds and seas from the southwest as well as being very shallow.

13 Whaleboat Marine Park

Whaleboat Island, only seven acres in size, was established as a marine park in 1981. Temporary anchorage is possible behind a five-foot drying rock between Whaleboat Island and Ruxton Island.

14 Pylades Island

Pylades Island is steep-sided and does not afford good anchorage except in a small shallow patch at the northeast end. This island was named after HMS *Pylades*, 21 guns, on this station from 1859 to 1862 and commanded by Captain Michael De Courcy. Other islands in the De Courcy Group were named after junior officers aboard the *Pylades*.

15 Boat Harbour

Boat Harbour was once known as Flewett's Harbour after a marine engineer who lived here and operated a steam launch in the Nanaimo area in the 1870s. Coal was shipped from the peninsula near the head of the harbour where the remains of a grey slag pile, the old wharf, a huge sailing vessel's anchor and an abandoned railway line can still be seen. This railway line right-of-way is now protected as a recreational reserve. Although the harbour is fairly open to the east, good anchorage is possible in fair weather behind Reynolds Point or just off the private floats at the south end of the harbour. A miniature cannon — used by Mr. Kenary, an earlier resident, to "welcome" visitors, can still be seen near the tip of Flewett Point. Just south of Flewett Point, Pylades Drive provides access from the upland onto a sand and gravel pocket beach. About a mile inland is the Crow and Gate, one of the first and finest of Vancouver Island's country pubs.

16 Cedar

North of Boat Harbour the coastline is fairly shallow and fringed with drying sandbanks. Opposite Round Island one finds the tiny settlement of Cedars-by-the-Sea with a paved launching ramp and sandy beach. This attractive, pastoral area was once the headquarters for the Aquarian Foundation, before Brother Twelve sought more privacy and moved his colony onto the De Courcy Islands.

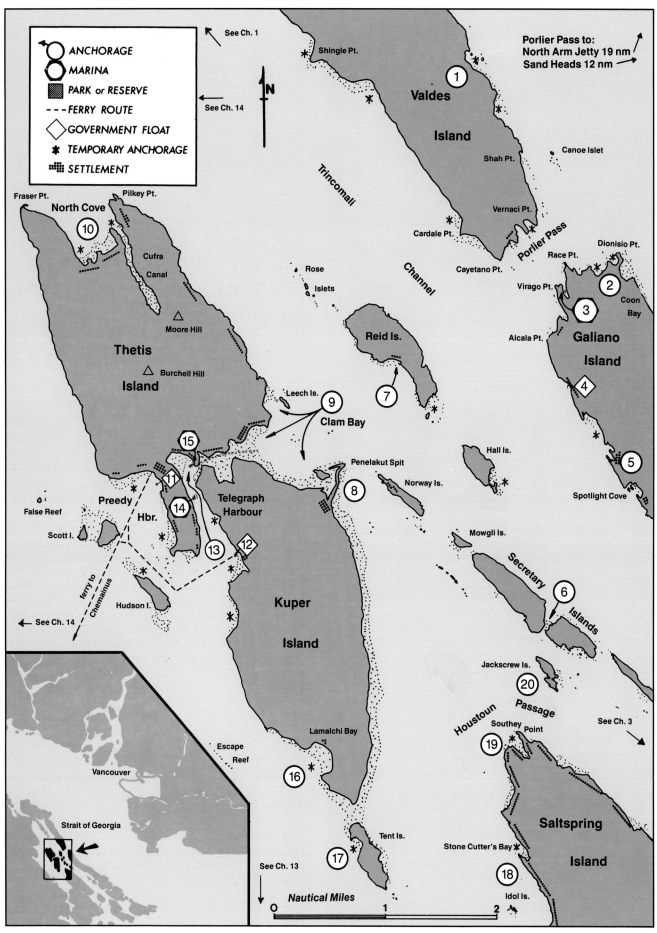

Porlier Pass to:
North Arm Jetty 19 nm
Sand Heads 12 nm

ANCHORAGE
MARINA
PARK or RESERVE
- - - **FERRY ROUTE**
◇ **GOVERNMENT FLOAT**
✳ **TEMPORARY ANCHORAGE**
▦ **SETTLEMENT**

N

Shingle Pt.

① Valdes

Canoe Islet

Shah Pt.

Island

Vernaci Pt.

Cardale Pt.

Porlier Pass

Dionisio Pt.

Fraser Pt.   Pilkey Pt.
North Cove
⑩

Cayetano Pt.

Race Pt.

② Coon Bay

Cufra
Canal

Virago Pt.

③

Moore Hill

Galiano

Rose
Islets

Alcala Pt.

Island

Thetis

Reid Is.

④

Burchell Hill

Leech Is.

⑨

⑦

Island

Clam Bay

⑮

Penelakut Spit

Hall Is.

⑤

Spotlight Cove

⑪

Preedy

Telegraph
Harbour

⑧

Norway Is.

False Reef

Hbr.

⑭

Scott I.

⑬

⑫

Mowgli Is.

Secretary

Kuper

⑥

ferry to
Chemainus

Hudson I.

Islands

Island

Jackscrew Is.

⑳

Houstoun   Passage

See Ch. 3

Lamalchi Bay

Southey Point

⑲

Escape
Reef

Vancouver

⑯

Stone Cutter's Bay

Saltspring

Strait of Georgia

Tent Is.

Idol Is.

⑰

⑱

Island

Nautical Miles

0   1   2

Not to be used for navigation

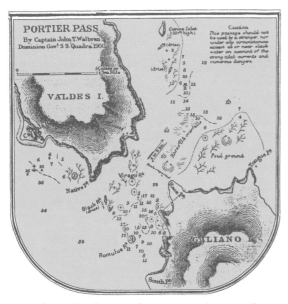

CHAPTER TWO

Early chart of Porlier Pass by Captain John T. Walbran.

Porlier Pass

Thetis and Kuper Islands

Porlier Pass leads between Galiano and Valdes islands to a group of smaller islands including Thetis and Kuper in the centre of the Gulf Island chain. On June 14, 1792 the Spanish explorers Valdes and Galiano were curious about this opening, which had been mapped as Boca de Porlier by their colleague Narvaez the year before. Suddenly, they were caught by the current and swept through the pass. It took them some time, fighting contrary winds and current, before they could extricate themselves from the Gulf Islands and return to the Strait of Georgia. A week later, Galiano and Valdes met Captain George Vancouver off Point Grey and established a strong friendship with him. They decided to combine forces to continue their exploration of the Strait of Georgia and circumnavigation of Vancouver Island together. It's sad that these two captains, who were to rise in the Spanish navy and become senior captains in the Battle of Trafalgar in 1805, were to lose both their ships and their lives at the hands of the Royal Navy. In 1858 the two islands separated by Porlier Pass were named in their honour by Royal Navy hydrographers.

Winds & Tides

While wind strengths in the Gulf Islands are considerably moderated during the summer months, this particular area does experience the occasional "Qualicum" type wind. This is a very strong westerly which blows off the Vancouver Island shore with little warning and is most common in spring or autumn. Generally, the area is noted for its dry, hot weather in the summer months with many calms and light winds. Stronger winds are often channelled by the surrounding topography, with northwesterlies bringing good weather and southeasterlies generally presaging a storm.

Currents run up to nine knots at spring tides through rock-infested Porlier Pass or Cowichan Gap, as it was also known by early settlers. Porlier Pass should be entered close to slack water, especially with spring tidal streams or when strong winds are likely to pile up dangerous seas at the entrance. It is best to line up the two lighthouses on Race Point and Virago Point, and to pass these lighthouses about 200 yards off the Galiano shore. Most of the dangerous rocks are on the Valdes side of the pass, with the exception of rocks 100 yards southwest of Virago Point and Race Point (Boscowitz Rock). Romulus Rock has had the top two fathoms removed by blasting.

Fishing

Because of the amount of feed churned up by the rapidly rushing waters, Porlier Pass is one of the best fishing areas in the Gulf Islands. Blueback fishing is good from April, especially around the bellbuoy at the east end of pass. Mooching for chinook peaks in August; bucktailing or trolling for coho is good in July.

CHARTS
3310 — Sheets 2, 3 and 4 (1:40,000)
3442 — NORTH PENDER ISLAND to THETIS
    ISLAND (1:40,000)
3473 — PORLIER PASS (1:12,000)
3477 — Plan of TELEGRAPH HARBOUR and
    PREEDY HARBOUR (1:15,000)

1 Valdes Island

Most of Valdes Island's few residents live along the outer shoreline south of Starvation Bay (Detwiller Point) and moor their boats in tiny coves which are somewhat protected from northerly seas by offshore reefs and islets. There is often a prevailing southward flowing current along this shore (strongest on the tidal ebb, a back eddy on the flood) which kicks up a rough sea in a southeasterly.

The inner shorelines of both Valdes and Galiano islands are noted for their remarkable sandstone galleries and caves, both above and below the water. Temporary anchorage is possible along the inner shoreline of Valdes close to three wide sand beaches which surround Blackberry, Shingle and Cardale points. These beaches are popular for swimming and picnicking and are the haunt of "Crazy Pete" and Misty, his faithful pointer. Pete is notable for his 10 motorcycles, pink-ribboned straw hat and knowledge of island history. He also acts as unofficial caretaker, watching over native burial grounds near locally-named Strawberry Point. Some of them have been desecrated by tourists and others searching for artefacts. Please remember that all visitors have a legal and moral responsibility to ensure that archaeological remains, as well as natural and historical features of value, are left undisturbed in this country (Cole).

Wrecks In Porlier Pass

There have been many shipwrecks in the vicinity of Porlier Pass as a result of the rocks, swift currents, occasional fogs and the steep seas which often pile up when a strong wind meets an opposing tide. Virago and Romulus rocks were named after the vessels which inadvertently discovered them by striking or grounding — HM Paddle Sloop of War Virago in 1853, and the German steamer *Romulus* in 1893. Among the wrecks were the schooner *Victoria Packet*, which disappeared without a trace in 1865. The 190-foot steamer *Del Norte* was carried onto the submerged reef south of Canoe Islet by a strong flood tide in 1868 while attempting to back out of the pass because of thick fog. A white-and-red can buoy here can be used for moorage while divers explore the wreck which is marked by a commemorative plaque. The steamtug *Peggy McNeil* went down in a boiling rip tide in 1923 while attempting to pull two scows through the pass. Only one of her crew of six survived, by climbing onto the bell buoy and then swimming to one of the scows. The 105-foot tug *Point Grey*, which slammed onto Virago Rock in the centre of the pass in dense fog in 1949, was visible until 1963 when a southeast gale swept her into deeper water. These wrecks are all described in more detail by Fred Rogers in *Shipwrecks of British Columbia*.

Opposite: Anchorage at Dionisio Point (Galiano Island) affords ready access to warm water swimming at Coon Bay (top left). Dionisio Point was named after the captain of 18th century Spanish vessel Sutil.

Canoe and Rose Islets

Rose Islets, to the northwest of Reid Island and Canoe Islet, just outside Porlier Pass, are two ecological reserves established in 1971 to protect representative samples of marine wildlife, particularly 212 nests of the double-crested cormorant. In the last few years these magnificent birds, which measure up to three feet in total length, have moved from this area but there is hope that they may return (Wayne Campbell 1985). Interested observers may have inadvertently caused the destruction of the colony. Even just approaching the islets by boat may startle the birds from their nests and expose the contents to predation by other birds. The cormorants' nests are particularly vulnerable from April to August. Please observe from a distance.

Porlier Pass between Galiano and Valdes islands provides access from the Strait of Georgia to islands in the centre of the Gulf Islands chain.

2 Dionisio Point

This point, and the one at the other end of the pass, were named after Commander Dionisio Alcala Galiano, captain of the *Sutil*. Good anchorage is afforded just within Dionisio Point or in the bay to the west, protected from southeasterly seas and out of the main flow of the current, but completely open to Georgia Strait northerlies. Coon Bay, a popular beach to the southeast, dries completely at low water, but at high tide offers warm bathing waters in an almost totally enclosed lagoon. Many tide pools offer opportunity to view an outstanding variety of invertebrate marine life. There are grassy bluffs, open meadows with arbutus-garry oak and juniper, and unique sandstone rock formations. Several driftwood shacks used by squatters and fishermen used to line the shores around Dionisio Point and Coon Bay. Some of the cabins were over 50 years old, originally built by Ladysmith loggers and coal miners who used them as temporary abodes when the fishing was hot in Porlier

Pass, but these buildings have been removed in order to open up the area to the public for camping and picnicking. Unfortunately, unrestricted road access through MacMillan-Bloedel property and a lack of maintenance have led to some degradation. Many hope that this beautiful area will one day become a park.

It is possible to hike from Coon Bay along the east coast all the way down to Whaler Bay at the south end of the island (Chapter 4). Certain sections can only be hiked at low tide and a mile south of Coon Bay there are three secluded beaches protected behind drying rocky spits (Molar).

3   Lighthouse Bay

Lighthouse Bay, formerly occupied by the Porlier Pass Marina, provides temporary shelter out of the tidal stream. A trail and cliff-side boardwalk constructed by the Ministry of Transport ("Use only at

At high water it is possible to row a dinghy across the shallow sand bank which joins the Secretary Islands in Trincomali Channel. Jackscrew Island is in the background.

your own risk") lead around the bay past the lighthouse on Race Point toward Dionisio Point and Coon Bay. Alcala Resort (539-5720) is located on Alcala Point and provides accommodation for scuba diving groups, plus boat charters and an air station. Porlier Pass is recognized as one of the top areas for diving in British Columbia and features basket stars, soft corals, underwater caves and up to 350 sea lions in the winter.

4   North Galiano

The northwestern shore of Galiano Island is broken in several places by tiny coves with several small projecting peninsulas and islets. Although moderately settled, the coves are interesting to explore by shallow-draught boat, but do not afford good anchorage as they are completely open to winds from the southwest quadrant. The public wharf at North Galiano is supported by many cross beams and pilings revealing the exposed nature of this landing. A small

50-foot float has space for one boat along the outside face. A large boulder which dries about two feet is located just off the northeastern corner of the float. At the head of the wharf is a launching ramp and the Spanish Hills General Store (539-2352) providing groceries, hardware, fishing supplies and a post office.

5   Spotlight Cove

This cove was once used as a log dump and booming ground. The next cove to the north contains pilings which you can secure to temporarily. Nearby is the Salishan Resort (539-2689), which provides a mooring buoy (shallow), gift shop, housekeeping cottages, showers and small boats.

6   Secretary Islands

These islands are joined together by a drying sand bank. Good anchorage is available in depths averaging two fathoms between the two islands, but beware of a rock pinnacle just off the north shore. At high water you can take your dinghy through the passage to explore the deserted farm with its old orchard and grassy overgrown meadows on South Secretary or to Jackscrew Island a few hundred yards to the south.

7   Reid Island

This island was originally bought for $2.60 in 1852 by Joe Silvey, the first Portugese in Canada to be given British citizenship. Queen Victoria gave him the fishing rights between Dodd Narrows and Sansum Narrows and he established salteries on the island. Although privately owned and subdivided, this wooded island is still largely undeveloped and natural. A few tiny chinks in the shoreline could be used for temporary anchorage at high water. An anchorage at the south end of the island carries three fathoms at low water and is protected from southerly seas by an encircling ring of drying rocks and islets, and by Hall Island, half a mile to the southeast. The rocks and islets are a provincial recreation reserve and also serve as a frequent haulout for harbour seals and sea lions. The best anchorage, with fair protection from southeasterlies, faces Clam Bay. The remains of a Japanese saltery in this bight is interesting to explore.

Mowgli, Norway and Hall Islands

A brass eagle which survived a Tokyo fire in the 1920s guards the shore of Norway Island (Van der Ree). Mowgli Island was previously owned by Annamarie Helene Menger-Morgan who lived in isolation on Hall Island from 1907 to 1933 and who was known as the "Mystery Duchess, Hermit of the Isle of Echoes."

Thetis and Kuper Islands

Thetis and Kuper islands — named after the 36-gun frigate HMS *Thetis* and her commander, Captain Augustus Kuper — are situated close together but are far apart in character and history. The two islands are separated by a dredged boat passage and by Telegraph Harbour, one of the safest anchorages in the Gulf Islands and the centre for many coastal explorations.

The harbour provides a convenient place to return to after spending the day exploring the many coves, islands and islets in adjacent waters.

Thetis Island is moderately settled with approximately 200 permanent residents. Early records reveal that of 77 residents in 1914, over 35 joined the services upon outbreak of World War I, seven were killed and only a handful returned to the island. Two small hills, Burchell and Moore, rise from the centre of the island and provide vistas north toward Valdes and the De Courcy group and south over the relatively flat-lying Kuper Island. Legend has it that caves beneath these hills extend under Trincomali Channel to Shingle Point on Valdes Island and were used as an escape route by Indians fleeing raids by the Southern Kwakiutl.

Kuper Island is the home of the once fierce and warlike Lamalcha, Yekoloa and Penelakut bands of the Cowichan Indians. Kuper is one of the few reserves which was large and isolated enough to retain a more or less separate identity in the face of encroaching white civilization. Many who have passed by the thickly forested shoreline have been thankful that here at least was one island which was still relatively natural, preserved in its undeveloped state by the first inhabitants of the land.

Cufra Canal cuts almost a mile into the heart of northern Thetis Island; it dries almost completely at low water.

41

Above: The boat passage between Clam Bay and Telegraph Harbour is best transited on a rising tide. Below: Penelakut Spit protects Clam Bay from the brunt of southeasterly seas.

8   Penelakut Spit

This recurved spit, known for a long time as White Spit owing to its clam-shell origin, protects Clam Bay from southeasterly seas. The village of Penelakut was the scene of one of the last unofficial potlatches in 1907, when hundreds of natives gathered to celebrate and give away their possessions. This native village is typical of many on the coast, with several small houses surrounding the church with its tall white spire; but unlike many others, it is still inhabited by a thriving community of approximately 200 individuals. The people are hospitable to visitors, but naturally resent being bothered by the merely curious and

Preceding page: Looking southwest over marinas in Telegraph Harbour; Boat Passage between Thetis and Kuper islands leads off to the left.

those tourists who encroach on their traditional oyster and clam beaches.

9   Clam Bay

Sheltered anchorage is possible in different parts of this bay, but beware of Centre Reef and Rocket Shoal between Penelakut Spit and Leech Island. The boat passage from Clam Bay to Telegraph Harbour should only be attempted with caution on a rising tide as depths are uneven, due to irregular silting, and the passage is curved, making it difficult to stay in the centre. The passage is periodically dredged, but dries approximately one to three feet above chart datum. Pass to the north of the marker piling at the west end of the passage before entering Telegraph Harbour.

10   North Cove

Excellent protection is offered from southerly winds, but the cove is completely exposed to the northwest. Shoreline farms and Pioneer Pacific Camp extend back from the head of the cove. At the eastern end a long, narrow arm — known locally as Cufra Canal — cuts one mile into the interior of Thetis Island. This beautiful inlet can be explored by canoe or dinghy, but since it dries almost completely it is only suitable for temporary anchorage at or about high water. Stone breakwaters at the entrance to Cufra Canal and just inside Fraser Point provide protection from northwesterly seas for moorage areas used by local residents.

11   Preedy Harbour

Good temporary anchorage is available at the north end of the harbour, although the area is moderately exposed to westerlies; and at the south end, sheltered behind a drying reef. Car ferries from Chemainus on Vancouver Island dock several times a day near the head of the harbour. Just south of the ferry dock is a public wharf with a small float on its north side for landing from small craft (150 feet of berthage space for three to five boats). On shore one can find the Capernwray Bible Centre and Overbury Farm Resort (246-9769) set in beautiful pastoral meadows. Camp Columbia, west of Burchell Hill, is operated by the Anglican Church as a summer camp and retreat centre. Hudson, Dayman and Scott islands, all privately owned, were named after junior officers aboard HMS *Thetis*. The centre of Hudson Island has been bulldozed flat to provide an airstrip extending the length of the island so that the lucky owners can have easy access to their Gulf Island paradise. A reef at the north end provides partial protection for a small anchorage area.

12   Kuper Island

A public wharf and ferry dock for passengers serves as the main access to Kuper Island. The harbour was once dominated by the impressive four-storey Indian residential school built of red brick at the turn of the century and demolished in October, 1985. This site was once the location of the Yoochelas Indian village. Temporary anchorage with good shelter from stormy

The view east over North Cove at the upper end of Thetis Island. Entrance to Cufra Canal is at centre top in the photo.

Picturesque Camp Columbia (Thetis Island) is a summer camp and retreat operated by the Anglican Church.

southeasters is possible in two wide bays just south of the public wharf, but both bays are open to the wash from power boats entering and leaving Telegraph Harbour.

13 Telegraph Harbour

Good anchorage is available near the head of Telegraph Harbour, safe from all dangerous winds and seas. In the summer months this harbour is often the most crowded in the Gulf Islands affording limited anchorage space. There are two large marinas here, each offering an excellent level of service. Rather than favouring one or the other, why not visit both?

14 Thetis Island Marina

Thetis Island Marina (246-3464). A breakwater protects moored boats from the wash of power cruisers on their way up the harbour. Fuel, repairs, moorage, bicycle rentals, charters, picnic area with barbecues, playground, showers, laundromat, licensed restaurant and a well-stocked store are provided.

15 Telegraph Harbour Marina

Telegraph Harbour Marina (246-9511) provides fuel, moorage, charts, bicycle rentals, laundry, showers, cafe and groceries. There is also a playground with teeter-totters, swings and other conveniences and amusements.

16 Lamalchi Bay

Fair temporary anchorage is possible in this bay which dries almost completely at low water and is open to the west. A memorial marks what was once a populous Indian village. In 1863 the village was bombarded by the gunboat *Forward* when the inhabitants

Above: Temporary anchorage is possible in Lamalchi Bay at the southwestern end of Kuper Island.

Left: Though Tent Island was once leased as a public marine park, permission must now be obtained from the Kuper Indians before camping ashore.

refused to disclose the whereabouts of the murderers of an American and his daughter on Saturna Island. The Indians fled to the opposite end of the island where they have stayed ever since. Cannon balls are still to be found ashore. In the 1880s a 100-acre tract of land (the only private property on the island) was established as a base for The Company for the Propagation of the Gospel in New England and the Ports adjacent in America. This land eventually became a farm well-known as Folded Hills and in the 1970s was used as the base for the Gestalt Touch Therapy Institute and an ecological centre.

17 Tent Island

This beautiful island is part of the Kuper Island Indian Reserve and is joined to it by a tombolo covered at high water. As the name implies, the island has long been a favourite overnight camping spot. Although the island was once a marine park, leased on a year to year basis, permission should now be obtained from the Kuper Indians before camping ashore. The main anchorage, safe in fair weather, is completely exposed to the west and a midnight wind shift occasionally sends boats scurrying for shelter to Telegraph Harbour. North Reef provides good opportunities for scuba diving because of minimal currents and generally good visibility in Stuart Channel.

18 Idol Island

Idol Island, at one time an Indian ceremonial bury-

ing ground, is now a park reserve. It is interesting to note the large number of other small islands similar to Idol Island which were used by the natives to bury their dead. Other examples are Coffin Island (Ladysmith), Burial Islet (Sansum Narrows), Senanus Island (Saanich Inlet), Deadman Island (Ganges), and Coffin Islet (Victoria Harbour).

19 Southey Point

The northern end of Saltspring Island is indented with several nooks such as Stone Cutters Bay and Southey Bay. These nooks could all provide temporary anchorage with good protection from southeasterly winds but all are surrounded by private homes and are filled with private moorings. Southey Bay is protected from all winds except northwesterlies. This area was the home of one of Canada's least-known heroes, Toronto-born Sir Charles Wright, an eminent scientist who was a hand-picked member of Scott's Antarctic Expedition, and was first to find the bodies of Scott's party after their ill-fated trek to the South Pole in 1911. Sir Charles Wright died in 1975 at the age of 88. His daughter Pat, a well-known wildlife artist still resides here. A boat launching ramp is located at Southey Point and two beautiful white shell beaches are located southeast of the point.

20 Jackscrew Island

The name Jackscrew is reported to be derived from its peculiar shape — miniature ridges and valleys are partially offset from one another like the threads of a jackscrew. The old home has been deserted by the original owner and the island is now looked after by caretakers. Visitors have reported strange feelings of uneasiness on this island, possibly the result of its earlier use as an Indian burial ground.

47

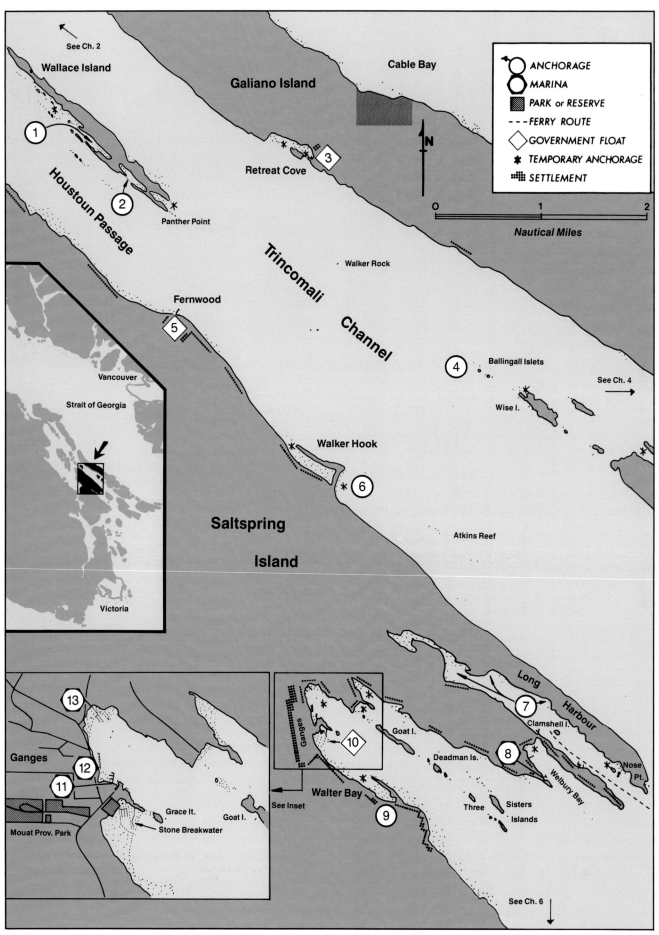

Wallace Island

See Ch. 2

Galiano Island

Cable Bay

ANCHORAGE

MARINA

PARK or RESERVE

- - - FERRY ROUTE

GOVERNMENT FLOAT

TEMPORARY ANCHORAGE

SETTLEMENT

N

0   1   2

Nautical Miles

①

Houstoun Passage

②

Retreat Cove

③

Panther Point

Walker Rock

Trincomali

Fernwood

⑤

Channel

④ Ballingall Islets

See Ch. 4

Wise I.

Vancouver

Strait of Georgia

Walker Hook

⑥

Victoria

Saltspring

Atkins Reef

Island

Long Harbour

⑦

Clamshell I.

⑬

Goat I.

⑩

⑧

Nose Pt.

Ganges

⑫

Deadman Is.

Welbury Bay

⑪

Ganges

See Inset

Walter Bay

Grace It.

Goat I.

Mouat Prov. Park

Stone Breakwater

⑨

Three   Sisters

Islands

See Ch. 6

Not to be used for navigation

48

Black settlers on Saltspring Island set up one of the first schools in British Columbia in the 1850s.

Trincomali Channel

Galiano to Ganges

Archaeological evidence has shown that the Gulf Islands, rich in wildlife and seafood, were of great significance in the food-gathering economy of the native Indians. Numerous bays and coves provided shelter, broad beaches gave easy landing from canoes, and the grassy knolls and meadows behind the beaches were ideal for temporary campsites.

There were few permanent settlements. In summer the islands were shared by groups of Cowichan and Saanich Indians from Vancouver Island, and Musqueams, Tsawwassens and Salish from the Fraser delta. Apart from the odd skirmish, these groups lived side by side in relative harmony. However, when raiding parties of Haidas and Bella Bellas would swoop down from the north ferocious battles were fought. The last of these battles was fought in Ganges Harbour on July 4, 1860, when several Bella Bellas were led into a trap and massacred by the local Cowichans.

Today many of the natural attractions that existed in Indian times are drawing similar invasions, this time from the south. While the battles for moorage and anchorage space are not quite as bloody as the earlier ones, they are no less frenzied, especially on sunny summer weekends.

These cruising waters are also ideal for the kayaker or canoeist — as long as he watches the weather. It is possible to carry your canoe onto a Gulf Islands ferry for the same fare as a foot passenger. From the island terminals there are a variety of sheltered paddling waters readily accessible, with numerous beaches and tiny, uncrowded coves to explore. Camping areas may be found near the top of a beach at neap tides, or where fir and salal give way to arbutus, garry oak and grassy backshores. Developed campsites are available at numerous parks.

The best time for paddling is in the spring and fall. If you choose July and August you will have to contend with the wake of many yachts powering their way at top speed in a massive invasion of the islands. Spring and autumn, while slightly cooler than summer, provide opportunity for savouring the solitude and quiet of undisturbed nature, and for observing migrating wildlife. It is possible in late autumn or early spring to spend a whole weekend in this area and see only B.C. ferries and the odd fishboat.

Winds

When the barometer is falling, southeasterly winds in the Strait of Georgia generally indicate that a depression with strong winds and rain may be coming. However, during good weather, particularly near the southern end of the Strait of Georgia, a southeasterly wind in the afternoon may also be a "dry southeaster", the result of daily heating of the Saltspring and Vancouver Island landmass drawing in winds from the Strait of Juan de Fuca.

CHARTS
3310 — Sheet 3 — EAST POINT to PORLIER
      PASS (1:40,000)
3442 — NORTH PENDER ISLAND to THETIS
      ISLAND (1:40,000)
3470 — Plan of GANGES HARBOUR and LONG
      HARBOUR (1:18,000)

1   Wallace Island

Wallace Island (formerly Narrow Island) was named after Captain Wallace Houston, RN, of HMS *Trincomalee*, a sailing frigate which served in these waters from 1853 to 1856. She was built in Bombay in 1819 and named after a river in Ceylon (Sri Lanka). Princess Harbour is a protected anchorage on Wallace Island, typical of many coves in the Gulf Islands, with a long narrow sandstone peninsula giving protection and a feeling of almost complete isolation. Nearby is the former home of David Conover, an American who "discovered" Marilyn Monroe and bought this island a number of years ago. Conover turned the island into a resort, wrote several prosaic books about his life — including *Once Upon an Island, One Man's Island, Finding Marilyn* and *Sitting on a Salt Spring* — and lived happily off the proceeds for many years. Most of the island is now owned by a band of Seattle teachers. Chivers Point and a point at Princess Harbour have been dedicated as reserves for public access. Unfortunately, several large signs reading "No trespassing" and "Any dogs caught chasing our sheep will be shot" warn anyone from attempting to explore ashore.

2   Conover Cove

This cove is a very good natural anchorage with the entrance partially protected from westerly seas by a dangerous, narrow reef running parallel to Wallace

A long, narrow sandstone peninsula provides protection for yachts overnighting in Princess Bay on Wallace Island.

Island a few hundred yards offshore. Conover Cove was once the location of the Wallace Island Resort. Temporary anchorage is also possible in a small bay inside Panther Point, which is exposed to the southeast and dries almost completely. At low water it is still sometimes possible to glimpse the outline of the U.S. clipper *Panther* which drifted ashore in a southeasterly gale and sank on Panther reef over 100 years ago.

3   Retreat Cove

The steep bluffs on Galiano's western shore are breached in only a few places. One of these, a tiny bight with wooded Retreat Island in the middle, is named Retreat Cove and affords good temporary anchorage immediately northwest and east of Retreat Island. A public float with 100 feet of berthage space is located in the eastern end of the cove. In a strong westerly wind this cove is not a safe retreat as it is dangerously exposed and many boats have taken a beating when caught unawares. Retreat Cove was once the site of an extensive Japanese herring saltery — large sheds and wharves were constructed just before the last war, but never used. The Pink Geranium, a unique restaurant located along Porlier Pass Road,

50

is a closely guarded secret of Galiano Islanders (phone 539-2477). A hiking trail near here leads across the island to Pebble Beach on Cable Bay.

4 Ballingall Islets

South of Retreat Cove lies Walker Rock, the beginning of an offshore ridge which emerges again as the Ballingall Islets and grows to become Wise and Parker islands, eventually joining up with Galiano to form the highest part of that island (1,121 feet). The Ballingall Islets (named after Second Lieutenant Alexander Campbell Ballingall of HMS *Trincomalee*) although only one acre in size, have been colonized by a variety of sea birds. Vancouver Island author Lyn Hancock described the nests in the following words:

> I for one appreciated the artistry of the bulky stick nests which sprouted starkly from the old dried and whitened Rocky Mountain juniper trees. Thousands of individual sticks had been expertly interwoven between existing branches to fix the bulky nests to the trees. One nest, complete with fishing lure, was actually reinforced with hundreds of feet of fishing line, probably scavenged from a helpless fisherman. The first cormorants found breeding on the Ballingall Islets were seen in the early twenties. By 1939 the pioneering tree-nesting colony had increased to 33 nests as still existed in 1967.

Here is one of the few places on our coast where double-crested cormorants find enough isolation and natural protection to nest and breed. The islets have been designated a provincial nature park, the second to be established on the B.C. coast — the first being Mittlenatch Island in the northern straits. In 1984 the number of nesting cormorants was greatly reduced by predation after cormorants were scared from their nests. This happens when visitors approach too closely during the nesting season, April to August. Please observe from a distance.

Saltspring Island

Saltspring Island (locals prefer *Salt Spring* Island), largest of all the Gulf Islands with over 77 miles of shoreline, was also one of the first agricultural communities in the new colony of Vancouver Island. The island was first known as Klaathem by the natives, then named Saltspring by officers of the Hudson's Bay Company for the brine pools near St. Mary Lake, one mile inland from Fernwood. There are about 14 brine pools in all, ranging from a few feet to almost a hundred feet in diameter and surrounded by marsh grass, sea blush and private property (Obee). In the last century Sir James Douglas referred to the island as Chuan, and the Royal Navy knew it as Admiral Island. In 1905 when the present name was officially adopted, the two words were joined together; but the local two-word usage of "Salt Spring" has persisted. The first permanent settlers were Negroes, who, while they had been technically freed from slavery, continued to suffer persecution in the "free" states. In the 1850s the Negro community in California sent a deputation to the Viceroy of Mexico and the Governor of British Columbia. Because of the welcoming reception they received from Sir James Douglas, they decided to emigrate, but before they came they drafted

A public float with 100 feet of wharfage is located in the eastern end of Retreat Cove, the site of a Japanese herring saltery before W.W. II.

Cormorant's stick-nests cling precariously to dead branches of juniper tree on Ballingall Islets, now a designated nature park. Please observe from a distance.

their own "Declaration of Independence" which included the following resolutions:

> Whereas we are fully convinced that the continued aim of the spirit and policy of our Mother Country is to oppress, degrade, and entrap us — we have therefore determined to seek an asylum in the land of strangers.
>
> Resolution (8): That we now unitedly cast our lots (after the toil and hardships that have wrung our sweat

and tears for centuries) in that land where bleeding humanity finds a balm, where philanthropy is crowned with royalty, slavery has laid aside its weapons, and the coloured American is unshackled; there in the lair of the Lion we will repose from the horrors of the past under the genial laws of the Queen of the Christian Isles.

(From an article by Judge F.W. Howay, originally published in *The British Columbia Historical Quarterly*, April 1939.)

The Negro community settled in the Fernwood area, set up the first regular school and played an active role in the island's development. Many Australians also came to the island in the 1860s after their luck had run out in the goldfields. In the next few decades people from various parts of the world who valued the isolation which island life brings, came to settle on Saltspring. In 1895 the first census recorded a population of 455, made up of: 160 English (mainly Canadian or Australian), 90 mixed-blood Indians, 50 Scots, 40 Negro Americans, 34 white Americans, 22 Portugese, 20 Irish, 13 Swedes, 10 Japanese, 6 Sandwich Islanders, 4 Germans, 2 Greeks, 2 Norwegians, 1 Egyptian and 1 Patagonian. Many of these early settlers were engaged in farming, which flourished on the islands in the nineteenth century when marine transport was considerably less expensive. Saltspring Island became famous for lamb, apples, peaches, dairy products and a variety of other farm products. Today over half of the Saltspring population of about 7,000 is settled around the Ganges area in the central part of the island where the weekly Saturday Farmers Market features island produce, crafts and artwork.

5 Fernwood

The northeast coast of Saltspring is low and featureless with a few beaches extending out into Houstoun Passage. The Last Resort (537-4111) offers waterfront cottages and camping and opportunities for kayaking, windsurfing and wildlife observation here. At Fernwood Point a pier stretches out over the tidal flats and a small public float provides a landing for small craft (180 feet of berthage space for three to four boats). A general store and gas station is located at the head of the pier. St. Mary Lake, with several resorts and opportunity for freshwater trout fishing, is one mile inland from Fernwood.

6 Walker Hook

A beautiful and relatively isolated beach, popular for *au naturel* sunbathing, fronts this sandy isthmus that joins a narrow wooded peninsula to Saltspring Island. This is a marvelous place for wildflowers, sea birds, song birds, eagles and viewing local scenery. Only temporary anchorage is available owing to shallow depths within the hook and exposure to southeasterly and northwesterly winds. The hook is, however, the only place on the northeast coast of Saltspring Island which offers some degree of protec-

Preceding page: Temporary anchorage can be found behind the islets just inside Nose Point at the Entrance to Long Harbour, Saltspring Island.

Walker Hook on the northeastern shore of Saltspring Island is the location of this remote and inviting sand beach. Temporary anchorage only.

tion when seas are running high in Trincomali Channel, and is a welcome stop, especially for canoeists and naturalists. Access by road is discouraged.

7 Long Harbour

This intriguing inlet, which extends northwest for about two and a half miles, provides abundant anchorage, safe from all winds except strong southeasterlies. Some protection from southeasterly seas is afforded by Prevost Island and the narrowness of the entrance which tends to dissipate the force of any waves entering the harbour. Just inside Nose Point a group of islets protects a tiny anchorage from the wake of boats on their way to the Royal Vancouver Yacht Club outstation (537-5033, members only) across the harbour.

Clamshell Island, located near the middle of the harbour facing the ferry wharf, has an abundance of prickly pear cacti, common on the steep, rocky ledges of the Gulf Islands (Jamie Little). The ferry terminal provides twice-daily service to Tsawwassen and connection with other Gulf Islands. It is possible to launch cartop boats alongside the ferry wharf or, in more shelter, from the head of Quebec Lane. At high water you can row your dinghy from a large bay near the head of the harbour through a narrow passage to a completely enclosed lagoon.

8 Welbury Bay

Spindrift Resort (537-5311) provides cottages and cabins here. Temporary anchorage with protection from all directions except southeast is available at the head of the bay. There is a portage for canoes and small boats between the head of Welbury Bay and Long Harbour.

Ganges Harbour

Ganges Harbour provides abundant anchorage, safe

Ganges Harbour

from all winds and seas except southeasterlies. The Chain Islands, with many rocks and drying reefs between them, line the northeastern shore. They include the three Sister islands, Twilight Island (located just inside the Second Sister and also known as "Islands 86" or "Lottery" Island), Deadman islands (so named because they were used as a mass burial ground for the Bella Bellas who were massacred in 1860) and Goat Island. At the head of the harbour is the town of Ganges, largest settlement in the Gulf Islands, and named for HMS *Ganges*, 84 guns, the last sailing line-of-battle ship in active commission in the Royal Navy. She was built of teak in Bombay in 1821 and served for almost 150 years, ending her years as a training ship for naval cadets.

9 Walter Bay

A low sand spit provides shelter from southeasterly seas for limited temporary anchorage and the floats of the Salt Spring Sailing Club (537-5112), which hosts several regattas including the annual Round-the-Island race in May.

10 Ganges Public Floats

Entrance into the well protected boat basin west of Grace Islet is sometimes perplexing for those unfamiliar with the area. The public wharf and floats are

The Ganges boat basin provides ready access to nearby stores, craft shops and restaurants. The town is the largest settlement in the Gulf Islands.

hidden behind the breakwater which extends south from Grace Peninsula and only the presence of sailboat and fishboat masts indicates its location. The narrow approach is marked by day beacons. Over 2000 feet of berthage space provides temporary moorage for over 80 small craft (more are often accommodated by tying alongside). Nearby there is a concrete boat launching ramp. A boardwalk promenade and bandshell are located along the water's edge, beneath Centennial Park. The town of Ganges offers a variety of services and facilities — interesting craft shops, general stores, grocery stores, hotels, restaurants, churches, etc. — all a short distance from the docks. Be sure to pick up the latest copy of the weekly *Gulf Islands Driftwood* for an entertaining review of local happenings. Mouat Provincial Park, behind the town, provides limited camping (15 sites) and picnicking (6 tables). The Bittancourt Heritage House (537-5302) includes a museum of early pioneering artifacts and is located on Rainbow Road. At the head of the wharf is an Information Centre (537-5252), Harbour Manager (537- 5711), public washrooms and a Coast Guard Station. Centennial Park, built on land reclaimed from the sea in 1966, hosts a Farmers Market with fresh vegetables, homemade bread, pastries and local handicrafts every Saturday morning. The Park also contains a war memorial and a stone cairn inscribed:

> HMS *Ganges*. This cairn with seat was erected July 1st, 1967, by HMS *Ganges* Chapter I.O.D.E.. Inset is the seat back from the captain's galley (or Gig) of HMS *Ganges*, the last sailing ship of the Royal Navy, after whom this harbour was named. She patrolled these waters 1857-1861.

One may ask why there was a need for such close protection by the Royal Navy when only a few hundred people lived here, but it must be remembered

The view southeast over the head of Ganges Harbour. Harbours End marina and Hastings House restaurant/Inn are in the foreground.

that this was the time of the San Juan boundary dispute and in addition, some of the local inhabitants were very afraid of the native Indians. Ganges Harbour had a history of Indian confrontations (usually skirmishes between different tribes). In 1862, while HM gunboat *Forward* was escorting some canoes filled with northern natives back to the north, they were fired upon by some local Cowichans at the entrance to Ganges Harbour. In *British Columbia Coast Names*), John T. Walbran notes:

> ... some of the shots passed unpleasantly close to the gunboat. Captain Lascelles stopped his vessel, cast off the canoes, sent an armed boat's crew on shore, who captured the rascals and brought them on board the gunboat, where they immediately received three dozen

lashes each, as a gentle reminder to keep their bullets at home in the future. It is recorded that this flogging exercised a very wholesome influence on other tribes along the coast, to whom the news was soon communicated.

It is also noted by Walbran that in 1862 the population of coastal natives was sadly decimated by smallpox, introduced by the white man.

11 The Wharf

Due north of the boat basin, on the other side of Grace Peninsula, lies a second public wharf, used mainly by cargo vessels. The fuel dock (537-5312) is located immediately south of the wharf and is exposed somewhat to southeasterlies. Floats for visiting boats are located north of the wharf. Floats for water taxi (537-2510) and float plane service (800-972-0212) are also located here. Just up from this dock is Mouat's General Store and a unique mall with many interesting craft and book shops. A fascinating display of early photographs of the harbour can be found in Mouat's store.

12 Ganges Marina

Moorage is available at this marina (537-5242) as well as fuel, rental boats, scuba equipment, air and fishing supplies.

13 Harbours End Marina

The Ross and Ganges Marine & Equipment (537-4202) here have a 2.5-ton hoist, marine ways and complete facilities for hull and engine repairs, as well as moorings and dry storage. The boatyard specializes in underwater salvage and repairs, dive boat charters and includes a scuba shop and ship's chandlery. The yard should be approached from the south as there are some offshore rocks (covered by less than six feet at chart datum) and a reef extending out from the shore, north of the floats, marked by two pilings. Nearby is the Harbour House Hotel (537-5571) with special rates for boaters, showers, laundry, a pub, lounge and restaurant and the Hastings House (537-2362), an exclusive country restaurant, bed and breakfast. The Hastings House estate comprises four historic buildings, including the original Hudson's Bay Company trading post, and is set in 25 acres of garden, pasture and woodland. The Manor House was modelled after a Sussex homestead and built in 1938 for Warren Hastings, a naval architect who needed an isolated retreat to work on secret designs for the Royal Navy. This retreat was not isolated enough, however, as his wife was befriended by a German-American girl who happened to be staying at the nearby Harbour House Hotel. Mrs. Hastings noticed tiny swastikas in the girl's bracelet and after the girl was questioned by local police, microfilms of Hastings' plans were found in her possession.

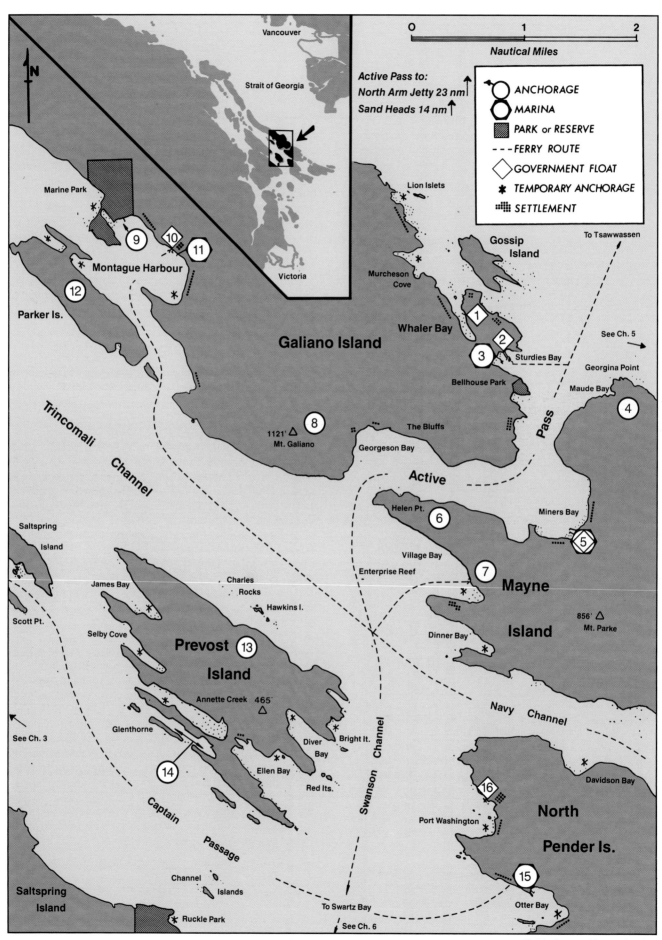

Vancouver

Strait of Georgia

Victoria

Active Pass to:
North Arm Jetty 23 nm ↑
Sand Heads 14 nm ↑

To Tsawwassen

0   1   2
Nautical Miles

ANCHORAGE
MARINA
PARK or RESERVE
--- FERRY ROUTE
GOVERNMENT FLOAT
* TEMPORARY ANCHORAGE
SETTLEMENT

Lion Islets

Gossip
Island

Murcheson
Cove

Marine Park

Montague Harbour

Parker Is.

(9)
(10)
(11)
(12)

Whaler Bay

(1)
(2)
(3)   Sturdies Bay

Bellhouse Park

See Ch. 5

Georgina Point

Maude Bay

(4)

Galiano Island

Trincomali

Channel

1121' △
Mt. Galiano

(8)

The Bluffs

Georgeson Bay

Active

Helen Pt.

(6)

Miners Bay

(5)

Saltspring

Island

James Bay

Charles
Rocks

Hawkins I.

Scott Pt.

Selby Cove

Prevost

Island   (13)

Village Bay

Enterprise Reef   (7)

Mayne

Island   856' △
Mt. Parke

Dinner Bay

Annette Creek   465
△

Glenthorne

(14)

Diver
Bay   Bright It.

Ellen Bay

Red Its.

Captain

Passage

Channel

Islands

Swanson   Channel

Navy   Channel

North

Port Washington

(16)

Davidson Bay

Pender Is.

See Ch. 3

Saltspring
Island

Ruckle Park

(15)

Otter Bay

To Swartz Bay

See Ch. 6

Not to be used for navigation

58

Mayne Island's Lady Constance Fawkes, "Lady of Culzean". (Watercolour by Colonel L.G. Fawkes, courtesy of J. Borradaile).

Active Pass

Montague Harbour, Prevost and North Pender Islands

Active Pass is one of the most constricted waterways in the Strait of Georgia, with regular ferry traffic passing within hundreds of feet of numerous coastal freighters, tankers and small fishing craft busily reaping their harvest at the entrances to the pass. Tidal currents run up to eight knots at springs, with a flood tide producing the most dangerous rips, so it is not the best place to develop engine trouble or to run out of wind. All small craft are strongly urged to stay out of the fairway when larger vessels are in the pass.

During spring and autumn migrations, Active Pass is a fascinating place for bird-watchers. It is a spectacular sight when thousands of birds — including ducks, gulls, terns, cormorants, ospreys, loons, murres and grebes come down to feed in the pass, resulting in the densest concentration of birds in the whole Gulf Islands. Up to 40 bald eagles have been observed at one time and there are seven nests, or eyries, near the tops of the highest trees in the pass. It is a common sight to see eagles circling overhead looking for fish churned up by the wake of the passing ferries. Occasionally the eagles will swoop down and pick up a fish which is being played by a fisherman. It has been estimated that there are 97 nesting pairs of bald eagles in the Canadian Gulf Islands, while in the adjacent San Juans only two pairs are known to produce young.

Fishing

The best salmon fishing is from June through August and mooching with cut plug herring is the favoured method. Helen Point is best fished on an ebb tide for coho. Miners Bay is a hot spot for chinooks at dusk. A big back eddy in Maude Bay is a good spot for chinooks on a flood tide and for jigging herring on slack tides. Gossip Island to Lion Islets is a consistent spot for coho and chinooks on both flood and ebb. Use Super Strip teaser or minnow and dodger. Special care must be taken to stay out of the way of all vessel traffic in the pass.

Galiano Island

This long, thin island has more shoreline in relation to land area than any other of the Gulf Islands. It is approximately 18 miles long and two miles wide, and reportedly receives less than 23 inches of rain a year, making it one of the driest (average is 30 inches in Gulf Islands) as well as sunniest of the islands. Seventy percent of the island is zoned for tree farming and much of it has been recently logged. Most of the permanent population of about 1,000 residents is concentrated at the southern end of the island, where there is easier access to the ferries and where higher elevations bring slightly more rainfall.

1   Whaler Bay

Rock-infested Whaler Bay, behind Gossip Island at the northern entrance to Active Pass, is a fair anchorage protected from all winds and seas except norther-

CHARTS
3310 — Sheet 3 — EAST POINT to PORLIER
    PASS (1:40,000)
3442 — NORTH PENDER ISLAND to THETIS
    ISLAND (1:40,000)
3470 — For WESTERN PREVOST ISLAND
    (1:18,000)
3473 — ACTIVE PASS (1:12,000), MONTAGUE
    HARBOUR (1:18,000)

lies. The entrance to this bay is also exposed to northeasterly winds, which prevail during the months of December and January. In summer, the safest temporary anchorage can be found in a few coves on the western side of the bay. These coves were used in the last century as anchorages for small whaling vessels, since they provided quick access to the Strait of Georgia where whales were more plentiful than nowadays. Today Whaler Bay is used mainly by local residents and by the owners of small craft waiting for a favourable tide in Active Pass.

The Murcheson Farmhouse, on the north side of Murcheson Cove, was built in 1882 and is one of the oldest residences still standing on Galiano Island (Ovanin). Murcheson Cove dries completely, but at high tide it is possible to land in a dinghy and take a ten-minute hike up the road, which passes a few feet above the cove to the Hummingbird Inn (539-5472) with its country pub, bed and breakfast. The inn also provides a courtesy bus for transport from Montague Harbour or Sturdies Bay. The nearby Corner Store provides a full line of groceries and household needs. The Galiano Golf and Country Club (539-5533) provides a delightful, well-maintained course. Visitors are welcome and breakfast, lunch and dinner are available.

A small public float on Cain Peninsula near the head of the bay provides limited moorage for small craft. The approaches to this wharf are somewhat shallow (one foot at a zero tide) but the float is perfectly sheltered behind some drying rocks and islets off Cain Point. An interesting fact to note about Whaler Bay is the large tidal range — almost 16 feet at springs. The maximum range for Miners Bay in Active Pass is two feet less; for Montague Harbour on the other side of Galiano, it is three feet less; and for Village Bay, only two miles to the south of Whaler Bay, it is four feet less.

2 Sturdies Bay

Sturdies Bay, the main settlement on Galiano Island, contains a ferry dock with twice-daily service to Tsawwassen. The ferry dock provides some protection from the wash of traffic in Active Pass for a small public float with 160 feet of float space for five to six small craft. Just up the road from here are a gas station, art gallery, deli, liquor store and Burrill Bros. Store with general produce and coffee shop. From Sturdies Bay it is a short walk to Bellhouse Provincial Park on Burrill Point, where one can watch the ferries churn through the tide rips in Active Pass only a few hundred feet offshore.

3 Galiano Lodge

Galiano Lodge (539-5211) is open all year and provides groceries, limited moorage, rental boats, a swimming pool, showers, sauna and coffee shop as well as accommodation. Moorage is free while dining at Entre Amis.

Mayne Island

Mayne Island was one of the earliest summer resorts on the west coast. In particular, Miners Bay was

In the last century vessels used Whaler Bay (Galiano Island) as a temporary anchorage when hunting whales in Georgia Strait.

Georgina Point light on Mayne Island guides vessels into the eastern entrance to Active Pass. Mount Baker is in the background.

very popular around the turn of the century, with several hotels and boarding houses, stores, pubs, tennis courts and teahouses. Some of these buildings still survive.

Mayne Island is credited with being the first place in British Columbia to grow apples. It may be a myth, but according to Mabel Foster, an island historian:

A Captain Simpson was ordered to the Pacific coast on survey work, and at a dinner party in England before sailing, a lady jokingly slipped a few pips into his waistcoat pocket. The incident was forgotten by Simpson until he arrived at the west coast. When wearing the same waistcoat at a formal dinner, the pips were found, duly planted and produced apple trees. Hence the delicious King apple still growing on Mayne Island.

Looking north over Sturdies Bay (right) and Whaler Bay.

4 Georgina Point

The first light in the Gulf Islands — on Georgina Point, was established in 1885 and cared for by Henry "Scotty" Georgeson from the Shetland Islands. His descendants have operated many other Gulf Island lights since then. Visitors are welcome from 1 p.m. to 3 p.m. every day. The light station was supplemented by a fog signal in 1889, since fog occasionally spills through the pass on late summer and early autumn mornings. In 1881 a settler found an English penny dated 1784 and the remains of a seaman's knife buried under a stone on this point — possibly left by a boat party from Captain Vancouver's *Discovery* in 1792. For the most part, Vancouver kept to the mainland side during his exploration of the Gulf of Georgia and this is the only record that some of his party may have visited the Gulf Islands.

Near the lighthouse is the site of the old Point Comfort Hotel or Cherry Tree Inn, also known as "Culzean" when it was the home of Colonel and Lady Constance Fawkes. This massive 35-room Tudor-style hotel was built in 1893 and was a familiar sight to ferry passengers until it was destroyed in 1958. The Hotel was owned by Commander Eustace Maude (note Maude Bay) and family from 1900 to 1924 when

The ferry landing at Sturdies Bay is the jumping off point for twice-daily service to Tsawwassen on the mainland shore. Just up the road is a store, gas station, liquor store and coffee shop.

Maude (age 77) sold it to the Fawkes prior to setting out on a round-the-world voyage in his 22-foot sailboat, *Half Moon*. He returned home after being hit on the head by the boom off the coast of California. (Hamilton).

The obscure but touching and frequently hilarious story of Culzean and the people who lived and visited here is related in a beautiful little booklet by John Borradaile titled *Lady of Culzean*. This book is absolutely essential for anyone who wishes to learn more about the Gulf Island mystique and the charm and graciousness of some of the early settlers.

5   Miners Bay

In the middle of Active Pass is Miners Bay, so called because in 1858 it was a convenient halfway camping place for the miners travelling by small boat from Victoria to the mouth of the Fraser River and passage up to the Barkerville gold rush. Many of these miners

Miners Bay (Active Pass) was one of the stopping points for gold seekers en route from Victoria to Barkerville in the late 1850s.

had come to British Columbia from the United States and were singled out by the native peoples, who repeatedly raided their boats and supplies, and made threats of bodily harm and finally murder, when they defied orders to leave (Bultman). Marie Elliott notes, however, that:

> "Despite the fact that the Indians outnumbered the white settlers [who came after the miners] they never attempted to take advantage of their strength and annihilate the intruders... [unlike other areas of North America]. White settlement here was achieved without

Immediately behind the wharf is the Springwater (formerly Grandview) Lodge (539-5521) "B.C.'s oldest continuously operated hotel," which provides informal accommodation and moorage for guests at a float south of the public wharf. Fuel, groceries, lodging, campsites, rental boats, restaurant, pub, liquor store, craft shops, picnic area and post office are also located here. The Five Roosters Restaurant (539-2727) is located near the post office. A short distance up the hill is the Plumper Pass Lockup or Mayne Island Gaol (1896) which now operates as a museum with a small collection of Indian artifacts, old farm implements, a geological display, and a diorama of the *Zephyr* — a sailing barque which sank off David Cove in 1872. The Church of St. Mary Magdalene, designed by the same architect who designed Victoria's Christ Church Cathedral, is located a quarter-mile north of the wharf. The church can be found in an attractive woodland setting above a waterfront cemetery. An attractive lych gate between the cemetery and churchyard was used to hold coffins prior to the burial service much as early natives stored their coffins in the limbs of trees. The unique 400-pound sandstone font was painstakingly transported from East Point, Saturna Island by rowboat in 1900 (Elliott, M).

Village Bay is the Mayne Island terminus for ferry service from Swartz Bay on Vancouver Island and Tsawwassen on the mainland.

a great deal of violence... Most of the early settlers deliberately chose Indian wives in order to protect themselves and their homesteads... Native women were trained from birth to live in the wilderness, a factor that added stability to their relationships with white men."

Owing to back eddies, flood tides generally flow clockwise around the bay and ebb tides, anti-clockwise. A public wharf with float space for about four to five small boats is located near the southern end of the bay. This bay receives considerable wash from the numerous ferries and other shipping traffic using the pass. Two ferries usually pass each other regularly at a quarter to every even hour in the winter and a quarter to every hour in the summer.

6   Helen Point

Archaeological diggings near Helen Point in 1968 have revealed that this site was occupied over 5,000 years ago - the oldest settlement yet discovered in the Gulf Islands. Sea lions, an unusual sight in the Gulf Islands, can occasionally be seen in the bay just east of this point.

*Montague Harbour Marine Park was established in 1959 —
the first in B.C. It continues to be one of the most popular.*

7 Village Bay

Village Bay is the terminus for the Mayne Island ferry. Both Village Bay and Dinner Bay are open to ferry wash and to seas and winds blowing down Trincomali Channel. A boat launching ramp is located about 100 yards past Dalton Drive on Mariners Way and an old wood pipe spews water from a sulphur spring onto the beach here. This spring, which was advertised as having "valuable curative powers," was accidently created in 1891 by prospectors drill-testing for coal (Elliott, M.)

Enterprise Reef is closely passed by ferries and other traffic travelling through Active Pass, but is very popular with experienced scuba divers who want to have a look at the interesting marine life here.

8 Mount Galiano

Mount Galiano, at over 1,100 feet above sea level, provides spectacular views of the southern Gulf Islands and is well worth the three-mile hike from Sturdies Bay or Montague Harbour. The steep south face of Mount Galiano rises almost sheer from the sea and the summit is covered with rock plants, colourful wild-flowers and some of the oldest and largest trees on the island. For those with less time for exploration ashore, Bluffs Park, located midway between Sturdies Bay and Mount Galiano, rises over 500 feet directly above Georgeson Bay and provides equally spectacular views of Active Pass. There are picnic tables and a shelter and a trail from the top of the bluffs to the beach.

Collinson Reef, in Georgeson Bay, marks the spot where the ferry *Queen of Alberni* ran aground in 1979. Concerned residents rowed out to the vessel to offer tea to the stranded passengers.

9 Montague Harbour Marine Park

Montague Harbour Marine Park, at the north end of this land-locked anchorage was established in 1959 — the first in B.C. — and remains the most popular and busiest of all marine parks in the Gulf Islands. The site was also extremely popular with the natives who had been camping here for over 3,000 years before the white man came. The only visible evidence of this long period of use is the beautiful white shell beach at the north end of the park. The area above the beach served as a garbage heap (known as a "kitchen midden" to archaeologists) where clam, oyster and abalone shells were discarded. Northerly storms have subsequently eroded the beach and crushed, bleached and re-deposited the shell fragments. These beaches, easily distinguishable at low tide throughout the islands because of their glistening whiteness, mark all the old native encampments.

Opposite: The long, sheltering arms of Prevost Island provide safe anchorage and a sense of pastoral serenity now rare in the Gulf Islands.

Gutsy youngsters contemplate a refreshing dip in the chill waters of Montague Harbour Marine Park.

Boat weary crews can stretch their legs on the shoreside trail which winds its way around the perimeter of Gray Peninsula, Montague Harbour Marine Park.

The view southeast over the long bays of southern Prevost Island; North Pender Island is at top.

The 240-acre marine park includes over 30 camp units, some for car campers arriving by road and others reserved for boaters. A wharf with floats (for boats under 20 feet), several mooring buoys, drinking water, toilets and a boat launching ramp are also provided. Trails lead from the wharf past an orchard, the campsites and around a tidal lagoon to white shell beaches and sandstone caves at the south end of Gray Peninsula. Care must be taken when anchoring in Montague Harbour as the bottom does not provide good holding ground in a strong southeaster.

The sandstone cliffs of Galiano Island are fascinating to explore. Wave erosion of some types of sandstone results in a honeycomb texture which may grow from pinhole to cavern size in a short distance. Just north of Montague Harbour this erosion has resulted in strange shapes (Mushroom Rock) and caves which are only accessible by boat or along the shore at low tide. One of these caves, whose entrance is extremely well concealed, opens out into a lofty and spacious hiding place that was used as such by natives in the old days. According to legend a secret passage climbs upwards to an exit above the bluffs overlooking Montague Harbour. This escape route was used by Indians fleeing a raid and was only discovered when the hunters saw an arm suddenly appear then disappear from a cleft in the cliff face.

10 Montague Harbour Public Floats

The Gulf Islands ferry from Swartz Bay docks at the southeast end of the harbour. This ferry dock also provides some protection from northwesterlies to public floats with about 160 feet of moorage space. Just a short walk up the hill is La Berengerie featuring fine french cuisine (539-5392 for reservations), bed and breakfast in rustic, tranquil surroundings.

11 Montague Harbour Marina

The Marina at Montague (539-5733) offers gas, diesel, moorage, fishing supplies, laundry, showers and groceries. Canoe and sailboat rentals are also available here.

12 Parker Island

Two coves at either end of a low isthmus near the north end of Parker Island are convenient places to escape to if the main anchorage in Montague Harbour is too crowded.

13 Prevost Island

This island is named after Captain James Charles Prevost, Commander of HMS *Satellite* which was on

The last rays of a setting sun peer through trees at the entrance to Annette Inlet, Prevost Island.

this station from 1857 to 1865. The bay and rocks at the northern end of the island honour the same person. Prevost Island is the largest of the southern Gulf Islands. It remains a quiet, natural and exceptionally beautiful island. Pastoral countryside and seven deep indentations all provide isolation from the clamour and confusion of the heavily populated commercial marinas and parks found elsewhere. The island has been farmed by the family of Hubert de Burgh since 1924. Farming as a way of life is not as common in the islands as it once was, since it takes a special breed of person to endure the hardships involved. It is doubly difficult when all transport is by boat, and sheep and cattle have to be loaded and unloaded several times before reaching the market. Nevertheless, this farm is one of the largest in the Gulf Islands, with 130 acres of seeded pasture and almost a thousand acres of rough pasture supporting over 100 breeding ewes, several beef cows and 40 Angora goats.

The Channel Islands in Captain Passage and Hawkins, Bright and Red islets off the north and east shores of Prevost are protected as park reserves.

The seven indentations (three bays on the southeast and a bay, cove, inlet and passage facing northwest) are all unique and have their own special character. The bays facing southeast offer temporary anchorage but are exposed to ferry wash. North Pender Island offers some protection from southeast winds and seas.

James Bay provides good temporary anchorage but is partially exposed to northwesterlies blowing down Trincomali Channel. At the head of the bay is O'Reilly beach and an extensive apple and plum orchard where cows can be seen rubbing their backs against the base of the trees and then gorging themselves on the fallen fruit in late October.

Selby Cove and Annette Inlet are more protected, but the latter is quite shallow near its head, which is separated by a low grassy isthmus from Ellen Bay at the southeast end of the island and Glenthorne Passage to the southwest. One should be wary of rocks which are covered near high water just off the tip of the point separating Annette Inlet from Glenthorne.

14   Glenthorne Passage

Glenthorne is the most popular anchorage and offers the most protection. Entrance is possible at the north end of the passage or in a small pass just north of Glenthorne Point only 30 feet wide, with three feet of water at low tide. In the early 1970s this anchorage was the home of a large float house, occupied by a group of University of Victoria students on an Opportunities for Youth grant. They were attempting to determine the feasibility of living afloat — existing only on what the sea and land can provide directly. Two managed to survive and continued to live an idyllic existence in beautiful surroundings for several years before moving up the coast. This anchorage is protected by Secret Island, a secret no longer since it has been subdivided into 38 lots.

Pender Islands

North and South Pender islands were originally one, joined by a rock isthmus which was removed by blasting in 1903. The islands were named after Captain Daniel Pender, who was actively engaged in surveying the B.C. coast from 1857 to 1870. There are approximately 1,300 permanent residents on the Pender Islands.

15   Otter Bay Marina

This marina (629-3579) is located at the west end of Hyashi Cove, a northerly extension of Otter Bay and the only anchorage on the west side of North Pender which is moderately protected from ferry wash. Emergency fuel and repairs, moorage, launching ramp, rental boats, laundry, showers, groceries and campsites are available. A quarter-mile west of the ferry landing is Pender Lodge (629-3221) directly across the road from the Royal Canadian Legion. The lodge provides accommodation, pool, tennis courts and waterfront dining facilities. There is a nine-hole golf course nearby. Roesland Resort (629-3565) is found just inside Roe Islet at the south end of Otter Bay.

16   Port Washington

Port Washington in Grimmer Bay is named after one of the first residents of Pender Island — Washington Grimmer — who settled here in the last century after emigrating from his native England. This settlement is the location of a public wharf which serves as an alternate dock for the ferry. Floats at both ends of the wharf provide moorage for small craft. The westernmost float is exposed to ferry wash twice an hour and to westerly winds, but is moderately protected from seas by Prevost Island, a mile and a half to the northwest. A store here (629-3423) provides groceries, fuel, mail service and marine hardware. A short distance up the road is the Pender Craft Store and St. Peter's Anglican Church.

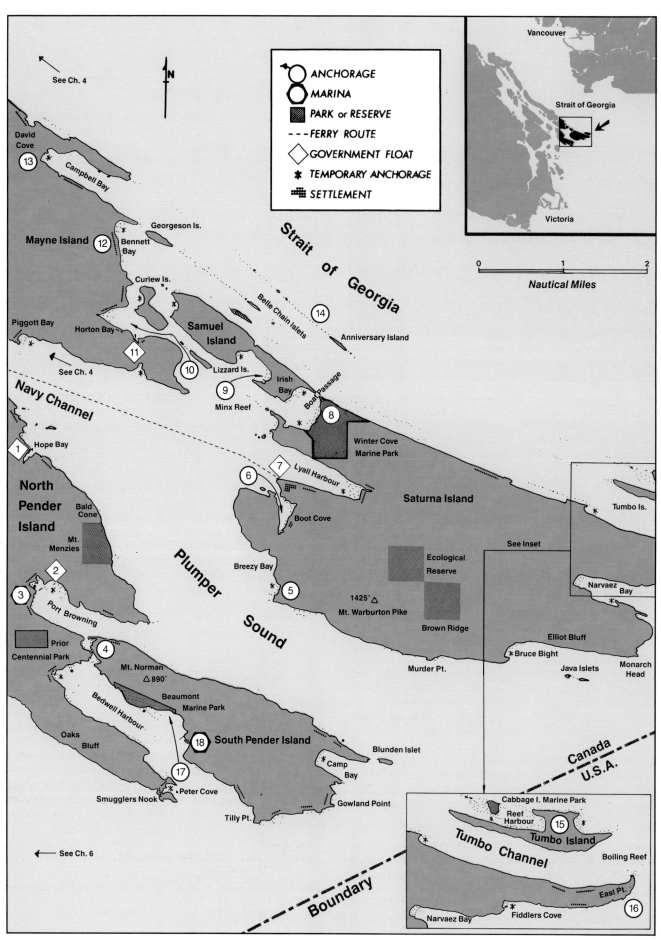

ANCHORAGE
MARINA
PARK or RESERVE
FERRY ROUTE
GOVERNMENT FLOAT
TEMPORARY ANCHORAGE
SETTLEMENT

Vancouver

Strait of Georgia

Victoria

0   1   2

Nautical Miles

See Ch. 4

N

David Cove

(13)

Campbell Bay

Mayne Island

(12)

Georgeson Is.

Bennett Bay

Curlew Is.

Piggott Bay

Horton Bay

(11)

See Ch. 4

(10)

Samuel Island

Lizzard Is.

(9)

Minx Reef

Belle Chain Islets

(14)

Anniversary Island

Strait of Georgia

Irish Bay

Boat Passage

(8)

Winter Cove Marine Park

Navy Channel

Hope Bay

(1)

(6)

(7)

Lyall Harbour

Saturna Island

Tumbo Is.

North Pender Island

Bald Cone

Mt. Menzies

(2)

(3)

Port Browning

Plumper

Boot Cove

Breezy Bay

(5)

Sound

Ecological Reserve

1425' △
Mt. Warburton Pike

Brown Ridge

See Inset

Narvaez Bay

Elliot Bluff

*Bruce Bight

Java Islets

Monarch Head

Murder Pt.

Prior Centennial Park

(4)

Mt. Norman
△ 890'

Beaumont Marine Park

Bedwell Harbour

(18)

South Pender Island

Oaks Bluff

(17)

Smugglers Nook

Peter Cove

Tilly Pt.

Camp Bay

Blunden Islet

Gowland Point

Canada
U.S.A.

See Ch. 6

Cabbage I. Marine Park

Reef Harbour

(15)

Tumbo Island

Tumbo Channel

Boiling Reef

Narvaez Bay

Fiddlers Cove

East Pt.

(16)

Boundary

Not to be used for navigation

68

CHAPTER FIVE

A lone fishboat finds peaceful moorage in tranquil waters off Cabbage Island.

Plumper Sound

The Penders, Mayne and Saturna

The lower outer Gulf Islands of North and South Pender, Saturna, Samuel and Mayne are considered by many to be the most charming of all islands in the Gulf. These islands offer a pleasing blend of natural beauty with pastoral countryside and older cottages which typify the quieter pace of life brought by greater isolation from the mainland.

Winds

Wind conditions for this area are sometimes difficult to predict as the nearest mainland weather stations are Tsawwassen (10 miles to the northeast) and Pat Bay on the Saanich Peninsula (10 miles to the southwest). The weather station at East Point lighthouse at the extreme east end of Saturna Island does, however, give a rough indication of what kind of winds to expect. Generally, the prevailing summer winds blow from the south and southwest over 60% of the time. Northwesterlies are the next most common wind with a frequency of 20%, increasing to 25% in the spring and autumn. In winter months the most common winds are the northeasterlies (20% to 35%) and the southeasterlies (20%).

Fishing

Troll off the kelp beds on the west end of Tumbo Island using strip or minnow on the flood or slow moving ebb. Boiling Reef is a favourite spot for moochers who let their herring drift along the outside border of the kelp. At East Point, fish on an ebb and first of a flood from the lighthouse out to Boiling Reef, or on any tide from Shag's Nest (cormorant roost in cliffs) in to Fiddler's Cove. At Monarch Head, troll with strip or minnow close along the cliffs on a flood tide.

Navy Channel

In Navy Channel between Mayne and North Pender islands, the tidal streams flood to the east and ebb to the west at rates up to three knots. The flood tide flowing north through Plumper Sound usually meets the opposing flood tide in Navy Channel off Hope Bay, occasionally resulting in tide rips.

The beach at Piggot Bay, Mayne Island is shallow and sandy at low tide. Car top boats can be launched here or at Gallagher Bay on the other side of the headland.

1 Hope Bay

The Hope Bay public floats provide 450 feet of moorage space. Although the floats are somewhat open to the east, winds from this direction are infrequent in summer. The bay is named after an early Pender resident, Rutherford Hope. The store at the head of the wharf was closed in 1984. Just a quarter mile north of here is Cliffside Inn-on-the-Sea which features bed and breakfast and a gourmet restaurant (629-6691). Seventy-five acres of recreational reserve

CHARTS
3310 — Sheet 3 — EAST POINT to PORLIER PASS (1:40,000)
3442 — NORTH PENDER ISLAND to THETIS ISLAND (1:40,000)
3441 — BOUNDARY PASS (1:40,000)
3477 — Plan of BEDWELL HARBOUR to GEORGESON PASSAGE (1:15,000)

between Bald Cone and Mount Menzies provide opportunity for hiking with vistas down Plumper Sound.

A floating breakwater offers protection for the marina at Port Browning on North Pender Island. On shore is a store, showers, dining room and pub.

2   Port Browning

Port Browning provides good temporary anchorage, but is exposed somewhat to winds and seas from the southeast. The best anchorage is found in the northern end of the harbour near a public float that provides 250 feet of berthage space.

3   Port Browning Marina

This marina (629-3493) is protected by a floating breakwater and provides extensive berthing facilities as well as fuel, provisions, minor boat and engine repairs, marine hardware, accommodations, heated pool, showers, laundromat, rental boats and a licenced dining room. The Sh-qu-ala Inn pub here is named after the local watering hole. The Driftwood Centre (fuel, deli, post office and liquor store) is located a few minute's walk up the road from the marina. Hamilton Beach, a popular local swimming area, is located to the south of this marina and The Maples (629-3282) provides rustic housekeeping cabins behind the beach.

4   Shark Cove

On the Port Browning side of Shark Cove, Mortimer Spit provides a nice sand and gravel beach. The cove itself, though shallow, affords good shelter for small

boats. Mortimer Spit marks the spot where two campers were attacked and one murdered by a band of Lamalchi Indians from Kuper Island in 1863. The other escaped and notified the police in Victoria, who dispatched a gunboat to chase down the suspects.

It is theoretically possible for small boats, including sailboats with masts no higher than 36 feet, to pass into Bedwell Harbour from Port Browning. Originally the two Penders were one island, but in 1903 a canal was successfully excavated. A highway bridge across the canal reunited the two islands in 1955. Tidal streams run up to four knots at springs, so it is wise to negotiate the canal close to slack water, since it averages only 70 feet in width (40 feet at the highway bridge). Small sailboats with mast heights higher than 27 feet should *only* attempt the pass at low slack water (the channel has been dredged to a depth of six feet below chart datum). Boats that don't follow this advice may be in for disaster. Assuming the posted 27-foot clearance was taken from high water, I attempted the pass a few hours before high water and watched, horrified, as the tip of my 29-foot mast caught the underneath of the highway bridge. Fortunately the tidal stream was against me and I quickly reversed with no damage other than a strained forestay, a cracked spreader and a red face. The clearance at high water is now charted at 8.5 m (28 ft). The maximum tidal range is 11 feet.

Beside the bridge on North Pender Island there is a midden which has revealed evidence of over 5,000 years of human occupation of the site. Among the artifacts discovered by a recent archaeological dig are arrow and spear heads, a slate box or prehistoric cist (receptacle with fitted lid), and one of the first miniature totems carved on the coast dating from 500 B.C. Power boats traversing the canal should slow down so that their wash does not cause further erosion of the midden site.

Half a mile up the hill from the bridge is landlocked, 40-acre Prior Centennial Provincial Park with 17 campsites.

Saturna Island

For those who enjoy solitude, Saturna is one of the most interesting islands to explore, for it is the least populated of the major Gulf Islands with less than 300 permanent residents and no major resorts or marinas. An ecological reserve of 324 acres on the gentle slopes east of Mount Warburton Pike protects a virgin stand of coastal Douglas fir. The island is named after the Spanish naval schooner *Saturnina* which was commanded by Jose Maria Narvaez, engaged in exploring this area in 1791.

Subtle hints of mauve tint this moody yet typical photo taken in the Gulf Islands.

Saturna Beach is the site of the popular Dominion Day Lamb Barbecue on Saturna Island. As many as 400 boats anchor off as their crews enjoy the annual feast ashore.

5 Saturna Beach

Saturna Beach to the south of Breezy Bay is the site of the now famous Dominion Day Lamb Barbecue. This annual feast — with bingo, darts, tug o'war, a beer garden, children's races and assorted country fair activities — attracts up to 400 boats which anchor off or are accommodated on two long floats. The beach is at the western end of a long thin farm that runs for several miles along a bench above the south coast of Saturna below the steep grassy slopes of Mount Warburton Pike.

The mountain is named after a young man who arrived here straight from Oxford in the early 1880s and eventually owned most of the land on Saturna and Mayne. He is remembered not only for his generosity in donating land for St. Mary Magdalene Church on Mayne, but also for his eccentric and colourful personality. He was a reticent man who would often disappear for months on end without warning. He wore well-tailored suits until they fell off his back and went barefoot so much he could use his toes like his fingers. Rated as one of the top six big game hunters in the world, Pike acquired an international reputation as an explorer after making two great journeys into the Canadian north. His two books, *The Barren Grounds of Northern Canada* (1892) and *Through the Subarctic Forest* (1896), are considered classics. He almost reached the Arctic Circle and had several perilous adventures, including a rescue by a sealer in the Bering Sea after a 3,000-mile canoe trip (Kneebone). Mount Warburton Pike provides excellent views from its summit (1,425 feet) and opportunities for observing turkey vultures and bald eagles. Its wide open slopes turn a brilliant burnt ochre colour with the setting sun, and Brown Ridge is a familiar landmark to anyone approaching Saturna from the south. This ridge was known as Prairie Hill in the 1880s, when Billy Trueworthy, a notorious but usually placid native shepherd, used to run up and down the steep open slopes herding the sheep with blood-curdling yells, causing the sheepdogs to cringe with terror (Reimer).

The waters off Elliot Bluff are popular with scuba divers for the sheer rock cliffs and some of the largest sea anemones in the Gulf Islands.

6 Boot Cove

Boot Cove would appear to be a perfect natural harbour with a narrow, obstruction-free entrance and a large basin of suitable depth for safe anchoring inside. This is normally true for the summer months, but during the winter the enclosing topography tends to produce a funneling effect into the cove when there are strong southerly, southwesterly or northerly winds. Winds up to 80 mph have been reported in this cove and it is not uncommon to have 40 to 50 mph winds go through during the spring and autumn. This cove does not provide convenient access to shore as most of the shoreline is privately owned. The Boot Cove Lodge (539-2254) provides a homey atmosphere with bed and breakfast and is located at the south end of the cove.

7 Lyall Harbour

Lyall Harbour provides plentiful anchorage, but is exposed to the northwest. A public wharf with over 400 feet of float space is located just behind the Sa-

Though Boot Cove (on right) usually provides safe, protected anchorage in summer, it can be less hospitable in winter when winds funnel forcefully through the surrounding topography.

turna ferry dock. Gas and diesel are available and provisions, fishing supplies and charts can be obtained from the store (539-5725) at the head of the wharf. The Lighthouse Pub, located beneath the store, serves meals, offers light entertainment and exhibits a relic of the *Zephyr*, a 190-foot barque which sank off Mayne Island. Up the road, within a mile of the wharf, are a medical centre, fire hall, St. Christopher's Church, liquor store and the Saturna General Store (539-2936).

At Samuel Island, boats anchor in protected waters at the southeastern end of Irish Bay. The upland area is private property.

8 Winter Cove Marine Park

At high water care should be taken to avoid Minx Reef at the entrance to Winter Cove between Saturna and Samuel islands. Church Cove, a tiny bay indenting the southwest shore of Winter Cove, is the site of St. Christopher's, a church that was rebuilt over 70 years ago from what was originally a Japanese-built boathouse.

Winter Cove is quite shallow in places and is somewhat exposed to winds from the northwest. The deepest anchorage (10 feet) appears to be directly off the marine park landing. This 228-acre marine park was established in 1979 after one of the last major industries in the Gulf Islands ceased operations. The B.C. Light Aggregates Plant operated an open pit quarry and furnace here, producing chipped stones for road-building. The park has a water pump, picnic area and launching ramp and is a delight to explore, with well laid out trails following the shoreline. Boardwalks pass over the bullrush covered outlets of two lagoons draining into the cove and reach an outlook over Boat Passage. Boat Passage is safe to navigate by small boats only at slack water. Tidal streams run with considerable force at rates up to seven knots through this very narrow passage. The Saturna shore should be followed closely as there is a drying reef which extends 100 yards east from Samuel Island at the entrance to the passage. Underwater rocks are often difficult to spot here because of the silty opaqueness of Fraser River runoff.

9 Samuel Island

Irish Bay almost cuts Samuel Island — which is privately owned — in half and provides excellent anchorage in its southeast corner. The northern half is suitable as a temporary anchorage when the wind is not blowing from the south. Visitors to this bay are occasionally entertained by the conscientious caretaker who uses a powerful megaphone to broadcast

Looking southeast over Samuel Island and Winter Cove. Take care when piloting the area around Minx Reef (centre-right).

In recent years Winter Cove Marine Park has been upgraded and now has picnic facilities and an attractive shoreside trail.

his stern admonishments to anyone he spies trespassing above the high tide line (the owners discourage visitors because the island is something of a wildlife preserve, and because of the ever-present danger of fire in the dry summer months). It is interesting to note that the tidal range on the Strait of Georgia side at the centre of Sameul Island is two feet greater than the range only a few hundred feet to the south, inside Irish Bay. This island has many sand and white shell beaches as well as protected anchorages at both ends.

Another interesting feature of this general area is the wide variety of marine plants, animals, birds and shellfish, such as the rock-burrowing clam which are uncommon and are possibly a result of the meeting of the cold, clear blue saline waters from Juan de Fuca Strait and the warmer sandy-turquoise waters of Georgia Strait. Georgeson Passage and Boat Passage are often good places to watch the mixing of waters take place, especially during the month of June when muddy waters from the Fraser River ebb through the Gulf Island passages.

10   Horton Bay (Mayne Island)

The tidal streams between Samuel, Curlew, Lizard and Mayne islands are fairly swift (up to five knots) making the passages somewhat tricky for smaller craft. Horton Bay provides good anchorage and there is a small public float (11) at the south end of the bay

Horton Bay offers sheltered anchorage and a public float at the south end of the bay.

Bennett Bay, which has one of the best bathing beaches on Mayne Island, is somewhat exposed to the southeast.

with 160 feet of float space for four or five boats. This area of Mayne Island was well populated with Japanese prior to World War II. They originally came to the area in the last century and were very successful at cultivating tomatoes, for which Mayne Island became famous. During the war the Japanese were deported inland and their property confiscated as they were not permitted to live within 100 miles of the coast. Today the permanent population of Mayne is over 700, but this number more than triples in the summer.

12 Bennett Bay

If you get tired of listening to the shrill, jungle-like screams of the peacocks on Curlew Island, you can take your boat through the passage and anchor (be-

ware of crab traps and mooring buoys) in Bennett Bay, which is somewhat exposed to the southeast. The offshore islets and reefs provide some degree of protection from southeasterly seas, but there is virtually no protection from southeasterly winds. One can also moor for a short time at the Mayne Inn wharf and walk ashore over a wobbly "Use at your own risk" pier that is supported by a line of single pilings. The pier was constructed in 1979 after a protracted dispute involving local residents and the Islands Trust, which were concerned about protecting what is said to be one of the best bathing beaches on Mayne Island. The Mayne Inn was originally constructed in 1911 by the Franco-Canadian Company as a boarding house for workers at a nearby brick plant, but was closed down prior to 1914. The inn, which was once the scene of wild weekend dances that attracted the locals for miles around, was closed again in 1985. Nearby are local handicraft and art shops, the Blue Vista Resort (539-2463) and Marisol Village Cabins (539-2336).

13 David Cove

David Cove, a small indentation on the north coast of Mayne, is surrounded by private homes but provides a convenient launching ramp or anchorage while waiting for the tide to change in Active Pass. Care should be taken to avoid the cables in the northern part of the cove. This cove is completely open to winter northeasterly winds. The wreck of the sailing barque *Zephyr*, which hit Georgina shoals and sank in a blinding snowstorm off this coast in 1872, is the first in B.C. to be designated an historic wreck. The *Zephyr* was carrying a sandstone column five feet thick by 30 feet long to the San Francisco Mint; this has since been salvaged for display at Newcastle Island Marine Park. Campbell Bay is seldom used as an anchorage because of its dangerous exposure to the southeast. There is a beautiful swimming beach here and sandstone caves are located along the northern shoreline.

14 Belle Chain Islets

The Belle Chain Islets are interesting to explore, especially by canoe in good weather or by scuba diving. One can find seal haulouts, bird roosts and wind-contorted juniper-like garry oaks. The islets were named after Isabel (Belle), the youngest daughter of Captain Jeremiah Nagle, Harbour Master for Vancouver Island in 1865. Anniversary Island has reefs which were discovered in a 1918 snowstorm by the *Kin Kon Maru*, a Japanese ship bound for Russia with a cargo of railway ties and barbed wire.

15 Tumbo Island

Tumbo Island is also a fascinating place to explore since it is so far out of the way and tends to be ignored by most people. This isolation has helped to preserve what some consider to be the most outstanding natural area within the Gulf Islands. The low-lying area between the two parallel east-west ridges supports a

Tiny coves, prolific tidepools and craggy shores provide interesting territory for off-boat exploration at Pine Islet, west of Cabbage Island Marine Park.

Cabbage Island Marine Park

The south-facing sand beaches of Cabbage Island have long been popular with local boaters as a delightful picnicking area, and in 1975 the Parks Branch acquired this 11-acre island, established it as a marine park and placed mooring buoys in Reef Harbour. At low tide you can walk out along the exposed outer conglomerate beaches that link Tumbo and Cabbage to the islets to the west. These beaches are fascinating to beachcomb as they are sometimes littered with huge tree stumps from the Fraser, sea lion carcasses from California and crates from the other side of the world. Reef Harbour offers outstanding tidepools for close examination of marine life. Rosenfeld Rock marks the spot where the sailing ship *John Rosenfeld* sank in 1886 while carrying coal from Nanaimo to San Francisco.

16   East Point

Boiling Reef off the eastern tip of Saturna Island is very suitably named as the tide fairly bubbles around the point at maximum rates up to five knots. The direction and force of the tidal streams in this area and along the southeast side of Saturna are very deceptive,

Eleven acre Cabbage Island Marine Park provides cruising yachtsmen with a broad sandy beach, mooring buoys and rough picnic facilities.

natural grassland and marsh with a large variety of bird and small mammal life. Tidal streams in Tumbo Channel ebb and flood in the same direction — to the east, because of back eddies as the flood tide curls around East Point.

75

The East Point lighthouse was established in 1888. It is said to be one of the best locations in the Gulf for sighting killer whales.

usually travelling in the opposite direction to what one would expect. This is probably due to the unique position and configuration of East Point — at the tip of the Gulf Islands chain — with an east-west rather than north-south orientation. The lighthouse here was established in 1888 and is open to visitors. There is a wildlife sanctuary on the point, a good place for observing ducks, loons, grebes, cormorants, auklets, guillemots, oystercatchers and raptors. This point, which was named Punta Santa Saturnina by Pantoja in 1791, is also said to be one of the best locations in the Gulf for whale watching.

Three indentations in the eastern Saturna shoreline, including Fiddlers Cove, Narvaez Bay and Bruce Bight, provide reasonable temporary anchorage, especially in the summer months when the prevailing winds are from the southwest or northwest. Monarch Head is named after HMS *Monarch*, 84 guns, a sister ship to H.M.S. *Ganges*, on this station from 1854 to 1857, and flagship of Rear Admiral Henry William Bruce, after whom this bight and the tallest mountain in the Gulf Islands (on Saltspring Island) are named. Taylor Beach, at the head of the Bight is said to be the nicest sand beach on the island (Roberts). Stone from this bay was quarried for use in construction of the Parliamennt Buildings in Victoria. Taylor Point and Java Islets are popular scuba diving locations.

Further along this coast (below Brown Ridge) is Murder Point where two Americans, a man and his daughter, were killed by the same band of Indians who had killed another American at Mortimer Spit only a few days before. No one knows why these apparently innocent people were murdered. B.J. Spalding Freeman, author of *A Gulf Islands Patchwork*, has noted that "Murder [of white settlers] was seldom perpetrated by the Indians. There was probably plenty of justification, but innocent people often suffered for the wrongs of others." Eleven natives implicated in the crime were eventually hunted down. Some were found at Kuper Island, two in a cave above Montague Harbour, and the others near Cowichan Bay and Kulleet Bay. After a careful trial three of the natives were hanged in Victoria on July 4, 1863.

Tidal streams at the southern entrance to Plumper Sound can reach maximum velocities of four knots, and a strong ebb meeting a southwesterly wind results in steep seas and tide rips off Blunden Islet.

Bedwell Harbour

The southern end of South Pender Island features an irregular conglomerate shoreline backed by extensive open grass headlands that mark a dramatic transition from exposed meadow with spring wildflowers to dense thickets of fir and salmonberry. There are caverns penetrating up to 15 feet 30 feet below Tilly

Bedwell Harbour Resort (centre -bottom) is one of the busiest marinas in the Gulf Islands. Facilities include customs clearance, restaurant, pub, store, fuel and accommodation.

Point, likely prospects for scuba exploration. In 1791 Pantoja, a pilot with the Eliza expedition, entered this harbour and named it Punta (Puerto) de San Antonia. The island was named Isla de Sayas but charted as Isla San Eusebio. The harbour, which separates the southern tip of North Pender from the northern tip of South Pender, is well known to United States' vessels that come here to clear customs and to local boats from the Sidney-Victoria area. Although anchorage is generally possible anywhere in Bedwell Harbour, the favoured location is between Bedwell Resort and Skull Islets. Temporary anchorage is also possible at the head of the harbour, off swampy Medicine Beach.

17   Beaumont Marine Park

This 143-acre park is named after the man who donated it to the province in 1961, Captain Beaumont of Victoria. A grassy isthmus, the site of an old Indian encampment, is flanked by gravel and sand beaches

Beaumont Marine Park, adjacent to Bedwell Resort, provides visitors with mooring buoys, trails and some picnic and camping facilties.

linking a small rocky peninsula to the park. Steeply dipping strata of thinly bedded shale and sandstone along the shore north of Skull Islets are interesting to investigate. Mooring buoys (east of Skull Islets), picnic tables, campsites, toilet facilities and a water supply are provided. Rough trails snake along the shoreline to Ainslie Point and the "canal" and up through the woods and a steep ravine to Mount Norman. Very good views are available from this mountain, which, at 890 feet, is the highest point of land on the Penders.

18   Bedwell Harbour Resort

The Bedwell Harbour Resort (629-3212) provides moorage, fuel, groceries, post office, rental boats, bikes, washrooms, showers, laundry, games room, the Bouquet Garni restaurant, cottages, lodge and heated pool. This well-run resort is one of the busiest in the Gulf Islands with over two-thirds of all U.S. recreational boats entering B.C. waters stopping here. Flowers fill the resort area and one can relax under the umbrellas in an outdoor courtyard while enjoying a light snack from the Ships Galley Snack Bar or sip a cool one in the Copper Whale Pub. Over 700 feet of float space at public floats south of the marina are provided for boats clearing customs.

Good temporary anchorage is possible in Peter Cove at the southern tip of North Pender. The cove is partially protected from southeasterly seas by South Pender Island. The foreshore is protected by a 17-acre park reserve. Although the upland area is developed there is public access onto Wallace Point.

Oaks Bluff was frequently used for target practice by ships of the Royal Navy in the last century, while Smugglers Nook, just around the corner from Peter Cove, was a convenient stash for rum-runners during Prohibition in the United States.

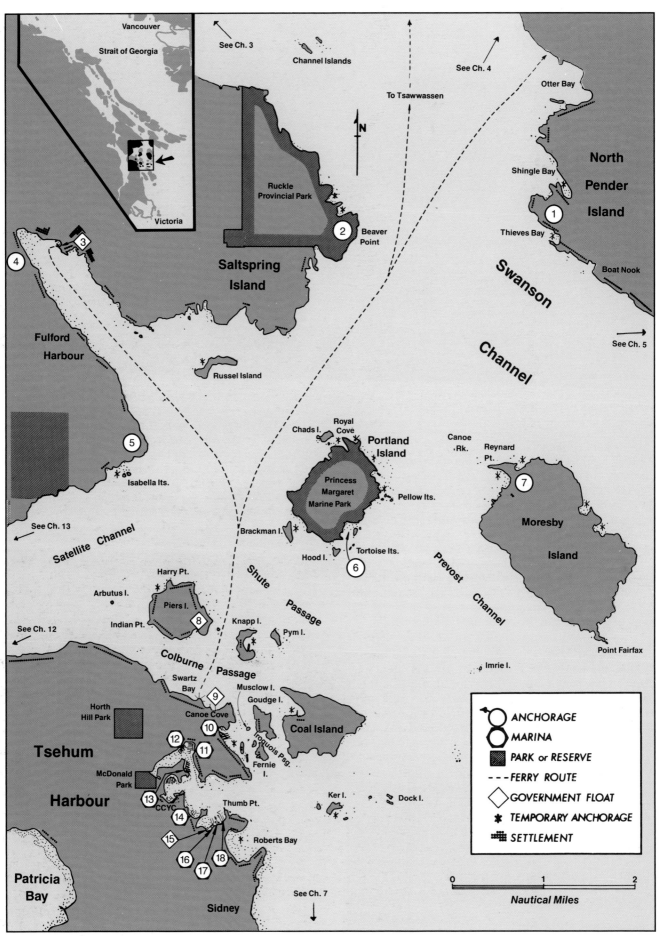

Not to be used for navigation

Inset map labels:
Vancouver
Strait of Georgia
Victoria

Main map labels:
See Ch. 3
Channel Islands
To Tsawwassen
See Ch. 4
Otter Bay
North Pender Island
Shingle Bay
①
Thieves Bay
Boat Nook
Ruckle Provincial Park
②
Beaver Point
Saltspring Island
N
Swanson Channel
See Ch. 5
③
④
Fulford Harbour
⑤
Russel Island
Chads I.
Royal Cove
Portland Island
Canoe Rk.
Reynard Pt.
⑦
Isabella Its.
Princess Margaret Marine Park
Pellow Its.
Moresby Island
See Ch. 13
Satellite Channel
Brackman I.
Hood I.
Tortoise Its.
⑥
Prevost Channel
Point Fairfax
Harry Pt.
Shute Passage
Arbutus I.
Piers I.
⑧
Indian Pt.
Knapp I.
Pym I.
Imrie I.
See Ch. 12
Colburne Passage
Swartz Bay
Musclow I.
⑨
Horth Hill Park
Goudge I.
Canoe Cove
⑩
Coal Island
Tsehum
⑫
⑪
McDonald Park
Iroquois Psg.
Fernie I.
⑬
CCYC
Harbour
⑭
Thumb Pt.
Ker I.
Dock I.
⑮
⑯
⑰
⑱
Roberts Bay
Patricia Bay
See Ch. 7
Sidney

Legend:
⚓ ANCHORAGE
⚓ MARINA
▰ PARK or RESERVE
- - - FERRY ROUTE
◇ GOVERNMENT FLOAT
✳ TEMPORARY ANCHORAGE
▦ SETTLEMENT

0   1   2
Nautical Miles

Kayakers pitch camp on Portland Island — Princess Margaret Marine Park — in the southern Gulf Islands.

Swartz Bay

Swanson Channel to Tsehum Harbour

Winds

In summer months, winds in the Swanson Channel to Tsehum Harbour area are predominantly light with southeasterlies and easterlies having the greatest frequency, blowing 45% of the time. The westerly is primarily an offshore night-time or morning wind with a frequency of 25% in summer and 30% in winter. The strongest winds come from the southeast and northeast in the winter with a mean speed of 12.5 mph.

Fishing

Fishing for salmon or cod is fairly good between the Little Islands, especially around Coal Island where strong tides cause turbulence and mixing which attracts the feeding sport fish. Use Super Strip Teasers, minnows, anchovies or drift lures. Fish the bottom of underwater valleys southeast of Coal Island for big chinooks.

1   North Pender Island

Boat Nook, a tiny indentation in the North Pender coastline, is used only by local craft and does not offer good anchorage as it is completely open to the southwest. Thieves Bay is headed by a nice beach with a grassy, tree-shaded public picnic area behind it. A stone breakwater provides protection from northwesterly winds for a boat lauching ramp at the head of the bay, some private floats and a small temporary anchorage area. This bay is used primarily by residents of Magic Lake Estates, but does provide protected access to this portion of North Pender Island. Hiking trails and roads lead from here past two artificial lakes to Prior Centennial Park. The cove at the head of Shingle Bay is suitable for temporary anchorage, but shelves rapidly and is exposed to the northwest.

2   Ruckle Provincial Park

Beaver Point has long been regarded as one of the most beautiful areas on Saltspring Island; its many tiny coves, rocky headlands, grassy backshores and pastoral farmland extend in a narrow hidden valley for almost a mile behind the point. Owing to the generosity of the Ruckle family, who have been farming here since 1875, 1,200 acres of the point were established as a provincial park in 1974, making it the largest park in the Gulf Islands. Mr. Ruckle has allowed people to wander freely or picnic along the waterfront of his property for many years. Visitors should respect the privacy of the members of the Ruckle family still living in the park. They have a "tenancy for life" agreement with the government. Dogs should not be allowed to run free as there are sheep in the central part of the park which is still being farmed. There are six heritage buildings in the park, built from 1876 to 1938, but only one, the Norman Ruckle House, is currently open to the public and serves as the park headquarters. This fine building was built in the

CHARTS
3310 — Sheets 1, 2 and 3 (1:40,000)
3441 — HARO STRAIT to SATELLITE
CHANNEL (1:40,000)
3470 — FULFORD HARBOUR (1:15,000)
3476 — Approaches to TSEHUM HARBOUR
(1:10,000)

The Fulford Harbour ferry terminal provides protection for boats moored at the public floats behind. Nearby are a store, post office and coffee shop.

The Fulford Inn with pub, dining room and accommodation is at the head of Fulford Harbour — a 20 minute walk from the public wharf.

1930s for Norman Ruckle's wedding. The wedding did not take place, however, and the house was never lived in, but used for storing potatoes instead (Ovanin).

At one time the cove just north of Beaver Point contained a large wharf and this was the main landing for steamships from the mainland. Very little evidence of the wharf remains today. These coves are all fairly exposed to winds and seas from the east and northeast. The coves to the south of Beaver Point are exposed to the southeast. All coves are open to the wash from ferries which pass by the point at least twice an hour and are therefore rather uncomfortable for small boats, except when the ferries are not operating — between midnight and 7 a.m.

There are 30 walk-in campsites and 20 vehicle campsites. The grassy meadows south of the point are usually dotted with a colourful array of tents — a popular place for kayakers and canoeists exploring the Gulf Islands. Be prepared for an early morning wakening as the deafening noise of passing ferries vibrates through the point beginning just after 7 a.m.

3 Fulford Harbour

The second largest community on Saltspring Island is still quite small with less than 200 permanent residents, a store, post office and a small coffee shop. The Fulford Inn (653-4432) is located at the head of the harbour and features pub, dining room and accommodation. A public wharf with 250 feet of float space is protected behind the ferry dock which serves as the main link between Saltspring and Vancouver Island. Another tiny float (40 feet) on the outside of the ferry dock is more exposed, but could be used for temporary berthage. Fulford Harbour is not particularly favoured as an anchorage owing to its open exposure to the southeast. Wilsons Marina provides fuel, emergency repairs and limited moorage (656-4261).

The harbour is named after John Fulford, Captain of HMS *Ganges*, and is familiar to many as the primary tidal reference station for the southern Gulf Islands. Near the head of the harbour is the conspicuous but tiny St. Paul's Roman Catholic Church. This church was built of stone hauled by Indian war canoe, stone boat and oxen from the site of the "Butter Church" in Cowichan Bay, via Burgoyne Bay between 1880 and 1885. This is the oldest church on Saltspring Island.

4 Drummond Park

Sand and gravel beaches, picnic sites and an adventure playground share a home with a large petroglyph boulder, relocated from the Fulford beach. The face of a seal, carved in sandstone by Tsaoult Indians, is said to represent a woman who was changed into a rock to protect this area.

5 Isabella Islets

The Isabella Point area was settled in the last century by several Kanaka families. These Kanakas were native Sandwich Islanders (Hawaiians) who had left their homeland when the United States began administering their islands. The Kanakas were part of a large group loyal to King Kamehameha, the hereditary chief, who objected to the new administration because he was not a republican. Some of the Kanakas went to San Juan Island, which at that time was still under the Crown, where they worked for the Hudson's Bay Company. Following the Pig War and realignment of the boundary in 1868, the Kanakas had the choice of remaining or moving to Canada. The majority chose to move to Portland Island and southern Saltspring because they found the republican system confusing and preferred to live under a monarch (Bea Hamilton). At the turn of the century many of the local landmarks had Hawaiian place names, but unfortunately, since they were difficult for the hydrographers to pronounce and spell properly, none ever appeared on any charts or maps. In 1971 some of the descen-

Pretty blue camas and cactus brighten the rocks near a small cove in the Isabella Islets. The Fulford Harbour ferry is in the background.

dants of the original Kanakas visited Hawaii for a reunion with the descendants of King Kamehameha.

In calm or easterly weather temporary anchorage is possible in a tiny area behind Isabella Island which is joined to Saltspring by a white shell and gravel spit at low water.

A 627 acre ecological reserve to protect marine wildlife and a unique southern Gulf Islands stand of dry zone Douglas fir is found along the shoreline west of Isabella Islets on the southeast face of Mount Tuam. Beautiful red-limbed arbutus, broadleaf maples, western red cedar and solitary pines can also be seen stretching up the otherwise barren hillside near Cape Keppel at the southernmost tip of Saltspring Island. The shoreline is occasionally used as a sea lion haulout. A marine ecological reserve of 837 acres south of Cape Keppel protects underwater plant and marine life for study by scientists.

6   Princess Margaret Marine Park

This provincial marine park, also known as Portland Island and over 450 acres in size, is one of the gems of the Gulf Islands. In the last century it was inhabited by Kanakas (note Kanaka Bluff at the western tip of the island) from the Hawaiian Islands. In the 1930s it was the home of Major General Frank "One-Arm" Sutton, who was reported to have died in China during World War II, leaving a beautiful orchard of over 50 plum and apple trees and an immense barn which once reputedly stabled 42 race horses.

The island was given to Princess Margaret in 1958 to commemorate our centennial, but she later graciously returned it to the province in 1961 so that it could be designated a marine park. Access is possible by anchoring in moderately well-protected Princess Bay at the south end of the island (enter close to Tortoise Islets) and rowing ashore. The offshore islets (one of which is private) do not offer much protection in a strong southeasterly. From this anchorage a narrow, open grass field extends one mile across the island to a small cove indenting the northern shoreline. Royal Cove behind Chads Island at the north end of the island is also a good anchorage if you do not mind bobbing to the regular wash of passing ferries.

For local people who become familiar with the reefs and rocks off the eastern end of the island, temporary anchorage is possible inside Turnbull Reef or Pellow Islets. A Kanaka, Johnny Palau, used to live at this end

81

Princess Bay at the southeastern end of Portland Island is the primary anchorage for visitors to Princess Margaret Marine Park.

of the island and the islets were named after him, his name being Anglicized in the process. Temporary anchorage is also possible inside Brackman Island.

Several white shell beaches surround the island and exploring inland is facilitated by a network of park trails and areas where thin underbrush is kept cropped by a few foraging sheep. Unfortunately, these sheep also destroy much of the grass land and many of the wildflowers which are unique to these islands. The four largest islands surrounding the park, including Chads, Brackman and Hood, are privately owned. Brackman Island has been proposed as an ecological reserve and boasts an incredible variety of wildflowers in the spring. White fawn lily, chocolate lily, harvest brodiaea, blue camas, sea blush, blue-eyed mary and western buttercup can be found.

7 Moresby Island

Moresby Island and the southernmost island of the Queen Charlottes are named after the same man — Admiral Sir Fairfax Moresby — who was Commander in Chief on this coast from 1850 to 1853. His flagship was HMS *Portland*, Captain Henry Chads commanding.

The island is privately owned and has a fascinating history. In 1887 Captain Horatio Robertson, a river pilot and merchant, retired from the China station and

Campers often pitch their tents in the open benchland opposite Brackman Island on Princess Margaret Marine Park.

built a unique house in the Chinese tradition on the island. Two three-storey octagonal towers were built, one for himself, his wife and three daughters, the other for his eight sons. The towers were joined by a 100-foot long verandah which was later glassed in. The Captain could be seen occasionally riding through Victoria in a rickshaw drawn by one of his coolies. Two of his Chinese servants escaped from Moresby Island on a log raft and were picked up half

82

Services at Canoe Cove include a store, coffee shop, fuel, showers, repairshop, marine ways and pub. The Swartz Bay ferry terminal is three minutes away by foot.

dead, several days later, near Foul Bay, Victoria. The circumstances surrounding this incident aroused much controversy as Captain Robertson was known to be very strict. In the 1900s the island was a prosperous farm, with a variety of owners. An old government wharf which was used to ship farm products to Vancouver Island has fallen into disuse and disappeared almost completely. At the south end of the island on Point Fairfax there is a conspicuous international boundary monument, erected in 1910.

Temporary anchorage is possible in a few tiny coves on the northeast shore and within the bight south of Reynard Point. The bight is open to westerlies. A small boat basin is found between the rocks at the south end of the bight.

Tiny one-acre Imrie Island, between Moresby Island and Coal Island, is fascinating for bird-watchers. It is not advisable to go ashore on this island, however, for it is one of the few areas where sea birds such as the black brant and glaucous-winged gull are able to nest and breed. Because Imrie is more than one mile distant from nearby islands, otter, mink, racoon, and other predators find it difficult to swim the tide-swept passages to raid the nests.

8   Piers Island

The approaches to the northeast end of the Saanich Peninsula are bordered with several islands and islets. Pym, Knapp and Piers Islands are named after officers of the Royal Navy at the time this area was first charted. In 1900 Sir Edward Clive Odnall Phillipps-

Wolley, a direct descendant of Robert Clive of India, established an estate here. In 1932 the island was used as a prison for over 600 Doukhabours who had been convicted of parading in the nude. The island was split in half by a double barbed wire fence to separate the men from the women. This experiment proved unsuccessful, however, as nearly 800 prisoners were released in 1934 (Arber).

A public float provides access to this island which has been subdivided into over 100 lots and is surrounded by 17 individual pocket beaches. Good temporary anchorage is possible, sheltered from ferry wash and afternoon southeasterlies, just south of Harry Point on the northwest side of the island.

9   Swartz Bay

A tiny public float here (87 feet of berthage space) provides a temporary landing place for residents of nearby islands and for small craft picking up or leaving passengers at the B.C. Ferries terminal. Small craft should stay well clear of ferries in Colburne Passage as there is very little manoeuvering room and tidal streams can reach maximum rates of two knots. The majority of ferries enter Swartz Bay between Piers and Knapp islands, but occasionally use the entrances between Piers Island and Saanich Peninsula, or between Pym and Coal islands.

10   Canoe Cove Marina

For those unfamiliar with this area, entrance to Canoe Cove Marina (656-5515 or 656-5566) is best made from either north or south via Iroquois Passage. When entering from the north it is best to keep between Goudge and Musclow Islet. Sailors familiar with the location of the many rocks in this area frequently pass inside Musclow Islet and use Page Pass, inside Fernie Island, when entering from the south.

The Canoe Cove Marina includes a large boat yard with a 12-ton hoist and ways capable of hauling out boats of up to 50 tons. Full facilities for repairs including do-it-yourself maintenance is available as well as fuel, berthage, launching by crane, dry land storage, marine hardware, charts, fishing supplies, showers, restaurant and a traditional pub — The Stonehouse (656-3498). This marina is within two minutes walk of the B.C. ferries terminal in Swartz Bay.

Tsehum Harbour

Tsehum Harbour, the location of most of the marinas serving Saanich Peninsula and the greater Victoria area, was formerly known as Shoal Harbour due to the extensive stretches of mud flats which used to be found at its head. These are gradually being dredged to provide sufficient depths for more float space. *Tsehum* is the Indian word for "clay" — the bottom material in much of the harbour — and is properly pronounced "Hws-se-kum" according to the Cowichan Indians.

11   Westport Marina

Limited transient moorage, showers and facilities for boat repairs (elevator lift) are available at this ma-

rina (656-2832). The B.C. ferries terminal is a five-minute walk to the north.

12   Cedar Grove Marina

This marina (656-1428) provides moorage and brokerage services and is located next to the mudflats at the head of Tsehum Harbour, just south of the Royal Victoria Yacht Club outstation floats (656-3413). McDonald Provincial Park, located half a mile to the south of Cedar Grove Marina, was established in 1948, one of the first on Vancouver Island, and has 30 campsites. Although the park fronts onto the head of Tsehum Harbour, it does not have a developed beach. Horth Hill Regional Park is located half a mile to the west.

13   North Saanich Marina

This marina (656-5558) which has recently expanded into Blue Heron Basin provides moorage, launching ramp, gas and diesel. The Sidney North Saanich Yacht Club is located in a turn-of-the-century house at 10735 McDonald Park Road (656-4600). The

Tsehum Harbour has become the centre of yachting activity on the Saanich Peninsula, home to numerous marinas and associated businesses.

Capital City Yacht Club (656-4512) is located at the south end of Blue Heron Basin.

14   Marina Park

This marina (656-0454) lies due west of Resthaven Peninsula at the southwest end of Tsehum Harbour. The approach channel is marked by log piling day beacons. This marina provides moorage, showers, washrooms, brokerage and a large cruising charter fleet (656-1611). Visitors are welcome when space is available — a very quiet moorage.

15   Shoal Harbour (All Bay) Wharf

The Shoal Harbour Public Wharf (656-3114) has 1,680 feet of float space for 50 to 60 small craft. These floats are mainly used during the winter months by fishermen. In summer months there is usually space for visiting boats, although some of the floats are

84

Facilities at the northern end of Tsehum Harbour include the recently expanded North Saanich Marina with new floats in Blue Heron Basin (centre left).

The clutch of marinas along Tsehum Harbour's southern shore include Shoal Harbour Public Wharf, All Bay Marina and Van Isle Marina.

removed for use at Sidney Public Wharf, two miles to the south.

16 All Bay Marina

This tiny marina (656-0153) tucked in behind the public wharf specializes in dinghies and assorted chandlery. There is a least depth of four feet in the approaches to the marina. McKinnon Marine (17) provides haul-outs, hull and engine repairs (656-2612) and the Blue Peter Pub (656-4551) is nearby.

18 Van Isle Marina

This large marina (656-1138) is protected from northeasterly seas by a stone breakwater extending north from Thumb Point. Facilities provided include fuel, moorage, a launching ramp, chandlery, charts, yacht charters, coffee shop, laundromat, showers and fishing supplies. Philbrooks Boat Yard (656-1157) immediately inside Thumb Point is one of the largest small boat shipyards on the island with full repair facilities including a 40-ton capacity ways.

The Latch Restaurant (656-6622) is one of Van- couver Island's finer eating establishments and is located at the base of Thumb Point in a former Lieutenant-Governor's summer residence made entirely from materials native to British Columbia.

Roberts Bay, to the south of Thumb Point, is very shallow and exposed to the wash of power boats on their way into Tsehum Harbour. It is generally only used by local residents, but would be a good temporary anchorage in a period of high tides and offshore winds.

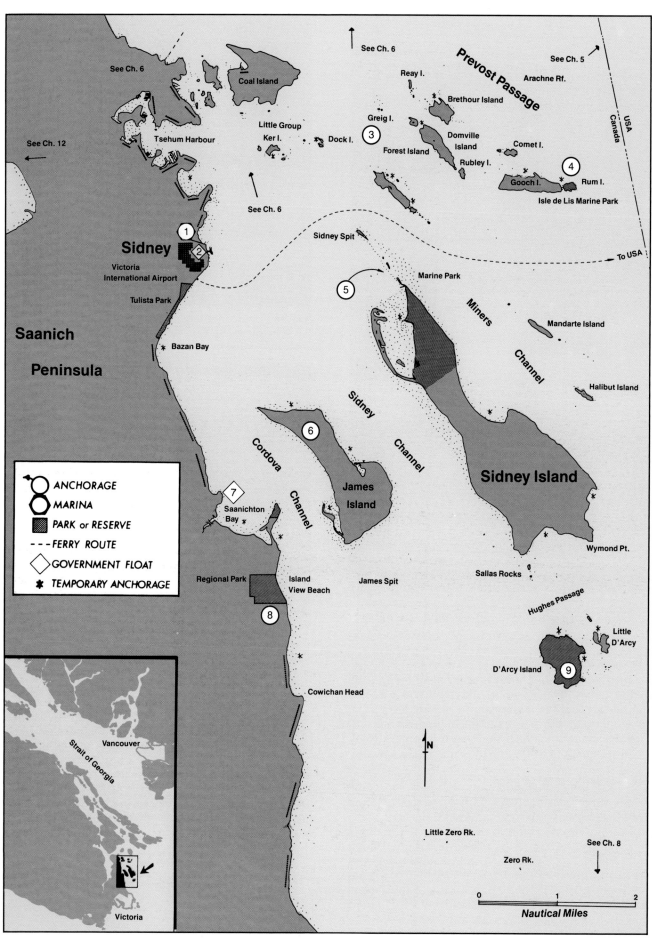

See Ch. 6

Prevost Passage

See Ch. 5

Reay I.

Arachne Rf.

Brethour Island

USA

See Ch. 6

Coal Island

Greig I.

③

Domville Island

Canada

Little Group

Ker I.

Dock I.

Comet I.

See Ch. 12

Tsehum Harbour

Forest Island

Rubley I.

④

See Ch. 6

Gooch I.

Rum I.

Isle de Lis Marine Park

①

Sidney

②

To USA

Victoria International Airport

Sidney Spit

Marine Park

Miners

Mandarte Island

Tulista Park

⑤

Saanich

Channel

Bazan Bay

Halibut Island

Peninsula

Sidney

⑥

Channel

Sidney Island

Cordova

James Island

ANCHORAGE

Channel

MARINA

⑦

Wymond Pt.

PARK or RESERVE

Saanichton Bay

Sallas Rocks

FERRY ROUTE

GOVERNMENT FLOAT

James Spit

Hughes Passage

TEMPORARY ANCHORAGE

Regional Park

Island View Beach

Little D'Arcy

⑧

Cowichan Head

D'Arcy Island

⑨

Vancouver

Strait of Georgia

N

Little Zero Rk.

See Ch. 8

Zero Rk.

Victoria

0 1 2

Nautical Miles

Not to be used for navigation

86

Sidney Spit Marine Park is a popular destination for crews from the Victoria/North Saanich area.

CHAPTER SEVEN

Sidney

Sidney and James Islands

The Sidney area at the north end of the Saanich Peninsula is the home of several active sailing and cruising clubs and marinas. It is ideally situated as a base for exploring the Gulf Islands because of its proximity to Victoria International Airport, the Swartz Bay ferry link to the mainland and the attractions offered by the town of Sidney.

Winds

This area has a preponderance of calms. The calms are possibly due to the fact that the Sidney area is in the transition zone of the strong southwest-northeast wind pattern which prevails around Victoria, and the northwest-southeast wind pattern found in the Strait of Georgia region. Off Sidney the northwesterly wind seldom occurs and the southeasterly wind is generally a fair weather, onshore wind, occurring most frequently in the summer months. Diurnal trends are dominant in summer with easterly and southeasterly winds blowing 80% of the time from noon to 4 p.m. and less than 20% of the time at night. Westerly and southwesterly winds blow over 50% of the time at night and less than 10% of the time from 10 a.m. and 5 p.m. In winter, when diurnal trends are not as important, strong southeasterly winds generally bring bad weather, while strong northeasterly winds bring colder, more stable weather.

Fishing

Use Tiny Teaser for trolling or Sildas, Pirks, Pirkens for drift fishing. James Island powder wharf (east side) is often hot for chinooks in April to May, September to October. The south and east edge of James Spit should be fished on a flood tide. Spin-cast from Saanichton spit for coho and big chinooks.

1 Port of Sidney

This marina (formerly Smitty's, Sterling or Island View) provides dry and wet berths, launching ramp, engine repairs, marine hardware and is protected from southeasterlies by a stone breakwater. The facility is to be tripled in size following breakwater extension and dredging.

2 Sidney Public Wharf

A log piling breakwater extending north from the end of this wharf provides limited protection in an area with several floats for small craft. In summer when strong southeasterly winds are uncommon, additional floats are attached to the pilings south of the wharf. However, the open exposure to powerboat wash can make this moorage uncomfortable and plans are afoot to construct a breakwater. The wharf also serves as a wholesale fish outlet (Satellite Fish Co.) and is located at the foot of Beacon Avenue, Sidney's main street and the gateway to several stores, gift shops, hotels and restaurants. The Sidney Museum is also

CHARTS
3310 — Sheet 1 — VICTORIA to ACTIVE PASS
     (1:40,000)
3441 — HARO STRAIT (1:40,000)
3476 — Approaches to TSEHUM HARBOUR
     (1:10,000)

Public floats at the foot of Beacon Avenue provide moorage for visitors to the town of Sidney on the Saanich Peninsula.

located at the foot of Beacon Avenue and has many interesting artefacts as well as a maritime display. The town of Sidney was named after Sidney Island which had been given this name around 1850 by officers of the Royal Navy.

Bazan Bay, to the south of Sidney, is a popular shorefront recreation area with a sand and gravel beach. There is a launching ramp at Tulista Park.

3   The Little Islands

Most of the larger of the little islands to the north and east of Sidney are privately owned — Ker, Forrest, Domville, Rubly, Comet, Brethour and Gooch — and on some the only permanent residents are a few sheep. Several of the islands offer temporary anchorage, generally on their northeast flanks or ends. Care should be taken to avoid the many rocks and shoals surrounding the islands. Other hazards include the tidal streams which flow at rates up to three knots and the wash from passing power boats. Brethour Island is named after one of the founding fathers of the town of Sidney.

There are also several islets, many of which are reserved by the crown for public recreational use, which are interesting to explore — Reay, Greig, Dock, etc. Dock Island derives its name from its earlier use as a location for careening of ships when there were no ways to haul out a boat in the vicinity. The sixteenth-century Hudson's Bay Company vessel *Nonsuch* used this island to careen when she was touring the B.C. coast in 1972.

An old breakwater which covers at high water pro-

Above: Rum Island (Isle de Lis Marine Park) makes an enchanting lunch stop, though overnight anchorage is not advised. Opposite: A pebble beach at the south end of Sidney Island.

tects a tiny anchorage area at the northeast end of Forrest Island from southeasterly seas, but care should be taken to avoid the many rocks at the entrance.

4   Isle de Lis Marine Park

Rum Island, now 11-acre Isle-de-Lis Marine Park, has the dubious distinction of being the closest Gulf

Island to the U.S. and is said to have been used as a stash for rum-runners crossing the border during Prohibition years. Temporary anchorage is recommended only in calm conditions. This park is best explored by those who have reached it in a beachable boat. Larger craft should anchor in the small, open bay on its northern flank.

Sidney Island

This island is often referred to as "the pearl of the Gulf Islands," with over 12 miles of sand or pebble beach encircling its 17-mile shoreline. Sidney Island was originally named Sallas Island by officers of the Hudson's Bay Company, but was renamed Sidney by Captain Richards of HM Surveying Vessel *Plumper* in 1859. The name Sallas lives on in the group of rocks at the southern end of the island. Both Sidney and James are geologically unique — they are the only Canadian Gulf Islands which are almost entirely composed of quaternary drift deposits: unconsolidated sands and gravels deposited by glaciers about 10,000 years ago

Miles of fine sandy beaches, wooded trails and extensive picnic facilities make Sidney Spit one of the most popular marine parks in the Gulf Islands.

and easily eroded, resulting in a sandy and constantly shifting shoreline.

5 Sidney Spit Marine Park

Sidney Spit Marine Park includes 350 acres of land and 374 acres of water. Mooring buoys are provided as well as float space (summer only) for landing from small boats or temporary moorage (nominal fee). Facilities are provided for camping (20 walk-in campsites and large open area with kitchen shelter for group camps) and picnicking. The sandy beaches and warm waters (up to 65 degrees F) provide excellent opportunities for swimming.

This park is also a very interesting area to watch the dynamic nature of shoreline processes in action over the years. Strong winds, high tides, longshore drift, erosion and deposition have all worked relentlessly to alter the area significantly. Recent charts show the northern spit is disappearing and the outer spit at the southern end of the park is now joined to the main island with the result that the anchorage area is filling in and is now shallower than previously charted. Where there were depths of one fathom at chart datum, now there is only one or two feet of water. The old government wharf, where a brickworks was once located, is still accessible at high water, but the approaches become shallower every year.

In a valiant effort, worthy of King Canute, the Parks Branch has attempted to hold back the relentless natural forces of wind, wave and tide by driving log piles into the spit. The purpose of the piles is to act as anchors for longitudinal logs in order to "stabilize the spit and prevent further erosion."

The lagoon at the south end of the park is well worth visiting by shallow-draught boat such as dinghy or canoe, especially at high water. This area is becoming a salt marsh now that the southern entrance has closed off and includes a solitary island, accessible by dinghy only at high water. Ducks, geese, gulls and many herons abound in this seldom visited area. The outer peninsula is covered with interesting sand dunes backed by interconnecting marshes and grassy islands. Temporary anchorage is possible near the old government wharf, but is not recommended south of this area due to shallows and underwater power cables.

The southern end of Sidney Island is privately owned and occupied by grazing sheep and imported exotic wildlife such as European fallow deer, peacocks, guinea hens, goats, wild turkey and Chinese pheasants. Wymond Point is backed by particularly attractive parkland. Temporary anchorage is possible at this end in several bays which are completely open to the southeast.

More protection from the southeast is possible in the large bight halfway down the eastern side of Sidney Island, but care must be taken to avoid the drying boulders which are plentiful on this side of the island. Miners Channel was used as the main canoe route through the Gulf Islands for miners on their way to the Cariboo gold rush in 1858 and 1859.

Mandarte Island, a steep-sided rock on the other side of Miners Channel, is said to hold the record of producing more Ph.Ds in zoology per acre than any other piece of real estate in B.C. The rock is the home for over 5,000 birds which have been studied intensively by ornithologists for over 50 years. Many species of birds share the island, with double-crested and pelagic cormorants generally perched on the steeper rock faces and pigeon-guillemots and glaucous-winged gulls sharing the more grassy flat areas. Anyone wishing to visit the island should first obtain permission from the local Indian band in Saanichton Bay, since the island is reserved by aboriginal right. Halibut Island, to the south of Mandarte, although similar in size is entirely different in character with few birds and many trees. It was formerly used as an Indian burial ground. A well and crumbling masonry indicate more recent habitation.

Facilities at Sidney Spit include a pay-for-use float and numerous red and white mooring buoys offshore.

At James Island, temporary anchorage is possible in the small lagoon off Cordova Channel. Recent depositions of sand and gravel are making the lagoon shallower with each passing year.

6 James Island

This island was named by the early settlers after James Douglas, Governor of Vancouver Island. For many years it was a farm and later became the isolated base for an explosives plant. Trespassers risked a heavy fine if they ventured ashore, since a fire on this land would have disastrous consequences.

Temporary anchorage is possible in a small lagoon which is gradually filling in south of where the old

D'Arcy Island Marine Park (foreground) was the site of a leper colony from 1890 until 1924 when it was moved to Bentinck Island southwest of Victoria.

CIL wharf in Cordova Channel was located. James Spit, south of the island, is also becoming shallower, with recent depths of one foot reported, where previously charted depths of three feet and one fathom were recorded. The "feeder" bluffs which are the source of sand and gravel for the recent deposition around the island, are a distinctive sight when viewed from the south, especially in the spring when the broom coats the upper slopes with a mass of golden yellow.

7   Saanichton Bay

The tiny float in Saanichton Bay (45 feet of moorage space) has the record of being the smallest public float on the B.C. coast. It was constructed for use as a boat landing for workers commuting to the CIL plant on James Island. Just to the south of this float is the site of what was once to have been one of the largest marinas in B.C. The southern portion of the bay is Indian reserve and has been used for many centuries as a food-gathering area. Permission should be obtained before using Cordova Spit at the east end of the bay for camping or picnicking.

8   Island View Regional Park

Just south of Cordova Spit is Island View Beach Regional Park with a beautiful fine-grained sand beach exposed at low tide. Over 50 years ago the tusk of an Imperial Mammoth was found here. Similar finds have also been made on James Island. Sand dunes between beach and backshore cliff support a variety of plant life including sea rocket, beach pea, sedge, sand-bur, Hooker's onion, beach knotweed and yellow sand verbena. Although this shoreline is fairly

Island View Park provides visitors with one of the finest sand beaches in the area: temporary anchorage is possible in calm conditions.

exposed, temporary anchorage is possible in calm conditions. Anchorage south of Cowichan Head is not recommended as the sandy tidal flats give way to a boulder and reef-strewn beach.

9   D'Arcy Island Park

D'Arcy Island (207 acres), located one mile south of Sidney Island, is a provincial park that has not been developed primarily because of its proximity to Sidney Spit Marine Park, which provides better anchorage. Starting in 1890 this island was used as a leper colony with a population that varied from one to six. Visitors to the island during this time were appalled at the conditions; when the old shacks were burned to the ground it was noted "there can be no estimate of the distress, misery and the shattered dreams that lay in the ashes" (Salazar, *B.C. Historical News*, Vol.18 #3

The view south over Little D'Arcy Island. Numerous off-lying rocks and reefs are cause for caution when navigating in this area.

The attractive cove in Little D'Arcy dries at low water; is best for exploration by dinghy or kayak only.

1985). The colony was finally closed in 1924 and Bentinck Island, south of Victoria, was used instead. Temporary anchorage is possible off a meadow along the eastern shore. There is a lovely cove in Little D'Arcy which almost dries at low water. Visitors have reported spooky feelings here, especially at night: "I woke up thinking there was no escape ... I was trapped there forever ... a.most depressing feeling ... and yet at the same time ... oddly delicious" (Teece).

Navigators in this area should be wary of the many underwater rocks and reefs between and south of the D'Arcy islands, including Unit Rocks, Kelp Reefs, rocks to the north of Zero Rock and Little Zero Rock. While wind conditions in this area in the summer months are generally flat calm to light southeasterly, as you travel south the southwesterly wind pattern which prevails in the Victoria area gains dominance.

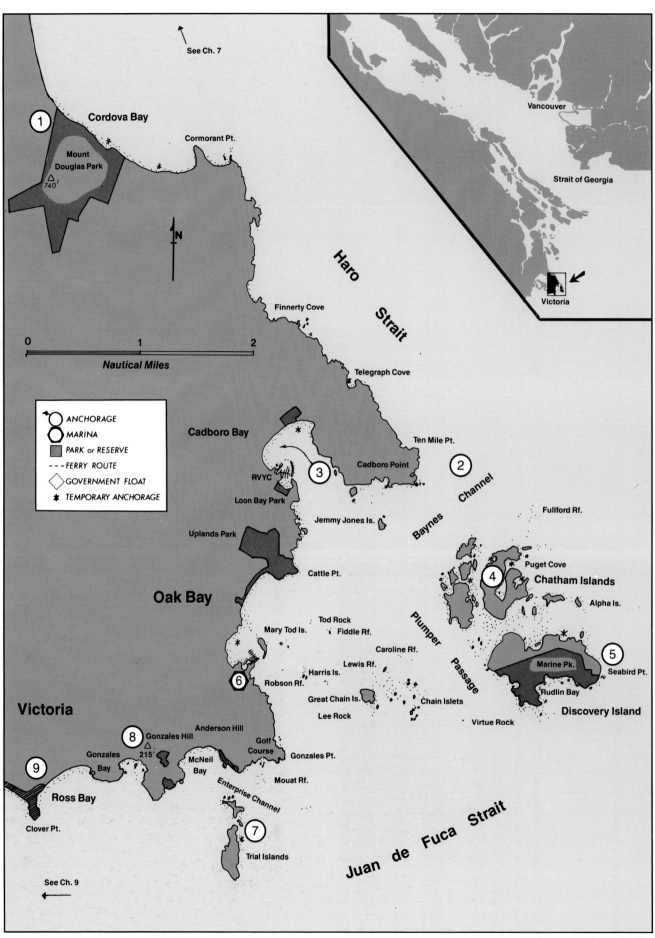

See Ch. 7

Vancouver

Strait of Georgia

Victoria

Cordova Bay

①

Mount
Douglas Park
△
740'

Cormorant Pt.

Haro Strait

Finnerty Cove

N

0   1   2
Nautical Miles

Telegraph Cove

○ ANCHORAGE
○ MARINA
▨ PARK or RESERVE
--- FERRY ROUTE
◇ GOVERNMENT FLOAT
✳ TEMPORARY ANCHORAGE

Cadboro Bay

Ten Mile Pt.

③

Cadboro Point

②

Baynes Channel

RVYC

Loon Bay Park

Jemmy Jones Is.

Fullford Rf.

Puget Cove

④

Chatham Islands

Uplands Park

Alpha Is.

Cattle Pt.

Oak Bay

Tod Rock

Mary Tod Is.   Fiddle Rf.

Plumper Passage

Caroline Rf.

Lewis Rf.

⑤

Marine Pk.

Seabird Pt.

Victoria

⑥

Robson Rf.

Harris Is.

Great Chain Is.

Chain Islets

Rudlin Bay

Discovery Island

Lee Rock

Virtue Rock

Anderson Hill

⑧ Gonzales Hill

Golf
Course

Gonzales Pt.

Gonzales   △
Bay   215'

McNeil
Bay

⑨

Mouat Rf.

Ross Bay

Enterprise Channel

Clover Pt.

⑦

Trial Islands

Juan de Fuca Strait

See Ch. 9

Not to be used for navigation

*The view southwest across Cadboro Bay in August, 1862.
(Watercolour on cardboard by E.C. Fellows).*

CHAPTER EIGHT

Oak Bay

Cordova Bay, Chatham Islands, Discovery Island

Oak Bay, home base of the Turkey Head Sailing Association, and Cadboro Bay, home of the Royal Victoria Yacht Club, provide protected havens for the many yachts taking advantage of the near perfect sailing conditions which prevail off the eastern extremity of Vancouver Island.

Winds and Tides

In summer this area has one of the lowest percentage frequencies of light winds on the east coast of Vancouver Island. Strong winds from Pacific Ocean high-pressure areas curl around from Juan de Fuca Strait as southwesterlies over 75% of the time from June to August, with a mean wind speed over 14 mph. Wind speeds tend to decrease slightly toward the end of the summer with September and October being the calmest months of the year. In winter, north and northeasterly winds prevail over 40% of the time, bringing colder arctic air from the interior of B.C.; and there are occasionally strong southeasterlies and very strong southwesterlies (mean wind speed over 19 mph).

The times of slack water in Baynes Channel vary considerably from the predicted times taken from the Victoria high and low waters. This is the area where the mainly diurnal tides (one low and two highs each day) of Victoria meet the mixed semi-diurnal (two highs, two lows) of Georgia Strait with confusing results. Slack water in Baynes Channel is supposed to occur about an hour and a half after high and low waters at Victoria. Local sailors have found, however, that the tidal current predictions for Active Pass are more accurate for this area, and the times for high and low water often follow the predictions for Fulford Harbour rather than Victoria. The main tidal stream passes close to the Chatham Island shore via Plumper Passage (maximum five knots). Streams between Oak Bay and Chain Islets seldom exceed three knots.

Fishing

Fishing from shore is possible at Ten Mile Point, the Oak Bay Marina breakwater, or the Golf Links (Gonzales Point). Try spin-casting for grilse, bluebacks and the occasional big chinook November to May. Oak Bay is hot in October and November and February to March for winter chinooks. Off the Gap (west side of Chatham-Discovery) use eight oz. weight, 30-50 feet of line, herring strip or minnow at normal trolling speed on an ebb tide. On a flood tide try Fulford Reef, north of Chatham Island, which is good for bucktail fly fishing in the fall coho season and for big chinook in May to June.

1   Cordova Bay

The name for this bay was transplanted about 1842 by officers of the Hudson's Bay Company from Es-

---

CHARTS
3310 - Sheet 1 — VICTORIA to ACTIVE PASS
    (1:40,000)
3423 — TRIAL ISLANDS to CADBORO BAY
    (1:12,000)
3440 — RACE ROCKS to D'ARCY ISLAND
    (1:40,000)

---

quimalt, which the Spaniards had named Puerto de Cordova in 1791. The northern shoreline of the bay (west of Zero Rock) has many offshore rocks and reefs eliminating the possibility of safe anchorage. The southern end of the bay is relatively free of dangers except for a few large boulders within 100 feet of the shoreline. Winds in the summer are generally offshore. On warm afternoons an onshore easterly or southeasterly breeze often counteracts the prevailing westerly, but this seldom lasts beyond nightfall.

Mount Douglas Park was named for Sir James Douglas, the first Governor of the colony of Vancouver Island and the "Father of British Columbia." This 365-acre park has a good sand and cobble beach and several trails which lead to the summit (740 feet), affording excellent views over the city of Victoria to the south, and the Gulf Islands to the north.

Several coves south of Cordova Bay could provide temporary anchorage, but are usually only used by local boats because of the high density of residential development along the shoreline. Finnerty Cove is a secondary tidal reference station with times of high and low water about an hour after Victoria. Back eddies in a flood tide often result in a south-moving stream for several hours after low water.

Telegraph Cove is the terminus of an underwater cable laid across Haro Strait, restricting anchorage to the western shore of the cove. In the 1800s this cove was the home of an explosives plant. In 1885 the ship *Western Slope* was loading dynamite here when she was witness to the collision of the steamships *Rithet* and *Enterprise* about a mile offshore in calm, clear, sunny conditions. Apparently the collision was the result of a misreading of the strength of the tidal streams through Baynes Channel. After the collision, survivors were picked out of the water and the *Enterprise* was towed into Cadboro Bay Beach by the *Western Slope*, where she was visible for over 20 years.

Anchorage between Cadboro Point and Ten Mile Point in tiny Maynard Cove is not advisable owing to the underwater radio cables which come ashore here ...unless you want to experience the full effect of radio station CKDA.

2 Baynes Channel

Entrance into Baynes Channel is often accompanied by an abrupt change in wind conditions. This can be accentuated by a real change in the actual wind strength and direction (from calm or light variable winds to a strong southwesterly), but is often the result of an increase or decrease in the apparent wind caused by the tidal streams. This "tide wind" will appear to increase the wind strength when wind and stream are opposed and to decrease the wind strength when wind and stream are in the same direction. With flat calm conditions and a strong tide, the "tide wind" will be of the same strength as the speed with which the boat is carried over the sea bottom by the tidal stream. In this situation it is possible to sail (beat diagonally across the tide) with no "real" wind. In cases where a sailboat is running with wind and stream of equal strength in the same direction, it is

possible to find oneself suddenly becalmed with no steerage way as the wind "disappears." This can sometimes prove to be quite embarrassing. These subtleties of wind and tide are unknown to some cruising sailors, who unless they are racing, often resort to the engine when the wind drops or they are faced with unfamiliar conditions.

Heavy tide rips with moderately-steep seas can also be experienced in this area whenever a strong tidal stream (maximum six knots) meets an opposing wind. As soon as one passes south of Jemmy Jones Island and out of the main stream, the seas will flatten and the "tide wind" will slacken noticeably.

Jemmy Jones Island is named after the "redoubtable" Captain Jemmy Jones, who, according to Captain Walbran in *British Columbia Coast Names* enjoyed sailing local waters in a variety of ships. His first ship, the schooner Emily Parker, burned near Clover Point in 1856. On December 31, 1858 his Wild Pigeon, 50 tons, capsized when leaving Victoria, but no lives were lost. His next vessel, the schooner Carolina, ran aground on the island now named after him. In 1864 he fitted his new schooner, the Jenny Jones, with steam power, but the ship was confiscated in the U.S. for non-payment of debts. At the same time, Captain

Offlying islands within minutes of marinas in Oak and Cadboro bays provide enchanting possibilities for yachtsmen from the Victoria area.

Jones was thrown into jail in Victoria for similar offences. He escaped, disguised as a woman with dress and bonnet, crossed to Olympia in the U.S. and took passage on his own vessel which was bound for Seattle to be sold. In Seattle, after the U.S. Marshal had departed, Jones took command, cast off his bonnet, dress and the ship's lines and steamed away. He then proceeded north through Georgia Strait stopping at a few places for fuel, supplies and extra crew, with both U.S. and B.C. justice officers in hot pursuit. He rounded the northern tip of Vancouver Island and sailed down to Mexico where he sold the Jenny Jones for $10,000. After the fuss had died down, Jones returned to local waters where he owned and sailed a small schooner named the Industry. In 1878 he nearly lost his life when the Industry swamped near Trial Island. He died in 1882. To this day kindred spirits

Cadboro Bay was named after the Hudson's Bay Company's brigantine Cadboro, 'crack' vessel on this coast for many years in the last century. Royal Victoria Yacht Club is centre right in the photo.

can be found enjoying the local waters in all variety of ships in all kinds of weather. There are even some who insist on sailing in the middle of winter storms and others who sail curious craft with hinges in the middle so that they can be folded in two to escape paying high moorage fees. Others rely on sailboards, kayaks, junk-rigs or whaler-hulled trimarans to challenge the wind and seas.

3 Cadboro Bay

This bay is named after the Hudson's Bay Company brigantine *Cadboro*, the first vessel to enter Victoria Harbour (1843) and the "crack" vessel on this coast for many years. The southeast exposure of Cadboro Bay is not a problem in summer since there are infrequent winds from this direction. In winter, the offshore islands and shoals seem to dissipate the force of incoming seas to some degree. The best anchorage is afforded in the western end of the bay, north of the Royal Victoria Yacht Club (592-2441) moorings. A

good beach lines the shore and Gyro municipal park is found at the northern end of the bay. Cadboro Bay Village with shops, restaurant and the Barley Mow Pub are behind the park.

Two launching ramps are located on either side of Cattle Point, the seaward extension of Uplands Park, just south of Cadboro Bay. This park provides an ideal vantage point to watch weekend yacht races just offshore.

4 Chatham Islands

These beautiful islands, less than two miles east of Oak Bay and Victoria, provide fascinating possibilities for exploring, but the many rocks, shoals, strong winds and tides tend to discourage most from venturing too close. Once you become familiar with local conditions you can sail between the two Chatham islands with a light following wind and a rising tide. This passage has a least depth of three feet at chart datum, but for those unfamiliar with the channel you can go aground at any stage of the tide. The main anchorage area is off the northwest end of eastern Chatham Island. Puget Cove, at the northeast end of this island, appears to be an ideal anchorage, protected from the prevailing southwesterly wind, but the shallow inlet which leads south seems to funnel winds from this direction into the cove.

Although the only visible signs of civilization on

97

Looking southwest over the Chatham Islands; Puget Cove on right, Oak Bay in the background.

these islands are the radio transmission towers, these islands are Indian reserve and should be respected as private property. Through the years there have been isolated incidences of vandalism and at various times the Songhees Indians have threatened to exclude all visitors from the islands. If you are interested in camping ashore, permission should be obtained from the Chief of the Songhees in Victoria. At present the only permanent residents of the islands are a few sheep.

5   Discovery Island

This island was named by Captain Kellet (1846) after HMS *Discovery*, commanded by Captain George Vancouver; Chatham Island was named after the *Discovery*'s consort. Neither of the two ships, however, came within 20 miles of these islands, since Vancouver was intent on finding the west coast entrance to the fabled "northwest passage" and followed the continental shore in his exploration of the Strait of Georgia.

The most protected anchorage from southwesterly winds is found south of Alpha Islet. This anchorage is exposed to easterly seas and winds and westerly or northwesterly winds, which are, however, relatively infrequent in summer. Alpha Islet is named after the British trading schooner *Alpha*, 58 tons, built at Nanaimo in 1859. It was the first vessel constructed there, hence the name *Alpha*. At 1 a.m. on February 12, 1863 the *Alpha* ran aground on Alpha Islet in a blinding snowstorm. She was floated off after discharging her cargo of coal, but in 1868 she was driven ashore on Flores Island, Clayoquot Sound and became a total wreck.

Persons wanting to camp ashore on the Chatham Islands should first seek permission from the land-holding Songhees of Victoria.

The northern portion of Discovery Island belongs to the Indians. A shallow cove which dries almost completely at low water is backed by beautiful salt marshes, providing a haven for shorebirds and resting waterfowl.

Heavy tide rips are often experienced just off the lighthouse at Seabird Point. Another hazard to watch for is the wash from ocean freighters which often pass very close as they turn the corner from Haro Strait into Juan de Fuca. The lighthouse at Seabird Point was constructed in 1886 and is worth a visit. The point is named after the American paddle steamer *Sea Bird*, which caught fire and was totally consumed after running aground here in 1858.

Gulf Island 29 Tumbo rests peacefully at anchor in one of the Chatham Island anchorages.

Discovery Island Marine Park

The southern 151 acres of Discovery Island were left to the province by Captain E.G. Beaumont when he died in 1967, at the age of 91. Captain Beaumont had lived here for almost 50 years and had shared the beauties of his island with generations of boy scouts, sea cadets and countless young people from other youth and church organizations. Mink, eagles and numerous other forms of small wildlife make their home on the island. There are no sheep on Discovery, so grass grows tall across the many meadows and through an abandoned orchard, in marked contrast to the Chatham Islands. Wind-contorted arbutus and garry oak with branches pointing northeast, reveal the dominance of the southwesterly winds.

In 1972 the property was proclaimed a provincial marine park and is maintained in a relatively wild and natural condition. The difficult access helps to protect the peacefulness and isolation on the island. Fires are strictly forbidden anywhere, since the grass and woodlands are often tinder dry and an unexpected gust of wind could take a spark from a well-protected beach fire into the woods with awful results.

Rudlin Bay, the primary access to this park is filled with rocks and shoals as well as being exposed to the southeast. With moderate or northerly wind conditions, temporary anchorage is possible for small craft behind a rock which dries three feet at the western end of the bay.

Chain Islands

There are several unmarked rocks between Discovery Island and Oak Bay. The most dangerous are Virtue Rock in Plumper Passage, under two feet of water at chart datum, and Lee Rock south of Harris Island which dries three feet at chart datum. Winter gales have foiled attempts to establish permanent beacons on these rocks. Carolina Reef which dries four feet north of the Chain Islets, can be located by lining up the three beacons which mark Robson Reef, north Harris Island and Lewis Reef. The Chain Islands are a noisy, smelly, guano-spattered breeding colony for thousands of glaucous-winged gulls, black oyster-catchers and pelagic cormorants. These islands are an ecological reserve and landing is discouraged.

A former lightkeeper at Discovery Island, Shotto Fox, also served at the lightstation at Fiddle Reef for two years prior to its automation. Apparently life at the tiny station could be quite lonely, even though over 100,000 people live within a few miles and hun-

Looking northwest over Discovery Island (foreground) with Chatham Islands and Cadboro Bay in the background.

dreds of boats pass within a hundred yards or so every day. Occasionally his mother would row out for a visit. The living accommodation in the base of the light tower was only 10 square feet — just big enough for a bed, an upper berth, a hot plate, a radio, a small sink and a toilet which consisted of a pipe draining straight into Oak Bay. His mother was quite happy with the cramped conditions until one morning a CPR ferry passed as she was using the facilities — a monstrous wake hit the reef and shot up the pipe . . . with disastrous consequences.

6   Oak Bay Marina

If the tide is not too low, small craft can enter this marina around the western end of Mary Tod Island. The caution sign in the middle of the passage should be passed fairly closely as shoals extend out from both Mary Tod Island and the Oak Bay mainland. The caution sign should tell you how much water there is in the passage, but below 10 feet it is sometimes hard to read behind the barnacles.

Seas can get a bit steep at the southern entrance to the marina when a strong southeasterly wind meets an ebb tide coming out of Oak Bay. Low water at Oak Bay generally occurs twenty minutes or so after low water Victoria, while high water at Oak Bay generally occurs an hour after Victoria.

The Oak Bay Marina (598-3366) and Boat Works (598-2912) provide complete facilities for small craft including fuel, moorage, boat and engine repairs with ways of 50-ton capacity and a 6-ton hoist, tidal grid, launching ramps, boat and fishing tackle rental, restaurant and cafe. The marina is also the home for Sailtrend (592-2711), the largest chandlery on Vancouver Island, with an extensive stock of boating equipment, clothing, books, charts and facilities for rigging repairs. The Lakewood Fishing Charters and Sealand (598-3373) with harbour seals, wolf eels, salmon, cod, sea lions, octopuses and a variety of other forms of marine life are on view here from both above and below the water. Visitors are also regularly drenched by an orca or killer whale performing airborne leaps and some other rather un-whalelike manouevres. The orca does not always obey the trainer's

will attempt to beat the stream by hugging the shore and passing north of Mouat Reef.

The first light on southern Trial was installed in 1906 on top of the lightkeeper's house at the south end of the island. This has since been replaced by a 100-foot tower with a green flashing light — kinder to its neighbours ashore. The old lens and lantern room are now located in Bastion Square, Victoria. The first lightkeeper, Howard O'Kell, made valiant efforts to

Discovery Island was once home to beloved local philanthropist E.G. Beaumont. His property was given to the province for a park upon his death in 1967.

commands (perhaps he gets bored with the standard routine) and sometimes delights in acting coyly and surprising the cautious watchers. Although many people have been introduced to these magnificent, gentle creatures by the killer whale shows, nothing can equal the excitement of a chance encounter with a pod of orcas in their native environment.

7 Trial Islands

These islands have long been used by naval vessels from Esquimalt and coastal ferries as a turning mark while undergoing sea-trials. To successfully round these islands against a strong wind (maximum speeds of 80 mph) and strong tidal stream (maximum six knots) constitutes a major trial of one's seamanship. With opposing conditions the majority of small craft use Enterprise Channel, where tidal streams are only half as strong. This is a somewhat intricate passage, since at low water it is necessary to pilot one's craft a quarter-mile south of Gonzales Point in order to miss Mouat Reef, which dries three feet at chart datum. With an opposing tide those with local knowledge

grow a garden and keep a cow on the island, but the cow kept attempting to swim back in the direction of the Oak Bay Golf Course where the grass appeared to be greener. The cow was rescued several times on the brink of being carried out to sea by the rushing tide until she finally ended up in the pot.

The strong winds, frequent tidal rips and steep seas around Trial Island have led many vessels to disaster. Among these were the *Arabella*, the tugs *Velos* (five lives lost), *George McGregor* (six lives lost) and the *Clallam* (54 lost).

The story of the *Clallam's* sinking is almost unbelievable, as related in a very terse and bitter account by Frank Davey entitled *The Clallam or Old Glory in Juan de Fuca*. The *Clallam* was an 168-foot American passenger vessel, which was on its way to Victoria from Port Townsend on January 8, 1904. She had over 80 people aboard, including 38 Canadians who were

The centre of attention at Oak Bay Marina are the killer whales which perform regularly for paying visitors to adjacent Sealand.

returning home after a Christmas holiday in the United States. At 4 p.m., the *Clallam* started sinking just off Trial Island in plain view of the city of Victoria, but the captain refused to send up distress signals or accept assistance from passing vessels. After 10 hours of horror the *Clallam* finally sank in American waters several miles to the east. Thirty-four of the passengers and crew, including the captain, were saved. There were no Canadian survivors.

Anderson Park, due north of the Trial Islands, provides excellent views over Oak Bay and the offshore islands. McNeill Bay was originally known as Shoal Bay. Immediately behind Harling Point is the Chinese Cemetery. Prior to 1944 it was customary for all Chinese in Canada to be returned to their homeland for burial. All the bodies were stored in wooden boxes in a crypt in Victoria awaiting shipment every seven years. When the new government in China refused to accept them, the remains of 849 Chinese were buried here in large graves marked by flat marble stones in 1961.

8   Foul Bay

Gonzales Bay was first charted as Foul Bay, an appropriate name since it is full of rocks and small islets and is completely open to the southwest, the most dangerous exposure. Local residents disliked the name because of its other connotations (it actually has quite a good sand beach) and petitioned to have the name changed to Gonzales. The original name lives on, however, in the name of a major road leading to the head of the bay.

The summit of Gonzales Hill is marked by a conspicuous white meterological observatory which is well worth a visit (open Monday to Friday, 10 a.m. to 4 p.m.). There is a museum of weather recording instruments and one can see how the wind, rainfall, sun-

Facilities and services at Oak Bay Marina include moorage, marine ways, repairs, fuel, yacht chandlery, restaurant and boat brokerage.

Southeast of the observatory is Walbran Park, which has two rocky knolls. The highest knoll is surmounted by a historic cairn commemorating the explorers of Juan de Fuca Strait and the lower by a World War II observation post. The park is named after Captain John T. Walbran, author of *British Columbia Coast Names*, the classic gazetteer originally published in 1909. This fascinating book is an absolute must for anyone interested in the history of the B.C. coast.

9   Ross Bay

A magnificent place to walk during a winter southeasterly storm. Be prepared for a salt water wash as thundering breakers send gallons of spray over the causeway and above the graves of many of Victoria's notable citizens in the cemetery beyond.

Yachtsmen should take care to avoid the treacherous shoals of Mouat Reef when making their way through Enterprise Channel between Gonzales Point and Trial Islands... .

light, etc. are actually recorded. The view from the top of the observatory is superb.

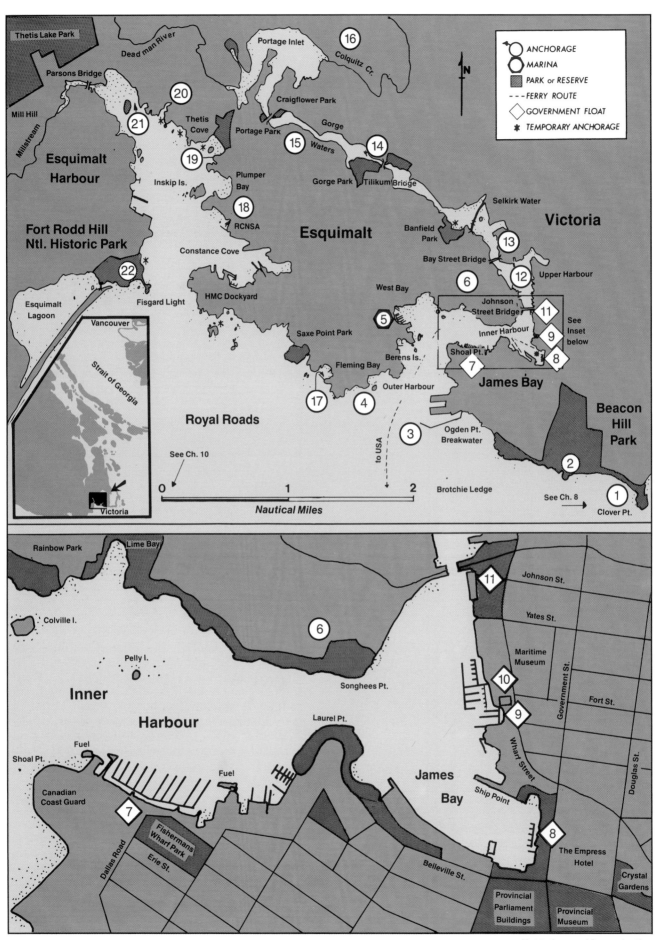

ANCHORAGE
MARINA
PARK or RESERVE
- - - FERRY ROUTE
GOVERNMENT FLOAT
* TEMPORARY ANCHORAGE

N

Thetis Lake Park

Dead man River

Portage Inlet

⑯

Colquitz Cr.

Parsons Bridge

Mill Hill

Millstream

⑳

Craigflower Park

Gorge

Waters

㉑

*

Thetis Cove

Portage Park

⑮

⑭

Esquimalt
Harbour

⑲

*

Inskip Is.

Plumper
Bay

Gorge Park

Tilikum Bridge

Selkirk Water

Victoria

Fort Rodd Hill
Ntl. Historic Park

⑱

RCNSA

Constance Cove

Esquimalt

Banfield
Park

*

⑬

Bay Street Bridge

⑫

Upper Harbour

West Bay

⑥

Johnson
Street Bridge

⑪

㉒

*

HMC Dockyard

⑤

Inner Harbour

See Inset
below

⑨

Fisgard Light

Saxe Point Park

Shoal Pt.

⑧

Esquimalt
Lagoon

Vancouver

Berens Is.

⑦

Fleming Bay

James Bay

Beacon
Hill
Park

Strait of Georgia

⑰

④

Outer Harbour

Royal Roads

③

Ogden Pt.
Breakwater

②

See Ch. 10

to USA

Brotchie Ledge

See Ch. 8

Victoria

0   1   2

Nautical Miles

Clover Pt.

①

Rainbow Park

Lime Bay

Johnson St.

⑪

Colville I.

⑥

Yates St.

Pelly I.

Inner

Songhees Pt.

Maritime
Museum

Government St.

Fort St.

⑩

⑨

Harbour

Laurel Pt.

Wharf Street

Douglas St.

Fuel

Shoal Pt.

Fuel

James

Ship Point

Canadian
Coast Guard

⑦

Bay

⑧

Fishermans
Wharf Park

Dallas Road

Erie St.

Belleville St.

The Empress
Hotel

Crystal
Gardens

Provincial
Parliament
Buildings

Provincial
Museum

Not to be used for navigation

104

Esquimalt Harbour circa 1860. (Watercolour on paper by Lieut. Bertram M. Chambers.)

Victoria and Esquimalt

West Bay, Inner Harbour, Portage Inlet

Victoria, Canada's oldest active harbour on the west coast, is a city worth visiting for its historical background as well as for its calm, unhurried pace and old world atmosphere. The charm of the city is greatly increased for those who have an opportunity to approach it by sea and to explore the shoreline. The upper reaches of both Victoria and Esquimalt harbours are accessible by shallow-draught sail or motorboat, but a dinghy or canoe is preferable.

Early explorers to this area were not impressed with Victoria Harbour because of the large number of rocks and shoals and the intricate entrance. Esquimalt Harbour, two miles to the west, was preferable as a port, but lacked the extensive tracts of level to gently sloping land suitable for farming and settlement. Together, with the help of the Royal Navy and the Hudson's Bay Company, the two harbours grew together to provide a viable community, transportation centre and capital city for British Columbia.

Winds and Tides

Winds off Victoria in the summer are predominantly from the southwest and there is a lower percentage of calms than in the Strait of Georgia. In winter, winds are either from the southeast (bringing rain), from the north (stable conditions with cooler temperatures) or from the southwest (short periods of rainfall followed by a clearing sky). During the summer months this area is the driest populated area in Canada, receiving less rain than the "dry belt" of Ashcroft, Kamloops or the Okanagan in the B.C. interior. The mean total precipitation for the Victoria

West-Esquimalt Peninsula area for June, July and August has been less than 2.1 inches. Only Lytton, B.C. has a lower mean — 2.03 inches, but it receives this rain on more days. The winter is another story . . .

The tidal range for Victoria averages only six feet for normal tides and nine feet for spring tides, with one low and two highs every day. With the exception of Seymour Inlet, this is the lowest range of all the ports on the entire B.C. coast. In summer, low water generally occurs in the morning and is followed by a rapid rise until mid-afternoon, then a slower rise and fall till about midnight. This pattern of tides is slightly different from that experienced in the Strait of Georgia with two highs and two lows every day.

Fishing

Troll to 30 fathoms from Brotchie Ledge to Clover Point or Albert Head. Fishing is best from December to February or September to October for coho or February to March for chinook as they follow spawning herring into Esquimalt Harbour. At Ogden Point try spin-casting when winter storms school bait close to shore. At Constance Banks (south of Clover Point) use anchovy, minnow or herring strip with revolving

---

CHARTS
3310 — Sheet 1 — VICTORIA to ACTIVE PASS
    (1:40,000)
3415 — VICTORIA HARBOUR (1:6,000)
3417 — ESQUIMALT HARBOUR (1:6,000)

flashers for salmon and halibut. Chinook season is best from December to March.

Open to the south, Victoria's waterfront homes regularly receive the full brunt of spectacular winter gales.

1   Clover Point

Hudson's Bay Company Factor James Douglas first landed at Clover Point in March 1843, coming ashore from the deck of the company steamship *Beaver*. Wading through clover two feet deep he climbed to what is now Beacon Hill Park, traversing open grasslands spread between isolated copses of thick forest to James Bay, in the Inner Harbour. It was here, in a place the Indians called Camosun, "place for gathering Camas," that Douglas began to build Fort Victoria with the cooperation of the local Songhees Indians and his French Canadian carpenters. He recorded his first impressions in this way:

> The place itself appears a perfect Eden in the midst of a dreary wilderness of the northwest coast, and so different in its general aspect from the wooded region around that one may be pardoned for supposing it had been dropped from the clouds into its present position.

A waterfront park and promenade follows the shoreline from Ross Bay all the way to Ogden Point at the entrance to Victoria Harbour. The Clover Point Anglers Association Boathouse (383-7492) was built deep into the rock after a 90 mph southeaster (1929) destroyed scores of individual boathouses along the shore. Clover Point is an excellent place to fly kites or watch world-class surfsailers and hangliders riding strong southwesterly winds. Ocean-going freighters pass close inshore here to meet speeding red pilot boats from Ogden Point.

2   Beacon Hill Park

Every spring this hill changes from green to yellow to blue to gold as over 100,000 daffodils, blue camas, broom and buttercups bloom through the grass. It was once known by the natives as *Meeacan*, roughly translated as "the hill that looked like the belly of a fat man lying on his back". A fortified Indian village was once located in front of the hill, at Finlayson Point. Threats of invasion in the 1800s, 1914 and 1942 also brought further fortification construction, trenches, batteries and searchlight towers, some of which still stand along the waterfront. Beacon Hill became B.C.'s first park when it was set aside for public use by Governor James Douglas in 1858. Two beacons were located on the hill, which, when in line, marked the position of Brotchie Ledge, a dangerous shoal at the entrance to Victoria Harbour. For a time horses raced around the hill on a track that is now Circle Drive. Today there are several small lakes with ducks, geese, and swans from Her Majesty's Swannery at Cookham-on-Thames. There are lawns for bowling and pitches for horseshoes, soccer, cricket, tennis courts, children's playground, wading pool and the Garry Oak Farmyard with lambs, chickens, rabbits, ponies, piglets, calves, goats, peacocks and pheasants. One can also view the world's largest totem pole (127 feet 7 inches) and listen to summer concerts at the Cameron Bandshell.

A lone yacht ghosts through grey seas and skies in eastern Juan de Fuca Strait.

3 Ogden Point Breakwater

Ogden Point breakwater, half a mile long, is great as a promenade, for fishing, observing marine traffic entering or leaving the harbour, or getting blasted by a winter storm. The waters just off this breakwater are also one of the most important scuba diving sites on Vancouver Island because of the exceptionally rich marine life (black rockfish, wolf eels, octopus, sea anemones, molluscs, herring and sandlance, dogfish and large concentrations of sponges) and relative safety (minimal currents, easy access). Divers are prohibited from removing sea life in this marine sanctuary and one may be guided along a signed, underwater nature trail. Brotchie Ledge, a half-mile offshore, is also popular for scuba diving, with many interesting artifacts up to 100 years old, dumped from garbage barges or shipwrecks such as the 1891 *San Pedro*. Nothing should be taken as this is part of the Ogden Point Marine Sanctuary.

Boats entering the harbour can use Channel 68 to receive assistance and information on moorage and marine traffic. Short, moderately-steep seas sometimes occur off Ogden Point when a strong wind meets an opposing tidal stream. In summer, with prevailing winds from the southwest, it is often possible to run or reach with full sail right up to the floats in front of the Empress Hotel. This can be an exhilarating experience, especially if the wind is strong. However, care should be taken to avoid freighters and ocean liners inside Ogden Point or coastal steamships, car ferries, float planes, schooners, brigantines and tugs pulling log booms or barges. Small craft should not insist on the right of way over larger ships which have difficulty manoeuvring in a constricted waterway. North of Ogden Point breakwater are the Pilotage Authority floats, CN ferry wharves, James Bay Anglers launching ramp, Canadian Coast Guard Base and Heliport on the site of the old Rithet/VMD wharves.

4 McLoughlin Point

Immediately southeast of Harrison Island, in 30 feet of water, is one of the oldest wrecks in British Columbia, the 97 foot *Major Tompkins* which sank here on February 25, 1855. Rose Bay, just to the north, contains breakwater-protected floats for members of the Canadian Armed Forces stationed at Work Point Barracks, home base for the Princess Patricia's Canadian Light Infantry.

At the entrance to Victoria's Inner Harbour is West Bay Marina, providing moorage, bait, ice and, nearby, groceries, marine ways and a pub.

5 West Bay Marina

This marina (385-1831) provides bait, ice and moorage for visiting small craft. A grocery store and pub are nearby. Just north of the marina is Outer Harbour Marine Ways (388-5632) with a boat yard capable of hauling out and repairing small craft up to 30 tons in size.

6 Songhees

A waterfront boardwalk promenade lines the north shore of West Bay linking several parks and public accesses around the new Songhees development area to the Johnson Street Bridge. At the head of Lime Bay (foot of Catherine Street) a thirsty traveller can find Canada's first neighbourhood brew pub — Spinnakers (384-2112). This venerable establishment features a nice view, "real" ale brewed on the premises and hearty meals. The north shore of the Inner Harbour, formerly the encampment for visiting natives from the north and latterly an industrial area, is now being redeveloped to include small marinas and residential communities.

7   Fishermen's (Erie Street) Floats

These public floats provide moorage for over 400 boats, the majority of which are fishboats secured three abreast in the winter time. In summer only a few fishboats remain, leaving ample space for visiting small craft. The floats are flanked on both sides by fuel barges, Esso (384-8712) to the west and Texaco (388-7224), Vinnies Eats, laundry and shower facilities to the east. Barb's Place (384-6515) on the floats is a handy place for Fish and Ships (sic) or you can wander the docks to find a fisherman with fresh fish for sale.

Looking north over Victoria's Inner Harbour; the parliament buildings are in the foreground, Empress Hotel on the right.

South of the floats is the Fisherman's Wharf Park and on Erie Street: Scott Plastics (382-0141) for fishing gear; Harbour Machine (383-6555) for engine and propeller repairs; Victoria Marine Electric (383-9731) for equipment, wiring and steering repairs; and MMOS (385-2251) for all your marine gear (chandlery).

Immediately east of the Texaco barge are the Capital City and Pier One floats providing private moorage. Russel Electronics (382-8632) on Kingston Street services marine equipment. A waterfront park and promenade surrounds the Laurel Point Inn.

8   Inner Harbour (James Bay)

The public floats in front of the Empress Hotel are available for public moorage for up to 72 hours at a time. Every year, during the last week in May, this entire basin is filled with as many as 400 sleek sailboats on the evening prior to the Swiftsure Race. This 136-mile race out to the Swiftsure Bank at the entrance to Juan de Fuca Strait and back again is the premier event for west coast yachtsmen. Thousands of spectactors crowd the shoreline to view the entrants and watch the start off Brotchie Ledge. Swiftsure Bank was named after HMS *Swiftsure*, the last fully-rigged sailing flagship of the Royal Navy, which was based here in the 1880s.

The Government Street causeway in front of the Empress was a bridge in the days when the mudflats of upper James Bay extended for several hundred yards beyond the Empress to the east. After the stone causeway was completed the bay was filled in, pilings were sunk into the fill and the hotel was constructed on top of the pilings. Apparently the Empress is now gradually sinking back into the mudflats at the rate of several inches a decade. Immediately south of the public floats is a private float which is used by small water taxis — Harbour Tours (381-1511). To the west is the Undersea Gardens (seals, barnacles, crabs, anemones, cucumbers, octopuses, sturgeon and scuba divers) and the Royal London Wax Museum located in the old CPR terminal building. The Parliament Buildings, built entirely of materials native to British Columbia, and the Provincial Museum south of the Empress, are both worth visiting. The museum, which is rated as one of the top five museums in the world, includes exhibits of early shipbuilding in B.C., a full-scale reconstruction of the stern cabin of Captain George Vancouver's *Discovery*, and lifelike dioramas of Gulf Islands and west coast habitats. Immediately next door is the Helmcken Heritage House and Thunderbird Park, with one of the largest collection of totems in the world. Here one can watch as the spirits of Bear, Beaver, Frog, Raven, Eagle and Whale are carved into red cedar by superb native craftsmen. Kitty-corner to the Park is the Crystal Gardens, with a variety of exotic birds, monkeys, tropical plants and afternoon tea. Three blocks to the east is the Beaconsfield Inn (384-4044) featuring Edwardian bed and breakfast.

North of the public floats is a Tourist Information Centre (382-2127), Chauney's Restaurant (385-4512) and the Ship Point Wharf. Here one can see traditional vessels including the *Robertson II*, the last original Grand Banks Fishing Schooner still actively sailing in Canada, the brigantine *Spirit of Chemainus* and topsail schooner *Pacific Swift*. These are operated by the SALTS — Sail and Life Training Society (383-6811).

The seat of government in British Columbia is at the parliament buildings in Victoria, seen here outlined in lights as they are each evening.

Public floats in front of the Empress Hotel are the moorings of choice for most visitors to Victoria - convenient to the downtown core.

9   Broughton Street Float

This public float is easy to miss as it is tiny and surrounded by large wharves. The southern side of the floats are reserved for fishery patrol vessels and the northern side for vessels clearing customs. Immediately south of here is the Air B.C. floatplane terminal (388-5151) and to the north are the floats of the Victoria Sailing School (384-7245). Directly above the float is Queen Elizabeth II Park, one of the smallest parks in Canada, measuring 28 feet by 70 feet. This park was originally intended to cover a larger area, encompassing the mooring rings embedded in the shoreline which are the only visible remaining portion of Fort Victoria.

South of Queen Elizabeth II Park is the first Customs House built in B.C., a distinctive pink building constructed in 1874. Formerly the home of HMCS *Malahat*, the building now houses offices for community groups including the Bastion Theatre Company, Greater Victoria Yachting Foundation and SALT Society.

10   Wharf (Fort) Street Floats

Extensive float space for visiting boats is now available at the foot of Fort Street. The B.C. Maritime Museum is located in Bastion Square (behind the floats, between Fort and Yates Street) in the old Provincial Court House. This museum has an outstanding collection of exhibits depicting the coastal history of British Columbia and is well worth the nominal admission charge. The prime attractions are the famous world-girdling vessels — *Tilikum* (Captain Voss's Indian dug-out canoe) and *Trekka* (John Guzzwell's tiny sailboat).

11   Johnson Street Floats

These floats on the east side of the Johnson Street Bridge provide access to Bosun's Locker (580 Johnson Street, ships chandlery, 386-1308) and the E&N rail terminal immediately adjacent (daily service to Courtenay). Four blocks to the north are North Sails (554 Herald Street, 385-9022) and Capital Iron (1900 Store Street, Navy surplus and a bit of everything else, 385-9703). The Johnson Street floats are not very popular because of their proximity to the constant drone of traffic over the bridge and the intermittent disruption caused by the wash from passing vessels. The floats can accommodate about 12 small craft, with the inside portion being the most protected. A floating log breakwater provides only minimal protection for the floats. The bridge is a bascule type with huge cement counterweights and opens regularly throughout the day and night (385-5717 or Ch. 12) to permit passage of vessels which cannot clear the closed bridge. The closed clearance is 19 feet at high water and 28 feet at chart datum. A large proportion of the vessels entering and leaving the Upper Harbour are tugs pulling barges; these pass the floats closely at maximum speed to clear the opened bridge and send up an enormous wash.

12 Upper Harbour and Selkirk Water

It is possible to sail, motor, row or paddle right up to Portage Inlet, subject to the clearance restrictions of five bridges and water depths which vary with the season as well as the state of the tide. It is advisable to make use of the tides, since contrary currents can impede progress, especially in the narrower portions of the waterway. In the summer months one should enter after low water (afternoon) and return when the tide is relatively stable in the evening.

The Upper Harbour, north of the Johnson Street Bridge and Selkirk Water, north of the Point Ellice (Bay Street) Bridge, are almost completely industrial-

A hardy dinghy sailor braves the turbulent Gorge waterway during the annual Gorge Race from Craigflower Park to the Inner Harbour.

ized but nevertheless interesting when viewed from the water. Among the many small scale industries are an iron and steel works (formerly a rice mill), gas works, cement company, machinery depot and shop, asphalt plant, shingle mill, barge and tug company, shipyard, sawmills and lumber companies, railway yards, ferry wharf and many warehouses. The Princess Mary Restaurant Vessel (386-3456) is also located here. The Point Ellice Bridge has a fixed span with a clearance of 30 feet at high water and approximately 38 feet at low water. One of the first crossings at this location collapsed on May 26, 1896, drowning 55 people who were trapped in a streetcar which fell through the bridge.

13 Point Ellice House

In the middle of all this industry is an oasis of arbutus and fir trees surrounding the historic home of the first gold commissioner of B.C., the Honourable

Peter O'Reilly. This home was built in 1861 and is still occupied by members of the O'Reilly family, with all the original furniture and household effects. Their home is open to the public (10 a.m.-4 p.m., Tuesday to Friday). Visitors who arrive by dinghy could beach in a small cove south of the home or tie to any of the numerous log booms which surround the shoreline.

Grassy Halkett Island, in the middle of the Selkirk Water, was used by the early Indians to bury their dead and is protected from industrial development by a park reserve. The railway bridge which splits Selkirk Water in two is usually left open on the weekends, but is closed during the week. If you are unable to clear the closed bridge (clearance of seven feet at high water and about 13 feet at low water) telephone 382-3170 or 384-3460 on holidays to request a raising of the span.

Just inside the railway bridge, on the southern shore, is beautiful Banfield Park; and between this park and the bridge, high up among the trees, is the old Warren Home. This home is surmounted by a unique glass-encased cupola known as a "widow's walk." In the old days the sea captain's wife would climb to this tiny room and spend the day staring out to sea, hoping to see the sails of her husband's ship returning.

14 The Gorge Waters

At Tillicum Bridge the Gorge narrows to 35 feet in width and a rock below the bridge is almost awash at low water, producing a reversing falls. With an extreme spring flood tide there is a two-foot drop; on the ebb, the drop is four feet coming out. Currents reach six knots. Because this constriction greatly retards the flow of water, high water above the bridge generally occurs one to two hours after high water in Victoria. Low water can occur anywhere up to six hours after low water in Victoria. The tidal range above the bridge seldom exceeds four feet. The Tillicum Bridge is a fixed span with a clearance of 30 feet above high water. Immediately above the bridge is the home base for the Victoria Canoe and Kayak Club (382-1077). The Gorge Waterway has been beautified and improved over the last few years and is now a very pleasant place to stroll or meander in a slow moving boat. Belted kingfishers and great blue herons are often seen along the waterway.

15 Craigflower Park

Craigflower Park is the site of Craigflower School, built in 1854 — the oldest remaining schoolhouse west of the Great Lakes. The school has many interesting nineteenth-century artifacts and is open to the public in the summer months. This park is usually the starting point for the annual Gorge Race for sailing dinghies that ends at the Inner Harbour. The fixed-span Craigflower Bridge (Admirals Road) has a clearance of only seven feet at high water and about 10 feet at low water, which effectively blocks all but the smallest of sailing dinghies. It is a common sight when the herring are running to see people fishing from this bridge. Boaters should watch that they don't get snagged by a wayward caster. Across the bridge is

In the 1800s navy men used Portage Inlet as a convenient, sheltered route between their Esquimalt base and the social whirl in Victoria.

Craigflower Manor National Historic Site. At first glance this white, moderately sized home is not really distinguishable from any other 1950-style suburban home. A closer look reveals it is substantially built and obviously older (it has lasted since 1855). The manor was built to serve as a fortress as well as a home for Kenneth McKenzie, who was bailiff for the Craigflower Farm. The farm was set up under the Hudson's Bay Company (HBC) to provide agricultural products for Fort Victoria and for the revictualling of HBC and Royal Navy ships. The Gorge provided a convenient waterway for the transport of goods down to the Fort. It is reported that some ocean-going sailing ships actually tried to make their way up to the farm and one is reported to have sunk directly across from Craigflower Park in 1856. The Manor is open to the public daily, except Mondays, from noon to 4 p.m.

16   Portage Inlet

Portage Inlet is a very shallow lagoon with a predominantly fresh-water environment in the winter, changing to a saltwater environment in the summer when the freshwater runoff dries up almost completely. The inlet derives its name from its use in the 1800s as a back-door entrance to Victoria by native Indians and by officers and men from the Royal Navy ships in Esquimalt Harbour when the outside passage was too rough for their small boats.

The inlet is now ringed with private homes and the drone of traffic on the Island Highway, which parallels the north shore, echoes across the water. At high

water in winter Colquitz Creek and Deadman River are navigable by canoe for a few miles upstream and offer a certain measure of peace and naturalness. The Colquitz Creek is bordered by trails, Tillicum Park, swamps, shopping centres, the Pacific Forest Research Centre and Hyacinth Park.

Royal Roads

The southern approaches to Esquimalt Harbour are used as a roadstead, where ships can ride at anchor while awaiting dock space. The roadstead (roads for short) was dubbed Royal because of the two Royal Personages whose names are honoured on either side — Victoria and her husband Albert. In 1790 Manuel Quimper had named the roads "Rada de Valdes y Bazan" when he anchored here while exploring Albert Head.

17   Fleming Bay

The mouth of the entrance channel to Fleming Bay is protected by the Gillingham Islands, but offshore rocks around these islands are a hazard, especially near high water when most of them are covered. Good anchorage is possible just inside the stone breakwater in Fleming Bay. Since there isn't much room in the bay it would be advisable to anchor from the stern with a bow line onto the breakwater. The breakwater was constructed to protect a boat launching ramp from southwesterly seas. Nearby is the clubhouse of the Esquimalt Anglers Association and tiny Buxton Green Park at the base of the breakwater. Overnight moorage at the floats alongside the launching ramp is permitted in an emergency only. This bay provides access to Macaulay Point, Saxe Point Park, the Olde

England Inn (388-4353) and Anne Hathaway's Cottage, part of an English village recreated on Lampson Street.

Esquimalt Harbour

Tidal streams at the entrance to Esquimalt Harbour are generally weak and variable, with both the flood and the ebb setting to the east. The name Esquimalt has nothing to do with the Eskimo, it is a derivation of the Indian *Isch-whoy-malth* which means "place of gradually shoaling waters." The harbour was also named Puerto de Cordova by the Spaniards after Quimper anchored here in 1790. Galiano and Valdes also stopped here while engaged in their circumnavigation of Vancouver Island in 1792. Galiano was quite taken with the place, for he opened the sixth chapter of his journal with the remark *El Puerto de Cordova es hermosa* (The Port of Cordova is beautiful). The Royal Navy established their Pacific headquarters here in the mid-1800s and the base was transferred to the Royal Canadian Navy in 1910. Many of the landmarks, islands and coves within the harbour are named after the officers of HMS *Fisgard* which first surveyed the harbour in conjunction with HMS*Pandora* in 1847.

Constance Cove is the home base for the Royal Canadian Navy's West Coast Fleet, Yarrows Shipyard and the Canadian Government Graving Dock (once the third largest in the world).

18   CFSA

A floating caisson breakwater north of Munroe Head provides protection from southwesterlies for the floats of the CFSA (formerly Royal Canadian Naval Sailing Association). Just inside the drying rocks north of here is a launching ramp operated by the Songhees Indians in what is known locally as Maple Bank Park. The natives hope to establish a campsite here for visitors. Plumper Bay is taken up almost exclusively by log booms which extend halfway across the harbour, almost encircling Inskip Islands.

19   Portage Park

The log booms of Plumper Bay provide some degree of protection from southwesterly seas for a beautiful anchorage at the entrance to Thetis Cove. This anchorage is an ideal winter haven when northeasterly and southeasterly winds predominate, but is partially exposed to strong southwesterly winds. Several drying rocks north of Richards Islands preclude the use of the north end of Thetis Cove as a safe anchorage, except at high water. Portage Regional Park was established to protect the historic portage trail across to Portage Inlet and includes Richards Island in the middle of Thetis Cove. The eastern boundary of the park is the Esquimalt and Nanaimo rail line and the portage trail from the western end of the park links up with this line where it bridges the old Island Highway. Park trails lead to the historic Four Mile House Pub (479-2514), now the House of Brougham Tearoom, Restaurant and Art Gallery, immediately west of the railbridge. At one time Thetis Cove was famous for

Fisgard light, oldest on the coast, marks the western side of the entrance to Esquimalt Harbour.

crabs which grew fat on the remains from an adjacent slaughterhouse. When the crabs were forced to switch their diet from cows innards to sawdust they quickly disappeared.

20   Limekiln Cove

At the head of Limekiln Cove is a cairn, erected in 1959 by the Thermopylae Club of Victoria, which is inscribed: "When Vancouver Island was an infant Crown Colony nearly a century ago it was here that the gallant sailing ships from the old world stopped to replenish their supply of fresh water". The cove is now used by local residents to moor their boats. Public access from the head of the cove leads up Helmcken Road to a junction with the old Island Highway, where there are several stores. Public access is easier in the cove immediately east of here.

21 Cole Island

The most protected anchorage from summer southwesterlies in Esquimalt Harbour is just east of Cole Island. Log booms south of the island could also be used as a temporary tie-up. Cole Island was used by the Royal Navy and Royal Canadian Navy as a safe and sheltered munitions magazine from 1860 to 1938. It could be directly shelled only from within the harbour and was far enough from centres of activity that little damage could result from the island exploding through accident or sabotage. Because of its historic significance local residents are campaigning to add this island to Fort Rodd Hill National Historic Park so that many of the stone and brick buildings may be restored.

At high water it is possible to row or paddle up over the tidal flats to Parsons Bridge where one can visit the historic Six Mile House Hotel (478-3121) and have a brew with the locals, if one fancies that sort of thing, or go shopping at the Farmers Market, south of the bridge. The upper reaches of Mill Stream are exquisitely beautiful and peaceful at high tide. A short trek above the limit of navigation is Thetis Lake Park to the north and Mill Hill Regional Park where Atkins Avenue crosses Mill Stream Creek. The summit of Mill Hill, at 650 feet, provides spectacular views over Victoria and Esquimalt Harbours.

22 Fort Rodd Hill Historic Park

This 44-acre park was originally constructed in 1895 to serve as a coastal artillery installation to protect the entrance to Esquimalt Harbour. Three separate batteries with a number of six-inch breech loading guns, 12-pounder quick-firing guns and a complete network of underground living quarters and communications were embedded into the hill. From the sea all you can see is a grassy hill, a flag pole and, at the entrance to Esquimalt Lagoon, an observation tower. The fort was greatly extended during World War II, but became obsolete in 1956. The park was established in 1962 and two of the batteries have been restored to their 1895 condition.

Fisgard Lighthouse, the oldest on the Pacific Coast of Canada, has also been restored to its 1860 condition and includes a museum. The causeway linking Fisgard Island to Fort Rodd is of recent construction.

Fort Rodd Hill Park is definitely worth a visit. Good anchorage is available just north of the lighthouse, in the lee of Fort Rodd, with protection from south and southwesterly winds and seas. There is also a good beach here and the backshore is exceptionally attractive, with grassy meadows, several shade trees and browsing Columbian blacktail deer. The cables which are shown on the chart running south of Fisgard Light and under the causeway are no longer active. At one time there was a landing float here and residents of Victoria could cross from Bronsons Pub near the head of Constance Cove by water taxi to picnic at Fort Rodd.

Esquimalt Lagoon

Temporary anchorage outside the entrance to Esquimalt Lagoon is possible in an area open to south-

erly winds but partially protected from southwesterly seas — by Albert Head. On the whole, however, this is not a good base for exploring the lagoon by dinghy. By the time the tide is flooding strongly enough to assist passage into the lagoon, the southerly wind has increased (as it often does in the afternoon), making the anchorage uncomfortable for small craft. Nevertheless, if wind and tide conditions are co-operating, the lagoon is well worth a visit. At chart datum there is only 12 feet of clearance under the bridge at the entrance (this channel is supposed to dry two feet). Motorboats are discouraged from entering the lagoon as it is a Canadian Wildlife Service sanctuary for resting waterfowl and shorebirds. The end of Coburg Peninsula is an interesting area to watch shore processes in action. The prevailing summer southwesterly wind causes longshore drift, moving sand and gravel

One of the most protected anchorages in Esquimalt Harbour is just east of Cole Island (centre), site of the navy's munitions magazine from 1860 to 1938.

to the end of the spit. If it were not for the scouring action of tide and winter runoff currents at the outlet of the lagoon, the spit would eventually link up with Fort Rodd Hill, eliminating access to the lagoon by water. This is what has happened to Albert Head Lagoon, a few miles to the south. Directly across Esquimalt Lagoon is the Royal Roads Canadian Service College for military cadets. Historic Hatley Castle, built by the Hon. James Dunsmuir, son of the man who built Craigdarroch Castle in Victoria, and a unique botanical garden south of the college, are both open to the public daily from 1 to 4 p.m.

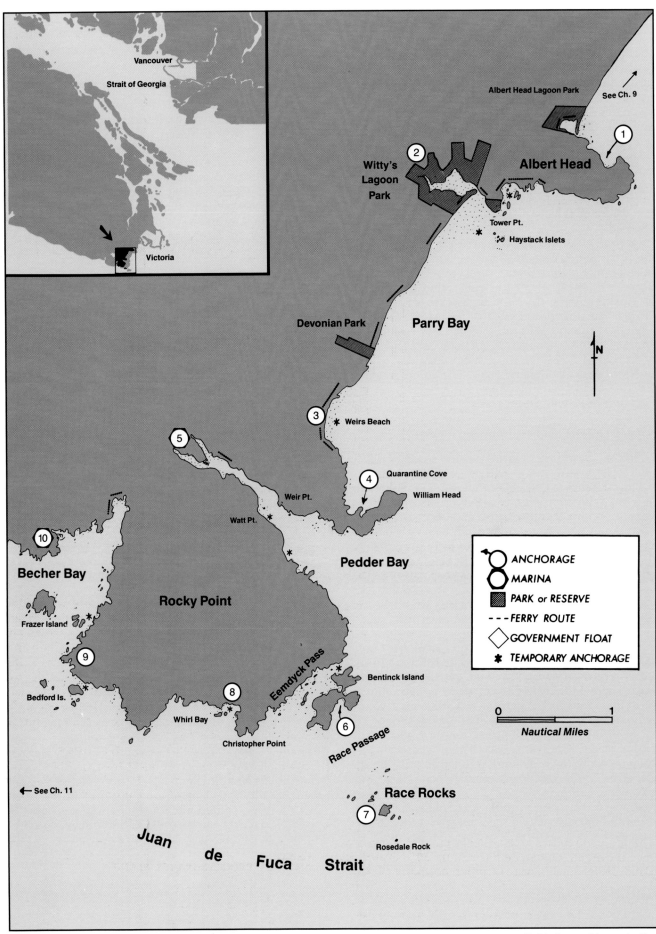

Vancouver

Strait of Georgia

Victoria

Albert Head Lagoon Park

See Ch. 9

(1)

(2)

Witty's
Lagoon
Park

Albert Head

Tower Pt.

Haystack Islets

Devonian Park

Parry Bay

N

(3)

Weirs Beach

(5)

Quarantine Cove

(4)

William Head

Weir Pt.

Watt Pt.

Pedder Bay

(10)

Becher Bay

Rocky Point

ANCHORAGE

MARINA

PARK or RESERVE

- - - FERRY ROUTE

GOVERNMENT FLOAT

TEMPORARY ANCHORAGE

Frazer Island

(9)

Eemdyck Pass

Bentinck Island

Bedford Is.

(8)

Whirl Bay

(6)

Race Passage

0   1

Nautical Miles

Christopher Point

← See Ch. 11

Race Rocks

(7)

Juan   de   Fuca   Strait

Rosedale Rock

Not to be used for navigation

114

The Olympic Mountains as seen from Pemberton's Rock. (Oil on paper by Thomas Bamford).

Albert Head to Becher Bay

Witty's Lagoon, Pedder Bay, Race Rocks, Becher Bay

The southernmost tip of Vancouver Island is a fascinating and challenging area to cruise and explore as it marks the transition between the relatively sheltered waters of the Strait of Georgia — with its predominant southeasterly-northwesterly wind pattern, and Juan de Fuca Strait — with its strong westerly winds from the open Pacific. Because westerly winds prevail throughout this area, the waters north of Bentinck Island are well protected with onshore winds occurring less than 10% of the time during the summer months.

If you decide to venture into the waters of Juan de Fuca Strait, remember you're approaching the open Pacific Ocean, where wind, sea and visibility are often entirely different from the more moderate conditions usual in the Strait of Georgia.

Winds

Winds are generally stronger in Juan de Fuca Strait. At Race Rocks the mean wind speed is 15 to 18 mph during the summer months and 80% of the time from the west. In winter, the westerly blows only 20% to 30% of the time, and the prevailing winds are from the northeast quadrant (50% to 60%). Southeasterly winds are infrequent at Race Rocks but more common near the mouth of Juan de Fuca Strait (30% to 40% at Cape Beale). In Victoria 12 miles northeast of Race Rocks, southeasterly winds occur less than 5% of the time during the summer months (still more than at Race Rocks). In winter with a full southeast gale blowing in Victoria with gusts up to 70 mph, Race Rocks

has recorded light winds of only 5 mph from the east.

During the summer months the prevailing westerly wind at Race Rocks is weakest during the morning. Since the tide is generally ebbing during the morning, this is often the best time of the day to plan an east to west passage.

Tides

The large tidal range which builds up within the Strait of Georgia provides impetus to the tidal streams which are very strong at the south end of the Island. The maximum six knot rate in Race Passage increases to seven knots south of Rocky Point and across the entrance to Becher Bay, but rapidly dissipates to less than three knots west of Sooke. Within the immediate vicinity of Race Rocks the tidal stream can reach up to nine knots due to channelization of the flow between the many rocks and islets.

The freshwater runoff in Georgia Strait and the coriolis force, which deflects currents to the right in the northern hemisphere, makes the ebb along the south coast of Vancouver Island stronger than the flood.

CHARTS
3440 — RACE ROCKS to D'ARCY ISLAND
    (1:40,000)
3641 — ALBERT HEAD to OTTER POINT
    (1:25,000)
3430 — Plans of PEDDER BAY (1:6,000) and
    BECHER BAY (1:15,000)

High altitude photo shows wisps of fog rolling past Becher Bay and Race Rocks in eastern Juan de Fuca Strait. Morning westerlies often disperse the haze by noon.

The time of slack water at Race Rocks is highly irregular and not necessarily coincident with local high or low water. At times, slack water can be up to two hours off the predicted time of high water as indicated in the standard tide and current tables (usually half to one hour before the change at the entrance to Juan de Fuca Strait). This time variation can be caused by prolonged periods of wind from one direction, or by differences in barometric pressure between the Strait of Georgia and Juan de Fuca Strait.

The secondary station at Race Rocks has recently been upgraded to a reference station with more accurate predictions for times of turn. It should also be noted that the predicted stream rates are about half of the actual current rate that one can expect, unless you are a supertanker, as the stream recordings were made 40 feet below the surface.

Seas

The prevailing westerly wind pattern in Juan de Fuca Strait helps drive ocean swells in from the open Pacific. These swells are sometimes noticeable once one has passed through Race Passage, even in calm conditions. The swells are generally of long wave length and not dangerous in deep water. In shallow water they tend to steepen and sometimes break (especially in bad weather with strong winds or against a strong current). Swells can be dangerous in shallow

116

coves where the surge may crash you down on the bottom several hours before you had expected low water.

Fog

Fog is very common off the west coast of Vancouver Island and occasionally moves up Juan de Fuca Strait into the Strait of Georgia, especially during the period from late summer to early winter. This fog sometimes builds up off the southern tip of Vancouver Island during the night then dissipates during the morning with the rising sun and westerly wind.

Fishing

Anglers from Pedder Bay mooch, drift fish and troll along the kelp beds in *all* weather and when the weather is calm they fish the south side of Bentinck Island to Becher Bay (see Fishing section in next Chapter).

Juan de Fuca Strait

In 1847 the Canadian artist Paul Kane attempted to cross Juan de Fuca Strait. His diary records that by 5 a.m.:

> ...the wind increased to a perfect gale and, blowing against an ebb tide, caused a heavy swell. We were obliged to keep one man constantly bailing to prevent our being swamped.
>
> The Indians on board commenced one of their wild chants, which increased to a perfect yell whenever a wave larger than the rest approached; this was accompanied with blowing and spitting against the wind as if they were in angry contention with the evil spirit of the storm. It was altogether a scene of the most wild and intense excitement: the mountainous waves roaming around our little canoe as if to engulf us every moment, the wind howling over our heads, and the yelling Indians, made it actually terrific. I was surprised at the dexterity with which they managed the canoe, all putting out their paddles on the windward side whenever a wave broke, thus breaking its force and guiding the spray over our heads to the other side of the boat.
>
> It was with the greatest anxiety that I watched each coming wave as it came thundering down, and I must confess that I felt considerable fear as to the event.

Eleven hours later they finally reached the safety of Fort Victoria.

Large portions of this coastline, particularly the headlands, are now owned by the federal government and have been used in the past primarily for quarantine, military or penal purposes. Over the years there have also been many proposals to open these headlands to the public for recreational purposes, but as yet little has changed.

1 Albert Head

This rocky promontory was named for HRH Prince Albert after his wife's name (Victoria) was given to the town on the opposite side of the bay. The first European to visit this region was Manuel Quimper, who landed at Albert Head in 1790, claimed the surrounding countryside for Spain and, after due ceremony, buried a bottle containing various documents underneath a large tree. This tree was marked with a large papal cross and the event described in Quimper's diary. In 1947 an old blaze mark was found on a tree here which matched the description in Quimper's diary. Attempts were made to retrieve the bottle, but it was never found.

Seventeen-acre Albert Head Lagoon Regional Park is a fascinating place to visit, with mute swans, ducks, loons, cormorants and a family of otters usually in residence behind a long gravel berm.

A small cove just north of Albert Head provides an

A small cove west of Albert Head provides good anchorage and access to Witty's Lagoon park on the left.

excellent summertime anchorage, but is exposed to northerly winds which prevail from October to March. A quarantine station which operated here from 1883 to 1893 was so inefficiently run that the Port of Vancouver banned all traffic from Victoria for a time. In 1893 the station was closed down and a new one built at William Head. This cove, now ringed with dilapidated World War II "No trespassing" signs, was a popular weekend picnicking and camping spot for Victorians who would arrive by excursion ferry in the 1920s when road transport was still relatively undeveloped.

The lighthouse and fog horn (discontinued 1984) on the point were constructed after the *Empress of Canada*, 21,000 tons, went aground in a fog on a Sunday morning in 1929. Many weekend campers were startled when they woke up to find the huge bow of the ship high and dry in the middle of a farmer's field.

During World War II massive self-contained underground fortifications were constructed here to guard the entrance to Esquimalt Harbour from Japanese warships. Three 9.2-inch guns were capable of lobbing shells across Juan de Fuca Strait into the United States, presumably in case the Japanese should attack Port Angeles. These fortifications are now abandoned, but Albert Head continues to be used spasmodically by the Department of National Defence as a training area and communications link.

Local residents anchor their boats in a tiny cove between Albert Head and Witty's Lagoon. Several islets and drying rocks guard the entrance to this cove, which also provides access to the peninsula portion of Witty's Lagoon Park (Tower Point).

2 Witty's Lagoon Park

This 126-acre park owes its popularity to the fine sandy beach which extends several hundred yards out into Parry Bay, almost reaching Haystock Islets at a zero tide. When low water occurs close to noon on a sunny day, the incoming flood waters of 40 to 45 degrees F are quickly warmed to 70 to 75 degrees F at

Services provided at Pedder Bay Marina include moorage, fuel, rental boats and launching ramp. Lester B. Pearson College of the Pacific is upland from the floats on right.

the end of the spit, resulting in ideal afternoon swimming conditions.

Good temporary anchorage is possible all along this shore in depths under four fathoms. Although offshore westerly and southwesterly winds prevail in this area, afternoon southerly winds can occasionally make the anchorage area west of Haystock Islets uncomfortable. Charts for this area indicate that anchorage is prohibited southwest of Albert Head for about two miles. This restriction is intended to discourage

larger vessels from snagging the cables which cross northern Parry Bay at depths generally greater than five fathoms.

The park itself is fascinating to explore, with trails leading behind the spit across grassy meadow and salt marshes to a beautiful waterfall at the head of the lagoon. This waterfall, referred to by early Indians as "The Sitting Lady," dries up almost completely by the end of the summer, but is a spectacular sight from late autumn to early summer. A nature house 100 yards east of the waterfall is open during the summer and trails lead around the lagoon shore to Olympic View Road and Tower Point. If tide and wind conditions are suitable, you can anchor close in and row by dinghy into the lagoon and up to the base of the waterfall. This procedure is greatly assisted when a strong flood tide counteracts the outflowing current at the end of the spit. Boats with outboard motors are discouraged within the lagoon as it is used by many nesting shorebirds and waterfowl, including mallards, buffleheads, Canada geese, sandpipers, curlews, plovers, herons, sanderlings and turnstones, as well as bald eagles, ospreys and belted kingfishers.

Devonian Regional Park

It is possible to walk along the beach from Witty's Lagoon and down to Sherwood Creek where 33-acre Devonian Park encompasses parts of Taylor Beach, Sherwood Pond and beautiful creekside trails which snake up the hillside to William Head Road. En route you will pass earthwork fortifications at the foot of Taylor Road, said to have been constructed by the Spaniards in the 1790s. A short distance along William Head Road is Fernie Farm (478-1682), famous for afternoon teas with scones and Devonshire cream in a country garden.

3 Weirs Beach

The south end of Parry Bay is more sheltered than the north end since it is protected by William Head from southerly seas. Care should be taken if anchoring here to avoid the underwater cables which cross Parker Bay at depths under four fathoms and come ashore at the south end of Weirs Beach. The Weirs Beach Resort (478-3323) boasts a fine sandy beach for swimming as will as a heated pool, tent and trailer campsites, showers, stores, boat rentals and launching ramp.

4 William Head

This headland and the bay to the north were named in 1846 after the famed Arctic explorer Sir William E. Parry by Captain Kellet, HMS *Herald*, an Arctic navigator himself. Several large "Keep Out" buoys surround the medium security prison at William Head. Mariners are requested to remain to seaward of these buoys at all time. Anchorage in Quarantine Cove is therefore restricted to the western half of the cove.

Quarantine Cove has a fascinating history since it was first used as an anchorage by sailing ships escaping the howling gales of the Pacific Ocean. Huge ring bolts can be found embedded in the rocky shoreline.

Race Rocks marks the southernmost portion of Canada west of Ontario. Granite used to build the 105-ft light was shipped around Cape Horn from Scotland in 1858.

These bolts were hammered into the rock by seamen of the Royal Navy and used by ships to secure extra lines ashore when strong southwesterly winds caused anchors to drag.

In 1894 a quarantine station was established here and all shipping to Canada's west coast ports had to stop and be inspected before proceeding. Massive wharves were built and internment and fumigation buildings constructed to house and clean any immigrants suspected of carrying "foreign diseases." At its peak of operation in 1927, 1,068 ships were inspected and during World War I a total of 80,000 Chinese passed through the station. Remnants of the wharves still remain. There is also a cemetery, but all the ghosts, including a seven-foot high Chinese with a benign expression, are reported to be happy and friendly. Apparently few of those who were interned here with incurable diseases minded spending their last days in such scenic surroundings.

In 1958 when the quarantine station was closed down, Dr. Jenkins, the medical superintendent, recognizing the inherent natural beauty and fine situation of William Head, suggested that the area be made into a park. This suggestion was ignored and today it is only the prisoners and their guards who benefit. Oddly enough, some of them try to escape. Most are caught, but one aspiring actor floated into freedom aboard a coffin after a prisoners' performance of "Dracula".

5 Pedder Bay

The safest anchorage within the outer portion of Pedder Bay is along the southern (Rocky Point) shoreline. Although this bay is completely open to the southeast, winds from this direction are unusual, occurring less than 5% of the time during the summer. The Rocky Point Military Reserve, presently used for munitions testing and storage, was established in the early 1950s amid much controversy. Several early settlers had their farms expropriated and many of the local people felt that the location of an arsenal close to populated areas and in a vulnerable position was unwise.

Lester B. Pearson College (United World College of the Pacific), with students from around the world, was opened in 1974 by HRH Prince Charles on a beautiful, tree enclosed site on the north shore of Pedder Bay. Students engage in a wide variety of arduous outdoor and community service activities as well as formal academic studies in several languages. They also operate an emergency land and sea rescue service during the winter months.

The Pedder Bay Marina (478-1771) at the head of the bay on Ash Point, provides fuel, moorage, rental boats, launching ramp and a trailer campsite with full facilities (showers, laundry, snack bar, groceries, fishing tackle). The approach to the marina appears very shallow on older charts, but an entrance channel has been dredged to a depth of 10 feet. Remnants of stone wall fortifications and trench embankments surround the grassy hill behind the marina revealing its earlier use as an Indian battleground. One mile inland is Matheson Lake Provincial Park which is now connected to Sooke Basin by Roche Cove Regional Park.

6   Bentinck Island

This island was once known as the Island of the Living Dead. From 1924, when D'Arcy Island was abandoned as a leper colony, until 1956, more than 20 lepers were confined here and lived out their existence in isolation. It wasn't until the widespread use of

A cruising sloop finds sheltered anchorage in a quiet nook behind large Bedford Island at the eastern entrance to Becher Bay.

sulpha drugs that leprosy became curable and it was learned that the disease is one of the least contagious of all diseases. Still, in 1956 when the last leper died of old age no one accepted the island when it was offered for rent at $40 a month. With no takers Bentinck Island finally reverted to the Department of National Defence in 1958 and is now used fitfully as a demolition range. Most of the old cottages used by the lepers have been destroyed and only vestiges of the past remain. Every spring beautiful flowers struggle

up from the underbrush that has encroached on the abandoned rock gardens and in a windswept deserted graveyard stand 13 unnamed white crosses.

Although several coves indent the island, only the one facing Race Rocks (Pilot Bay) is shoal-free as well as being relatively protected from the predominating westerly winds. Warning signs painted on rock bluffs read "RCN Blasting — Keep Off." Most of the blasting is confined to the area where the island's three peninsulas meet. A red flag is usually hoisted over the crude log cabin bunkers visible from the sea when blasting is taking place.

Eemdyk Passage is also known as Choked Passage due to the innumerable shoals, rocks, islets and kelp beds which clog the waterway. These obstructions, when combined with strong southwesterly winds and tidal currents up to four knots, can make this passage a nightmare to navigate. Temporary anchorage is advisable only in ideal conditions. A disused government float with space for one or two boats provides access to Bentinck Island.

Race Passage

Race Passage is subject to swift tidal streams of up to six knots which can form dangerous rips and overfalls, especially when there is a strong opposing wind which will tend to cause waves to steepen and break. Small craft should favour the Bentinck Island shore when conditions are rough in Race Passage.

7   Race Rocks

Race Rocks, the southernmost portion of Canada west of Ontario, was named by officers of the Hudson Bay Company. Captain Kellet of HM Survey Ship *Herald* wrote in his journal in 1846: "This dangerous group is appropriately named, for the tide makes a perfect race around it." Over 35 vessels have met disaster in the immediate vicinity of these rocks. Some of the more notable of these were the *Nanette*, a 385-ton barque which foundered only a few days before the light at the Rocks was first lit in 1860; the *Rosedale*, which ran aground on Rosedale Reef in 1862; the *Idaho*, a total loss; the *Rosamond*, the *Eemdyk*, the tugs *Hope* and *Tyee*; and the steamer *Sechelt*, on which all 48 aboard drowned. All of these disasters occurred during the winter months, predominantly October to December.

In addition to these larger vessels, a number of small craft have succumbed to the seas and rips, which can be very deceptive. At times the strong currents cause only a ripple on the surface, but a passing freighter may send in a swell which meets the tidal stream at a certain angle and causes huge breaking seas to develop without warning. The lightkeepers have rescued many who were close to disaster, but were too late several years ago when a Cub sailboat went down just south of Rosedale Rock. All four aboard drowned.

The 105-foot, black and white striped lighthouse, one of the most distinctive and attractive lighthouses on the B.C. coast is made from four-foot-thick granite blocks; cut, fitted and numbered in Scotland and brought around the Horn as ballast. This light and the Fisgard light outside Esquimalt were the first two lighthouses to be erected on the B.C. coast.

On Christmas Day, 1865, the first lightkeeper at Race Rocks, George Davies, watched helplessly as his wife's brother and his sister-in-law and three friends struggled and drowned before his eyes when their small boat overturned while trying to cross to the Rocks. His only boat had been withdrawn by the

Cheanuh Marina is owned and operated by the Becher Bay Indians and caters mostly to Victoria area sportsfishermen.

government a few days previously so he was unable to go to their assistance. Davies, aged 33, died within a year; many said from grief.

Thomas Argyle, lightkeeper here from 1867 to 1888, and the "first skin diver on the west coast", is said to have augmented his meagre wage with gold sovereigns from one of the many wrecks around the rocks (Graham). Race Rocks is a fascinating area for diving, but is safe only at slack water because of the strength of the tidal stream. An ecological reserve has been established to protect the many diverse forms of marine life. It is common to see up to 20 seals at one time, their heads bobbing in the current. Other visitors include as many as several hundred California sea lions basking on the smaller rocks, and Stellar sea lions in passage. Diverse marine birds, Dall porpoises and killer whales may also be spotted.

8 Rocky Point

Christopher Point is notable for its huge experimental wind generator. A small, shallow cove behind the Shelter Islets in Whirl Bay provides good temporary anchorage in favourable conditions. The tiny beaches of steeply sloped hard-packed sand that surround this cove are unlike anything found in the Strait of Georgia and are the product of Pacific Ocean swells which surge into the cove after a prolonged period of westerly winds. Large "No trespassing" signs surrounding the cove discourage the visitor from exploring ashore.

The scenic wonders of this area were outlined in somewhat flowery language in a brief to the Natural History Society of Victoria in 1952, which put forth some reasons for preserving Rocky Point as a national park:

> Consisting of over 3,000 acres, this magnificent peninsula known as Rocky Point, comprising the most southerly extent of Canadian soil on the Pacific Coast, is girded by approximately 12 miles of the most majestic ocean frontage to be found on the North American continent. Embellished with innumerable coves, beaches and islands, the entire panorama becomes almost indescribable against the backdrop of the Olympics to the south, the Sooke Hills to the north, Mount Baker to the east and the open Pacific to the west. Within this breath-taking perimeter lie open fields and meadows with the charm of an English countryside; two rugged mountains bearing the stern aspect of the Scottish Highlands, and between them large tracts of virgin timber as truly native as our own Vancouver Island.

9 Becher Bay

The eastern shore of Becher Bay is fascinating to explore, with many tiny coves and offshore islet groups — the Bedfords, Argyles, Villages, John Parkers, etc. The Indian reserve at Smyth Head was once well populated, but is virtually deserted today. Permission should be obtained from the Becher Indians at the head of the bay before camping ashore. Temporary anchorage is possible on either side of a tombolo which links Large Bedford Island to Vancouver Island. A petroglyph face is located on the precarious south slope of Large Bedford Island.

George Nicholson, author of *Vancouver Island's West Coast*, notes in his book that this area was the scene of an incredible massacre around 1820. Apparently a band of local Indians were surprised and almost totally annihilated by a combined force of Nitinats and Clallam Indians from across the straits. Of 300 local Indians, only three survived. Up to 100 years later human skeletons in great numbers, bleached by the sun and lying obviously where their former owners had met with sudden death or died of wounds, were to be found in the hills immediately behind Becher Bay.

Although there are several rocks and shoals in the area, in good weather temporary anchorage can be found behind Large Bedford Island and the Village Islets. Log booms behind Fraser Island can also provide temporary moorage if you secure alongside, but be prepared to move off if tugs arrive to remove the booms. More log booms and many deadheads abound in the northeast corner of Becher Bay.

10 Cheanuh Marina

This marina (478-4880), owned and operated by the Becher Bay Indians, is protected from southerlies by a floating log breakwater. *Cheanuh* is a local native word meaning "salmon," and this marina caters mainly to sport fishermen who try their luck in the productive waters outside Becher Bay. Fuel, rental boats, campsites, picnic tables, grocery store, laundromat and showers, hiking trails, fishing tackle, guides and charters and launching ramp are provided at this marina.

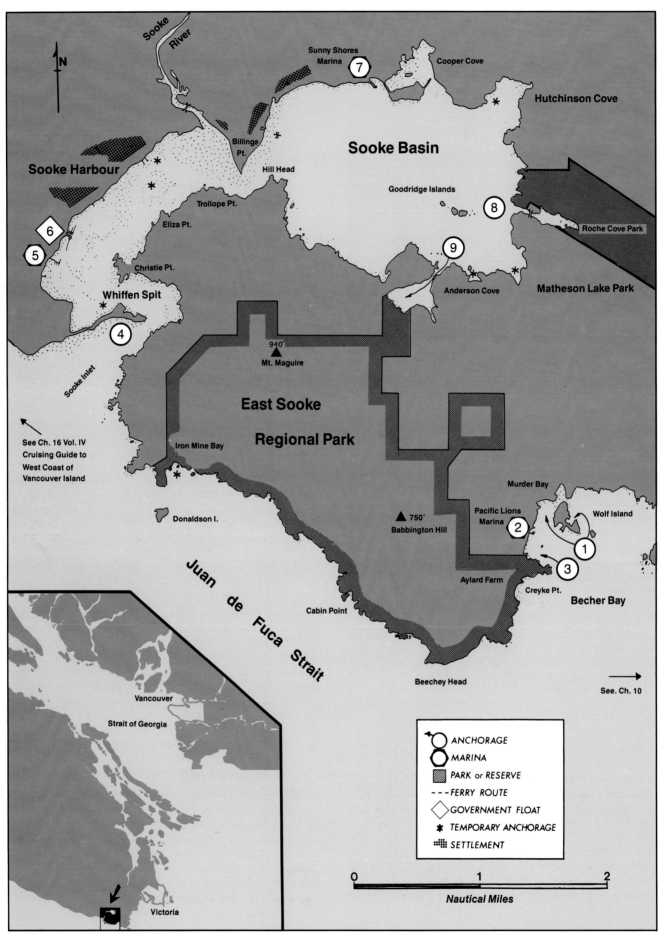

Sooke River

N

See Ch. 16 Vol. IV
Cruising Guide to
West Coast of
Vancouver Island

Sunny Shores
Marina
⑦

Cooper Cove

Hutchinson Cove

Billings
Pt.

Sooke Harbour

Sooke Basin

Hill Head

Goodridge Islands

⑧

Trollope Pt.

Roche Cove Park

Eliza Pt.

⑥
⑤

Christie Pt.

⑨

Matheson Lake Park

Whiffen Spit

Anderson Cove

④

Sooke Inlet

940'
Mt. Maguire

East Sooke

Regional Park

Iron Mine Bay

Murder Bay

Donaldson I.

▲ 750'
Babbington Hill

Pacific Lions
Marina
②

Wolf Island

①

③

Aylard Farm

Creyke Pt.

Becher Bay

Juan de Fuca Strait

Cabin Point

Beechey Head

See. Ch. 10

Strait of Georgia

Vancouver

Victoria

Juan de Fuca Strait

○ ANCHORAGE
◉ MARINA
▨ PARK or RESERVE
--- FERRY ROUTE
◇ GOVERNMENT FLOAT
✳ TEMPORARY ANCHORAGE
▦ SETTLEMENT

0   1   2
Nautical Miles

Sooke waters are some of the most productive in British Columbia, attracting large numbers of sport and commercial fishermen.

Sooke

Whiffen Spit, Wolf Island, Roche Cove

Sooke is an attractive area for those coastal explorers who do not want to venture into the open Pacific, but still want to get away from the more popular areas in the Strait of Georgia. For residents of Victoria, Sooke is a comfortable weekend sail with favourable tides and weather. To visit the entire Sooke area, however, a week would be required, for there are several places to explore, including Becher Bay, East Sooke Park and the inner Sooke Basin.

Winds and Tides

Hazards to watch for are the strong tidal streams and occasional rough water at Race Rocks (described in the previous chapter), strong westerly winds, shallows within Sooke Harbour, and early morning fogs — which predominate in late summer and fall but can be encountered throughout the summer season. Winds in Juan de Fuca Strait generally blow in from the Pacific during the day (strongest in the afternoon) and out at night.

Fishing

The Sooke area is one of the most productive sport salmon fishing areas in the world. There are often large concentrations of feeding salmon here and therefore, many fishboats — both sport and commercial. These fishboats, some only 12 feet long, fish the area constantly in all weather, including strong winds and fog. For winter chinooks (October to March) fish close to the bottom along the 20- to 35-fathom ledge using revolving flashers and anchovies, herring-strip and hoochy-type lures. From March to May, Race

Rocks banks yield 100-pound halibut. Migrating chinooks (May to July) are fished closer to the kelp beds using around 60 feet of line and two pounds of weight, no flasher and herring strip, or flasher and anchovy, minnow or hoochy-type lure and long six-foot leaders. Big chinooks may also be caught from shore with drift fishing lures. June is hottest for 50-pound fish while June to July provides lively fishing for resident coho as they move back in from Swiftsure Bank. For cohos and pinks in odd-numbered years (August to October) anglers shorten leaders and move out to fish along the second and third tide lines. The pinks like lures with a little red and the coho prefer green.

1 Wolf Island

Safe anchorage is available in the northwest corner of Becher Bay behind Wolf Island, with good protection from southwesterly winds, or in Murder Bay, west of Wolf Island. The passage between Wolf Island and the mainland dries two to three feet above chart datum. Murder Bay apparently derived its name from the untimely end of a local white resident who was in the habit of paying too much nocturnal attention to the girls from the nearby Indian village. He was found floating face down one morning in this bay, after

CHARTS
3641 — ALBERT HEAD to OTTER POINT
    (1:25,000)
3430 — Plans of BECHER BAY (1:15,000) and
    SOOKE (1:12,000)

several husbands had returned unexpectedly from a seal-catching expedition.

2 Pacific Lions Marina

Two cast iron lions from one of Victoria's historic buildings guard the landward entrance to this marina (642-3816), formerly known as the Becher Bay Marina. Fuel, launching ramp and limited moorage are available during the summer and there is a small cafe-store. Campsites for trailers or tents are also provided at this marina.

3 East Sooke Park

Good anchorage is available within Campbell Cove but care should be taken to avoid the six-foot drying rock in the centre of the cove. This rock is usually marked in the summer by kelp and a temporary white plastic bottle-buoy. Care should also be taken if anchoring in the south end of the cove. The mooring dolphins indicated on older charts have all fallen or been sheared off below the water line. Just inside Creyke Point are the remains of the steamtug *Faultless*, which was being used as a sawmill barge when she went aground here in 1968.

Creyke Point provides access to East Sooke Park, the largest shoreline park east of Port Renfrew (Pacific Rim) and south of Desolation Sound, comprising over 3,500 acres. Trails lead from here through Aylards farm (now part of the park) out past Alldridge Point and Beechey Head, where there is an international boundary monument, some Indian petroglyphs and magnificent views across the straits to the Olympic mountains. New park trails parallel the shoreline and old logging roads cut into the interior of the park toward Babbington Hill and Mount Maguire. Several old mine shafts are to be found on Iron Mine Road southeast of Mount Maguire. This area receives exceptionally low rainfall during the summer and fires are strictly prohibited within the park between April 30 and November 1.

The tidal streams run up to seven knots at springs across the mouth of Becher Bay and past Beechey Head. Although this stretch of coastline appears rugged and inhospitable, there are a number of excep-

In Becher Bay, safe anchorage can be found in the northwest corner, either behind Wolf Island (centre) or in Murder Bay (behind).

Twisted, peeling arbutus frame this view of a secluded beach on picturesque Wolf Island in Becher Bay.

tionally tiny nooks and crannies where it is possible to find shelter and beach a small boat. Cabin Point is the site of the "Trap Shack", used by men operating a "pot and spiller" fish trap in the early part of this century.

Iron Mine Bay, just north of Donaldson Island, is usually crowded with people on a sunny summer weekend as the beach here marks the seaward terminus of the major road and trail access into the park. This bay provides safe temporary anchorage protected from southwest winds. Although Iron Mine Bay is open to the southeast, winds from this direction are rare in the summer. Donaldson Island has always been known as Secretary Island by the locals but was changed by the hydrographers several years ago to avoid confusion with the Gulf Island's Secretaries.

4 Whiffen Spit

This uniquely beautiful recurved spit protects Sooke Harbour from southerly seas, but has been partially degraded by riprap, past road building and associated log storage and booming activities. The spit was broached by a winter storm in the early 1980s and access by land to the tip of the spit is not possible

near high tide. Access into Sooke Harbour is facilitated by entering close to slack water or with a flooding tide, as currents can run up to four knots at the end of the spit. Leading beacons have been erected to help one avoid Grant Rocks and a reef just off the tip of Whiffen Spit. Fog occasionally invades Sooke Inlet making navigation into the harbour somewhat awkward unless one is quite familiar with the landmarks, buoys and beacons. Anchorage north of the spit is possible, but a tripline should be used as the sea bottom here is littered with logging debris and old mooring dolphins.

The Sooke Harbour House Hotel (642-3421) at the base of Whiffen Spit features a gourmet restaurant, huge open fireplace, antique furnishings and ocean view rooms in a home-like atmosphere.

Around 1820 this spit was the scene of the T'Soke Indians revenge. The local Indians had been almost totally annihilated in Becher Bay. Only three out of over 300 had managed to escape the massacre — a mother, her son and a niece. The son called on the sacred Thunderbird to give both his mother and himself great powers to avenge the outrage. Meanwhile, most of the invading Clallams had returned to their homes across the Straits, and the Nitinats to Barkley Sound, leaving behind a small force at Whiffen Spit to guard the newly captured territory. The mother then made her way around Sooke Basin to the landward end of the spit while the son crossed from East Sooke to the end of the spit, on a log raft in the middle of the night. At a prearranged signal, an owl hoot, the son and the mother then proceeded to join each other in

Though often jammed with fishboats in winter, the public floats at Sooke often have moorage available when the fleet has gone fishing in summer.

the middle of the spit, clubbing and slaughtering every one of the sleeping Clallams as they went. The rest of the Clallams from across the Strait never returned to claim their territory and today the T'Soke (Sooke) Indians have greatly increased their numbers.

Sooke Harbour

The first white man to enter Sooke Harbour was Manuel Quimper who named it Puerto de Revilla Gigedo and claimed the surrounding countryside for Spain in 1790. A few years later, in the 1800s, officers of the Royal Navy seriously considered this harbour for their Pacific Coast naval base. The narrow entrance and strong currents around the end of Whiffen Spit were a determining factor against the use of Sooke Harbour and Esquimalt was chosen instead. The Hudson's Bay Company also considered this site for a trading post, but eventually decided in favour of Victoria. In the mid 1800s the narrow entrance was the major hindrance to Sooke becoming a major port and possibly the future capital of British Columbia. It may have been a good thing that Victoria was chosen, for throughout the last 100 years the outer basin has been almost completely filled in with silt and mud, making the inner basin only accessible to the smallest vessels. In 1847 there was a least depth of three fathoms through the harbour and into the inner basin.

Today the harbour is choked with a myriad of drying mud flats and shallow banks with a least depth of five feet along the tortuous passage into the inner basin. Massive logging of stream banks and placer mining in the Sooke River watershed have contributed much of the material now filling the harbour and overwhelming the natural flushing action of tide and river currents.

Sooke was named after the T'Soke (or T'So-uke, meaning "stickleback" — a small fish) Indians and was originally spelled "Soke". and pronounced "soak." The extra "o" was apparently added when the

Sooke Marine Industries northeast of Billings Spit has facilities for repairing boats up to 70 feet and 60 tons.

wife of one of the early settlers decided that "Sooke" sounded a little bit more civilized and used the new spelling in her correspondence with the outside world.

5   Sooke Harbour Marina

The approach channel to this marina (642-3236) is marked by large red-and-white mooring buoys, pilings and a green spar buoy to port; three red spar buoys to starboard; and a single range sector light marking the centre of the channel. The marina provides boat rentals, bait and tackle shop, launching ramp, fishing charters, campsites, showers and limited moorage. Free transport to the Sooke Harbour House (642-3421) can be arranged from here.

6   Sooke Public Wharf

Over 600 feet of moorage space is provided by two sets of public floats extending north of the public wharf (642-4431). These are periodically crammed with fishboats, but are quite often almost deserted during the summer. At the head of the wharf is a large warehouse where fishing nets and gear are stored. There is also an amazing variety of odds and ends of ships gear and chandlery at prices considerably lower than the standard yacht supply store (Pallisters, 642-3355). A block up from the government wharf is a small cairn commemorating Vancouver Island's first

independent settler, Captain Walter Colquhoun Grant of the Royal Scots Greys, who started farming here in 1849 and who introduced the Scotch broom. This shrub now grows wild over the whole of southern Vancouver Island, the Gulf Islands and much of the lower mainland, and is distinguished by its mass of yellow blooms in spring. In 1855 John Muir established Vancouver Island's first steam-powered sawmill here. Across the road is Buffy's Place Pub (642-3333).

Sooke Village

The centre of Sooke village, a lively settlement of over 5,000 persons, is a short walk east on the west coast road. Here one can find a variety of goods and services. Passage by boat from the government wharf into the inner basin involves returning to the main channel, unless your vessel is shallow draught and the tide is approaching high water. The average tidal range for Sooke is around six feet, which does not give much depth to play around with. For deeper draught vessels there are two possible routes from Christie Point into the inner basin. The direct route via Eliza Point has a least depth of one to four feet, depending on the location of the shifting mud banks and the quantity of water being discharged into the harbour by the Sooke River. The buoyed channel to the west of the Middle Ground is more circuitous and bypasses the Sooke Motel (642-5644), where there is limited moorage and charter boats for rent. Temporary anchorage is possible near here in a shallow patch north of the fairway or in a backwater in the Middle Ground.

Sooke River

An exploratory side-trip by dinghy can be made up the Sooke River, bypassing the Sooke River Hotel (642-9900) at the south end of the bridge. The original Sooke River Hotel was located at the top of the hill, but when it burned down many years ago the old stables and barn down by the bridge were converted into the new hotel. The old silo beside the barn now forms part of the pub and the Castle Cafe is adjacent. The Tourist Information Centre and the Sooke Region Museum (642-3121) are located across the road from the hotel. The museum (open 10 a.m. to 5 p.m. October to April; 10 a.m. to 6 p.m. May to September) houses historical artifacts and scale models and exhibits of pioneer logging, salmon traps unique to the Sooke area and the Leechtown gold rush plus weavings and carvings by Coast Salish and Nootka Indians. Nearby is Moss Cottage, an historic house, built in 1877. Right across the road from the museum is Shoreline Seafood (642-3153) on Belvista Place, distinguishable from the harbour by its huge white shell beach, the remains of Coopers Cove Oysters. Just up the river from the bridge is the Sooke Flats Community Park, which is the location for activities connected with All Sooke Day, taking place annually on the third Saturday of July. Included in the festivities are world-title competitions for traditional logger sports and re-enactment of pioneer activities including spar climbing, log birling, axe throwing, eating and drinking. Sooke River

Roche Cove is accessible only to shallow draft boats which are capable of squeezing under the bridge (12-ft clearance) across its entrance.

Potholes Provincial Park, where the river passes through a spectacular gorge,is located another two miles upstream. The potholes, ranging in size from a few inches to several feet, attract great interest from visitors to the park. They are a series of broken volcanic bubbles formed by a cooling lava flow and worn smooth by the action of the Sooke River.

Sooke Basin

Entrance into Sooke Basin is best made with a flooding tide as currents between Trollope Point and Hill Head are fairly strong. The southern shore should be favoured as the Sooke River delta extends to within a few hundred feet of Trollope Point. At low tide, Billings Spit — a wildlife sanctuary — is alive with bird life and clamdiggers. Northeast of Billings Spit is Sooke Marine Industries (642-3523) with facilities for repairing boats up to 70 feet and 60 tons, the Harbour Court Motel (642- 3528) and Ocean Village (642-5254) condos and canoes.

7   Sunny Shores Marina

Within Sooke Basin the Sunny Shores Marina (642-5731) provides a family resort with tent and trailer campsites, swimming pool, playground, shower and laundry facilities, boat rentals, launching ramp, fuel and limited moorage.

Coopers Cove, once famous for oysters which thrived in the warmer waters of the basin, is now the location of a large industrial forest products complex. Hutchinson Cove in the northwest corner of the basin is exposed to southwesterly winds, but these, while strong, are seldom troublesome (unless your anchor is prone to dragging), due to the limited fetch within the basin. A few hundred yards up the road from this cove is the historic hostelry — The Royal Ensign Hotel (or 17 Mile House), which was built in 1894 and still provides the weary traveller with rest and liquid refreshment.

8   Roche Cove Park

In 1985, over 287 acres south of the Grouse Nest Resort was acquired for a regional park linking Sooke Basin with Matheson Lake Park. Roche Cove is only accessible to shallow draught vessels (one foot of water at chart datum) which are capable of squeezing under the bridge (12 feet clearance). The waters here are noted to be unusually warm for swimming. An old rail line runs along the northern shore of this cove into Matheson Lake Provincial Park which is half a mile inland. The most comfortable anchorages in Sooke Basin are in the southeast corner, protected from the prevailing southwesterly winds.

Pretty Anderson Cove on the southern shore of Sooke Basin is completely enclosed, providing protected anchorage in virtually all conditions.

9   Anderson Cove

Entrance to Anderson Cove should be made close to the eastern shoreline to avoid the rocks at the entrance and a rock within the channel itself. This beautiful cove is completely enclosed, offering protected anchorage from all but the strongest winds. Access into East Sooke Park is also possible from the western end of the cove, but care should be exercised if anchoring in this area as there are a few snags and deadheads.

127

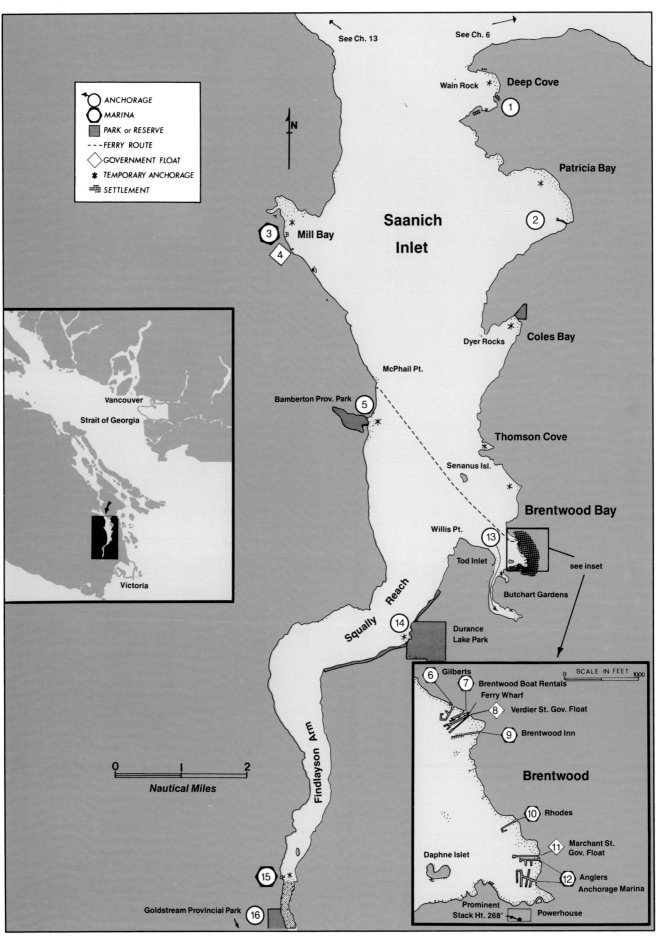

ANCHORAGE
MARINA
PARK or RESERVE
- - - FERRY ROUTE
GOVERNMENT FLOAT
TEMPORARY ANCHORAGE
SETTLEMENT

See Ch. 13

See Ch. 6

N

Wain Rock

Deep Cove
①

Patricia Bay

②

Saanich
Inlet

Mill Bay
③
④

Vancouver

Strait of Georgia

Dyer Rocks

Coles Bay

McPhail Pt.

Bamberton Prov. Park
⑤

Thomson Cove

Senanus Isl.

Victoria

Brentwood Bay

Willis Pt.
⑬

Tod Inlet

see inset

Butchart Gardens

0   1   2

Nautical Miles

Squally Reach

⑭

Durance
Lake Park

Findlayson Arm

SCALE IN FEET
0   1000

⑥ Gilberts
⑦ Brentwood Boat Rentals
Ferry Wharf
⑧ Verdier St. Gov. Float
⑨ Brentwood Inn

Brentwood

⑩ Rhodes

⑪ Marchant St.
Gov. Float

Daphne Islet

⑫ Anglers
Anchorage Marina

⑮

Goldstream Provincial Park
⑯

Prominent
Stack Ht. 268'   Powerhouse

Not to be used for navigation

128

Colourful gardens are the world renowned trademark of Butchart Gardens off Tod Inlet.

Saanich Inlet

Deep Cove, Brentwood Bay, Butchart Gardens

Saanich Inlet, B.C.'s southernmost inlet, has the distinction of being the only fiord-like inlet on the east coast of Vancouver Island and virtually the only inlet on the B.C. coast whose mouth is "above" (northeast of) its head. The entrance to the inlet has a shallow 40-fathom sill, but is unlike other fiord-inlets in that the surrounding shores are relatively flat and low-lying. It is not until south of Willis Point that the inlet takes on the characteristics of a typical fiord with steep, almost perpendicular bluffs and deep water close to shore. This deep water limits all the anchorages to the shallower, northern portion of the inlet.

Winds and Tide

Wind conditions in the inlet are generally light with a preponderance of calms, especially in summer. The inlet is fairly well protected from the northwest to southeast pattern which prevails throughout the Gulf, but occasional southwesterly winds blow into the inlet over the Sooke Hills from Juan de Fuca Strait. The main influence on wind direction is the diurnal heating and cooling of the Vancouver Island land mass with over 80% of all afternoon winds blowing from the east or southeast. At night calms, westerlies or southwesterlies predominate. Tidal streams in Saanich Inlet are fairly weak with a maximum range of 12 feet. The flood is slightly stronger along the west shore with the ebb slightly stronger off Pat Bay and Deep Cove.

Fishing

"Grief-free" fishing is found every day of the year in the quiet waters of Saanich Inlet. Most of the fish are very deep (up to 300 feet beneath the surface). In January, light lines can be used in mid-inlet wherever birds are spotted feeding on grilse. In June and July, chinooks move along Mill Bay to Bamberton shoreline and may be taken on anything representing small minnows. September is a prime time for drift fishing and in October short flies and spinners can be used when bucktailing for coho.

1   Deep Cove

This cove offers good temporary anchorage safe from all winds with an easterly component, but the northern portion is exposed to winds from the west or southwest. Winds from these directions are seldom strong and not particularly dangerous owing to the limited fetch across Saanich Inlet. The cove is lined with private homes and summer cottages. The Deep Cove Chalet, a conspicuous Swiss-style building at the head of the cove, is now a notable restaurant, but was originally constructed to serve as the B.C. Electric Railway terminal for North Saanich in 1914. Guests may anchor off or berth at any nearby marina and telephone to arrange free transport to the Chalet (656-3541).

Entrance to the Charthouse Marina (656-8185, fuel and moorage) is made with the red conical buoy to starboard and the standard day beacon to port. Care

CHARTS
3310 — Sheet 2 — TSEHUM HARBOUR to
      SANSUM NARROWS (1:40,000)
3441 — For SAANICH INLET (1:40,000)

should be taken when entering this marina to avoid some dangerous rocks: Deep Cove is not deep everywhere.

Facilities and services available in the vicinity of the Brentwood-Mill Bay ferry terminal include several marinas, marine ways, boat repairs, boat & tackle rentals, fishing guides, stores, cafe and a pub.

Angler's Anchorage Marina is the largest marina in Saanich Inlet. It offers many services and provides convenient overnight moorage for visitors to nearby Butchart Gardens.

2   Patricia Bay

Just south of Deep Cove is Pat Bay, which was once used by the Royal Canadian Navy as a test firing range, but is now used mainly by seaplanes landing at the head of the bay, by the Canadian Armed Forces and by Controlled Ecosystem Pollution Experiment (CEPEX). CEPEX is a study by a number of oceanographers of the effects of various pollutants on marine life. Giant plastic test tubes are submerged in the bay;

the mouth of each test tube, eight feet in diameter, floats on the surface and the body of the tube extends down 60 feet from the surface enclosing some 85 cubic yards of water. Each test tube is marked by yellow and orange striped scientific buoys and should be avoided (especially by trolling fishermen) as a tear in the plastic would destroy the experiment. Pat Bay is the site for the federal government Institute of Ocean Sciences and Pacific Geoscience Centre. Conducted tours of the institute are available, providing visitors with an interesting glimpse into chart production and some hydrographic and oceanographic displays (Tuesday, Wednesday, Thursday: 10 a.m.). If you phone in advance (656-8211), you can arrange to moor temporarily at the institute's wharf. If you do not mind the drone of low-flying aircraft passing close overhead, the northern portion of Pat Bay offers good temporary anchorage. Anchorage in the southern portion of the bay is prohibited.

Coles Bay

About a mile south of Pat Bay is Coles Bay Regional Park which offers good temporary anchorage, a pebble beach and a small regional park with trails and picnic sites.

Mill Bay

Mill Bay, on the western shore, provides the best overnight good weather anchorage in northern Saanich Inlet. In the summer, with high pressures predominating, this western shore is in the lee of any offshore westerly or northwesterly winds. However, in winter, or with changeable low pressure conditions, this bay may prove uncomfortable since it is completely open to the southeast. The bay derives its name from being the site for one of the first sawmills on Vancouver Island, constructed in 1861. The group of large buildings just south of the head of the bay is Brentwood College School, which moved across the inlet from Brentwood Bay when the original school burned down a number of years ago.

3   Mill Bay Marina

This marina (743-4112), located just south of the school, provides moorage, fuel, showers, laundromat, rental boats and a two-lane paved launching ramp. The marina is open all year although most of the floats are taken up in the winter because of the southeast exposure. Several stores are located a few hundred yards inland from the marina at the junction of the coast road — Deloume Road — with the Island Highway.

4   Mill Bay Government Float

This small government float provides temporary moorage space for three to four boats at a unique float which is actually four floats joined together in a square with a hole in the middle. The float provides access to shore for those who want to walk into the stores at Mill Bay.

The ketch Starshine *lies peacefully at anchor in Thomson Cove.*

5   Bamberton Provincial Park

About half a mile south of the McPhail Point ferry terminal is Bamberton Provincial Park, donated to the province by the cement company located another mile down the inlet. This park boasts the only all-sand beach in the inlet. Many visitors wonder how such a fine sandy beach came to be here, contrary to the geology of this coast. The beach was actually formed in this century — the result of dumping surplus sand from a now abandoned gravel pit located several hundred feet inland. The park contains 50 campsites as well as 41 picnic sites and changing rooms for swimmers.

Thomson Cove

Directly across the inlet from Bamberton Park is Thomson Cove, a delightful afternoon anchorage which narrows at its head to a tiny one-boat nook with about four fathoms of water. One mile inland from this cove on Mount Newton Cross Road is St. Stephen's Anglican Church, built in 1862 and reputed to be the oldest church in B.C. holding continuous services since that date on the same site. Just south of Thomson Cove is Senanus Island, referred to by early pioneers as the Island of the Dead. The island, named after a famous Tsartlip Chief, was used by the early Indians as a burying ground.

Brentwood Bay

This community, the largest in the inlet with an area population of over 5,000, is the centre for the very active Victoria and Saanich Inlet Anglers Association. The inlet is closed to commercial gillnetters and has the reputation of being the most consistently productive all-year fishing area on Vancouver Island. Brentwood has several stores, cafes and local craft shops. The Tsartlip Campground, located just north of Brentwood, is operated by the local natives and provides 32 campsites, showers, launching ramp, swimming beach and a store selling Indian handicrafts. Several marinas in the area cater mainly to sport fishermen, but many of the services provided may also be of use to coastal explorers.

6   Gilbert's Marine and Guide Service

Gilbert's (652-2211) offers a complete sport fishing service with professional guides. They will store, ice, freeze, wrap or smoke your catch. Other services include hull and engine repairs (covered marine ways), fuel, marine hardware, moorage, ramp, boat and tackle rentals. Telephone 652-2211 for weather, fishing and tide condition report.

A small float in the cove at the entrance to Tod Inlet provides temporary moorage for visitors to lovely Butchart Gardens (centre left) but overnight moorage is discouraged.

7 Brentwood Boat Rentals

This marina (652-1014) specializes in rentals of fishing tackle, inboard motorboats and canoes. A small cafe is located at the head of the wharf.

The Verdier Street Public Float (8), just south of the ferry dock, provides temporary moorage for six to eight boats. The access to shore was removed in 1983.

9 Brentwood Inn

Extensive float space just south of the government float is available for temporary moorage. The inn (652-2413) provides overnight accommodation, the Oak'n-'Barrel waterfront restaurant, and the Brig Marine Pub. Charter boats for fishing or cruising are available.

10 Rhodes Sportsfishing Service

Rhodes (652-1512) provides charter boats, fishing guides, limited moorage and fuel and specializes in custom canning or smoking of fish.

A 50 foot float at the foot of Marchant Street (11) provides temporary moorage for three to four boats.

12 Anglers Anchorage Marina

Anglers Marina (651-3531), just south of the government float, and the larger Anchorage Marina are now combined to form the largest marina in Saanich Inlet. Facilities include gas and diesel, charts, moorage, laundry, showers, boat ways (maximum 24 feet), repairs, charters, fishing guides, groceries, tackle shop and marine hardware. This is a popular moorage for visitors to Butchart Gardens.

The Butchart Gardens

The Butchart Gardens (652-4422) are a major attraction; visitors come to Vancouver Island from all over the world particularly to see them. The gardens began

as a hobby over 80 years ago when Mrs. Robert Pim Butchart decided to reclaim and beautify an abandoned limestone quarry originally excavated by her husband's cement company. The gardens have been gradually expanded and improved to include over 25 acres that reflect four distinct landscaping styles — Japanese, English, Italian and the unique Sunken Garden with lighted fountains and waterfalls in the deepest section of the old quarry. Special attractions include puppet shows, afternoon and evening concerts, pipe band tatoos, fireworks displays, afternoon tea and a restaurant. A small cove located on the eastern shore just inside the entrance to Tod Inlet serves as an anchorage area for visitors to Butchart Gardens who arrive by boat. A float at the head of this cove is also provided for guests who wish to tie up while they visit the gardens, but overnight moorage is discouraged.

13 Tod Inlet

The entrance to the southern portion of Tod Inlet is remarkable for the steepness of the encircling cliffs, which add to the atmosphere of isolation and peacefulness permeating this "mini-Princess Louisa Inlet." Several private moorings and a private wharf are found near the head of the Inlet and at night the lights and fireworks of Butchart's Gardens filter through and above the surrounding trees. This inlet provides the best all-weather anchorage in Saanich Inlet, but in winter it often freezes over completely due to local concentrations of freshwater.

14 Mount Work Regional Park

McKenzie Bight is a small indentation notched into the steep surrounding bluffs and offers virtually the only anchorage south of Willis Point. The head of the bight dries several feet and drops off quickly below the low water line, leaving little anchorage space. It is best to anchor with a rising tide. The 1025-acre park includes a 66-foot-wide strip of shoreline which extends south to Elbow Point and north to Mark Lane. A trail leads up the hillside past Cascade Falls (five minutes), Durrance Lake and Pease Lake (45 minutes) to Mount Work (two hours). This area is known as the Highland District and is characterized by oak- and arbutus-covered rocky knolls and pastoral farmland in the valleys. Good views are possible from several highpoints looking south over Victoria and Juan de Fuca Strait to the Olympic Mountains; north over Saanich Peninsula to the Gulf Islands; and west to the Malahat.

Squally Reach is curiously named. Wind of any kind is so infrequent in summer in this inlet that when some wind finally comes, no matter how light, it is considered a squall.

Scuba diving can be spectacular in Saanich Inlet. The steep walls support a variety of rock scallops, tunicates, anemones, boot and cloud sponges.

15 Hall's Boat House

Hall's Boat House (478-4407) at the head of the inlet is open all year, and provides fuel, moorage and fish-

Pretty summer flowers brighten a view north from Hall's Boat House toward Sawluctus Island in Finlayson Arm.

Hall's Boat House is located at the northern edge of Goldstream delta in Finlayson Arm; the 828-acre Goldstream Park is within easy walking distance.

ing supplies. There is a three-lane paved launching ramp and facilities for minor hull repairs.

16 Goldstream Provincial Park

Hall's Boat House marks the termination of the delta of the Goldstream River which extends for al-most a mile into Finlayson Arm with several intercon-necting distributaries separating the drying mud and marsh flats. This area is fascinating to explore by canoe or dinghy, especially with a rising tide or in the late autumn when returning salmon clog the river mouth as they prepare to fight their way upstream to spawn and die. There are few places on the east coast of Vancouver Island where one can wander beneath the cool evergreens of a mature, huge-treed rainforest. This is one of them. There are some splendid 500-year-old red cedars.

Mount Finlayson towers 1,365 feet above the head of Saanich Inlet and provides excellent views. The summit is about an hour's hike from the Finlayson Arm Road, which parallels the shore just above the point where the Goldstream River emerges from the trees onto the mudflats. The conspicuous Freeman King Visitor Centre overlooks the head of the estuary and houses interpretive displays of the areas natural and human history. Goldstream Park, one of the best maintained parks in B.C., is 828 acres in size, has 166 campsites, 46 picnic sites and several miles of trails. On the west side of the mouth of the river, the Gold Mine Trail leads up Niagara Creek to 100-foot high Niagara Falls and some old mine workings which include a 65-foot tunnel driven by early prospectors. The park has a naturalist who conducts walks, gives slide shows at the Visitor Centre and interprets the natural history of the area. Although birds are not usually seen in the park, one visitor, the water ouzel — commonly known as the dipper — can often be seen walking underwater up the bed of the river.

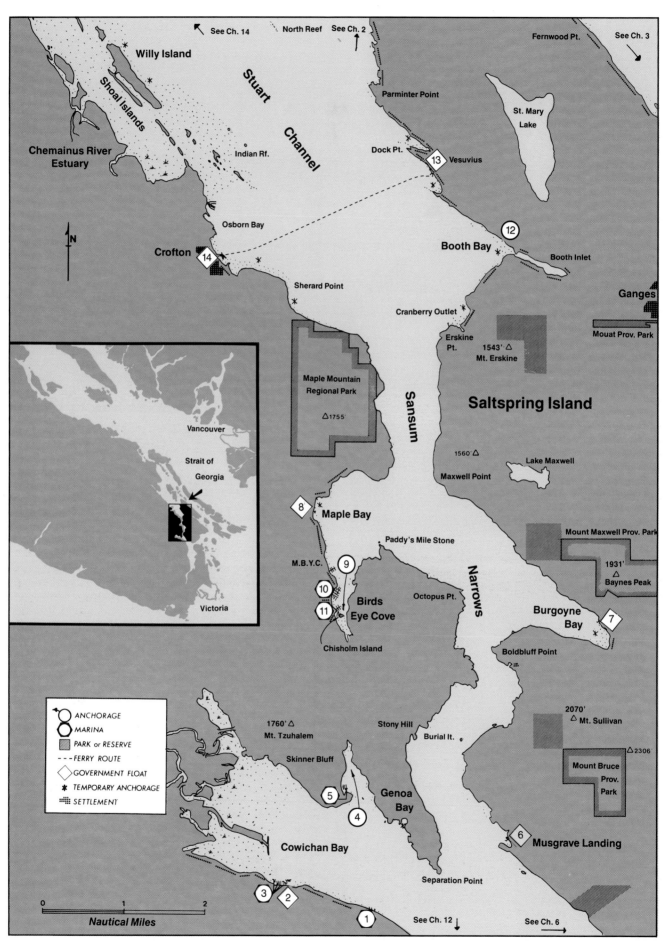

See Ch. 14
North Reef
See Ch. 2
Fernwood Pt.
See Ch. 3

Willy Island

Stuart Channel

Parminter Point

St. Mary Lake

Shoal Islands

Chemainus River Estuary

Indian Rf.

Dock Pt.

Vesuvius

13

Osborn Bay

Booth Bay

12

Booth Inlet

N

Crofton

14

Sherard Point

Ganges

Cranberry Outlet

Mouat Prov. Park

Erskine Pt.

1543' △ Mt. Erskine

Maple Mountain Regional Park

Sansum

Saltspring Island

△1755'

Vancouver

1560' △

Lake Maxwell

Strait of Georgia

Maxwell Point

Victoria

8

Maple Bay

Mount Maxwell Prov. Park

Paddy's Mile Stone

M.B.Y.C.

9

1931' △ Baynes Peak

10

Octopus Pt.

Narrows

11

Birds Eye Cove

Burgoyne Bay

7

Chisholm Island

Boldbluff Point

ANCHORAGE

MARINA

PARK or RESERVE

FERRY ROUTE

GOVERNMENT FLOAT

TEMPORARY ANCHORAGE

SETTLEMENT

1760' △ Mt. Tzuhalem

Stony Hill

2070' △ Mt. Sullivan

Burial It.

Skinner Bluff

△ 2306

5

Mount Bruce Prov. Park

4

Genoa Bay

6

Musgrave Landing

Cowichan Bay

Separation Point

3

2

1

See Ch. 12

See Ch. 6

0   1   2

Nautical Miles

Not to be used for navigation

134

A spanking summer breeze pushes this colourful sloop through Sansum Narrows.

CHAPTER THIRTEEN

Sansum Narrows

Cowichan Bay, Maple Bay, Crofton & Chemainus

Captain Walbran, writing in *British Columbia Coast Names*, notes that in 1854 this area was the home of one of the strongest Indian tribes on the coast:

> The tribe was fierce, turbulent and treacherous, but is now few in number, peaceable and quiet. Inordinate indulgence in spirituous liquors of the worst kind, and diseases largely incident to the transition from the savage to the quasi-civilized state, account for the decrease in their numbers during the early colonial days, 1850-1870. The waters on the east coast of Vancouver Island, inhabited by the small bands which together were known as the powerful Cowichan tribe, teemed with edible fish, and on the land deer and other fur-bearing animals abounded, which afforded the natives an easy and convenient means of providing their daily food. Sheltered as that part of the coast is from the heavy swell of the Pacific, it is also noted for the numerous coves and bays with sandy and shell-strewn beaches, which found favour with the natives as places of settlement, and wood and freshwater were in abundance. This natural wealth of the country led to a division of the Cowichans into small bands such as those known in the present day as Saanich, Somenos, Quamichan, Koksilah, Chemainus, Lamalchi and Penelakut, all derived from bands of the great Cowichan tribe.

In the local Indian dialect Cowichan means "between streams" and the head of this bay is the delta for two rivers - the Cowichan and the Koksilah. The delta is fertile land which has been farmed for over 120 years. On August 18, 1862 HMS *Hecate* dropped anchor in Cowichan Bay and landed 100 settlers. This event is commemorated by a cairn in the Robert Serv-

ice Wayside Park a few hundred yards above the southwest corner of the bay on the old Island Highway. Robert Service came to the Cowichan Valley from England in 1894 and lived here for over 10 years, working as a farmhand and assistant in the local store and post office before heading for the Yukon and writing the poetry which made him famous. Half a mile north of here is the South Cowichan Lawn Tennis Club, the oldest in North America and second oldest in the world (next to Wimbledon). A unique stand of mature broadleaf maples is found in the pastoral farmland behind the estuary.

The south shore of Cowichan Bay is lined with many small marinas and resorts, but the head of the bay is shallow tidal flat. If you can find your way through the maze of pilings, log booms and lumber storage piles, the estuary distributaries and channels behind provide some fascinating opportunities for small boat exploration. This part of the estuary contains natural and pastoral meadows and winding, bush-lined creeks with overhanging vegetation straight out of *Wind in the Willows*. The upland here has been preserved because much of it is designated

CHARTS
3310 — Sheet 2 — TSEHUM HARBOUR to
       SANSUM NARROWS (1:40,000)
3441 — SATELLITE CHANNEL to SANSUM
       NARROWS (1:40,000)
3442 — NORTH PENDER ISLAND to THETIS
       ISLAND (1:40,000)
3470 — Plans of COWICHAN BAY to MAPLE
       BAY (1:18,000), BIRDS EYE COVE and
       GENOA BAY (1:12,000)
3475 — OSBORN BAY (Crofton) (1:15,000)

farmland or Indian reserve and should be respected as private land. Native children can occasionally be seen playing along the river bank, swinging from ropes into the water or spearing fish from bridges across the river. The Cowichan and Koksilah rivers are navigable at times of high water by canoe, dinghy or kayak for several miles upstream, although it is much easier to bring a boat *down* the river with the assistance of the current. From the late 1880s until 1908 the Cowichan River saw enormous log drives of up to 14 million feet of timber at one time all the way from Cowichan Lake to tidewater (a drop of 527 feet in 35 miles of river). Snags, deadheads and the Skutz Falls are hazards for boaters today. It is also possible, with a few portages, to canoe down to tidewater from Somenos (four feet above sea level) and Quamichan lakes (26 feet above sea level). The B.C. Forest Museum is located at the west end of Somenos Lake. The north arm of the Cowichan bypasses the historic Old Stone ("Butter") Church, recently restored by the natives to serve as a craft centre. The city of Duncan with a population of 4,500 lies approximately three miles up the Cowichan River.

Winds and Tides

Strong westerly winds can blow out through Cowichan Bay. If the seas are high off Separation Point, smaller craft should head south and approach the marinas along the south shore of Cowichan Bay. Satellite Channel, south of Saltspring Island, often experiences brisk southeasterly winds on summer

Access to Cowichan Bay public boat basin (above and below) should be made close to the east end of the encircling piling-breakwater, taking care to avoid a sand bank which extends from the adjacent shore.

afternoons. These winds are generally a diurnal phenomenon caused by the heating of the Saltspring-Vancouver Island land mass and do not usually presage a storm. The south wind generally carries through Sansum Narrows, but appears to weaken if there is a strong flood tide.

Fishing

Cowichan Bay has an established reputation as one of the best sport fishing areas for salmon in British Columbia. Migrating chinooks provide good fishing along Skinner Bluffs, in the middle of the bay and along the village shore where anglers cast from the public wharf. This area is noted for the unique Cowichan Bay bucktail flies which are used with pearl spinners, little weight and light-test lines when fishing for coho. Anglers usually fish Sansum Narrows around Bold Bluff, using drift fishing lures close to the bottom or mooching with cut plug herring.

1 Cherry Point Marina

Fuel, moorage, three-lane launching ramp, campsites, a machine shop and 12-ton ways for repair work are provided at this marina (748-0453). Immediately to the west is the Wilcuma Resort (748-8737) providing heated freshwater pool, showers, campsites, accommodation and complete dining facilities in an English Tudor Lodge built in 1902.

2 Cowichan Bay Village

Cowichan Bay is a very lively little community with several facilities geared to an active sport fishing industry. Almost 2,000 feet of float space is provided for about 50 to 60 small craft at the Cowichan Bay Public Wharf (746-5911). Entrance into the boat basin should be made close to the east end of the log piling breakwater which almost completely encircles the floats as there is a sand bank extending out from the shore close to the entrance. The float space here is usually fairly crowded and visiting boats may have to tie alongside other boats. The huge five-storey Inn at Cowichan Bay (748-6222) provides accommodation, indoor pool, sauna, dining room and lounges with a spectacular view directly over the wharf and floats below. Immediately adjacent is the Black Douglas Inn Pub and The Masthead Restaurant (748-3714) and Harbour Front Craft Shop/Deli in Ordano's 1873 Hotel, a heritage building. The Coho Marina, home of the world record Coho salmon, was formerly located here. Immediately west of the public wharf is McDonell's floating Marine Hardware (secondhand, "Browsers Welcome") with accompanying sailboat, rowboat, kayak and windsurfer rentals. There are a number of other facilities nearby including: the Cowichan Bay Shipyard (743-2233) with moorage and repairs; Anchor Marina (746-5424) with moorage, boat rentals, Morgan charters/guides, repair shop, marine and fishing supplies, coffee shop, Simon Charlie Indian carvings, restaurant; Bayshore Seafoods with a fresh fish market and post office; Pier 66 (748-8444) with gas, diesel, moorage, repairs, boat rentals, marine and fishing supplies; Covey Marine and Coastal

Shipyard (746-4705) full-service marine ways and diesel repairs; Cowichan Bay Yacht Club; Bluenose Marina (748-2222) ship chandlers, tackle shop, provisions, moorage, restaurant and dining lounge featuring the "best crab in Canada." The Wessex Inn Seaside Motel (748-4214) is found a few hundred feet down the road.

Facilities and services at Genoa Bay Marina include moorage, fuel, store, cafe, rental boats and showers. The net-pens of one of B.C's salmon farms are next door.

4 Genoa Bay

Genoa Bay on Vancouver Island offers abundant anchorage, but the central portion of the bay is partially exposed to winds and seas from the southeast. Log booms are occasionally stored along the eastern shore of this bay. Genoa Bay has long been a favourite for coastal explorers and fishermen who have spent the day fishing the productive waters of Cowichan Bay and Sansum Narrows. The bay is named after the birthplace of an early settler, Giovani Baptiste Ordano, who came here in 1858 and built the first hotel at Cowichan Bay.

5 Genoa Bay Marina

Just inside this bay on the port hand is the Genoa Bay Marina (746-7621), formerly Captain Morgan's Lodge. Boats entering Genoa Bay should keep the red triangular day beacon on the starboard side and the green can buoy to port. This marina is in the location of one of the largest sawmills in the province from 1889 to 1928. Some of the remains of this immense operation can still be seen. The marina provides fuel, moorage, rental boats, launching, dry storage, campsites, showers, laundromat, cafe, groceries, craft shop, cookbooks and a friendly atmosphere. This marina is also a good starting place for a hike up Skinner Bluff to Mount Tzuhalem, where excellent views down Satellite Channel to the Saanich Peninsula are possible.

Mount Tzuhalem is named after one of the fiercest of the Cowichan war chiefs. G.P.V. Akrigg, in *1001 British Columbia Place Names*, writes:

Because of his frequent murders he was banished at last by his tribe, and took up residence in a cave on the side of Mount Tzuhalem. With him he had some 14 wives, most of whom had been widowed by him. Going to Kuper Island to acquire a new wife, Tzuhalem was slain...

Apparently Tzuhalem's fierceness stemmed from the early loss of his mother and brother, who were drowned by invading Indians. After his death an autopsy was performed to find the cause of his vileness — his heart was said to be only the size of a salmon's. Temporary anchorage is possible in a few tiny coves which indent the shoreline southeast of Genoa Bay.

Temporary anchorage north of Cape Keppel is exposed to afternoon southerly winds. Mount Tzuhalem is in the background.

Cape Keppel

Cape Keppel, the southernmost tip of Saltspring Island six miles southeast of Musgrave Landing (off the map), was named in 1859 after Rear Admiral the Honourable Sir Henry Keppel, the "Father of the British Navy" and author of *A Sailor's Life under Four Sovereigns* (see Walbran).

The steep west-facing upper slopes of Mount Tuam are almost completely grass covered — evidence of

past logging, fires and the scanty rainfall on this side of the island. "Tuam" is derived from an earlier name for Saltspring Island — "Chuan", which means "facing the sun." This mountain is an exhilarating hike from here or Musgrave Landing (6) and provides spectacular views of the lower Gulf Islands and down Saanich Inlet to Victoria and the Olympic Mountains beyond.

An 87-acre greenbelt reserve opposite Musgrave Island includes a beach, creek and waterfall. Trails from here lead up to Musgrave Road, past abandoned farms, log barns and split rail fences.

6   Musgrave Landing

Behind Musgrave Point one finds what was once a delightful nook sheltered beneath the steep southwest slopes of Saltspring Island. Limited moorage is available at a small government wharf with 80 feet of float space. From Musgrave Landing roads and trails wind up the mountainside past Musgrave Farm to Bruce Peak, the highest mountain in the Gulf Islands at 2,306 feet and Mount Tuam (2,000 feet). Bruce peak is named after Rear Admiral Henry William Bruce, whose flagship while on this station from 1854 to 1857 was HMS *Monarch*. Musgrave farm was once the home of Brigadier Miles Smeeton and family. This intrepid soldier and his equally intrepid wife, Beryl, sailed the oceans of the world for several years, with many narrow escapes from dismastings, broachings and pitch-polings before moving to Alberta to care for endangered wildlife. His books, *A Change of Jungles* and *The Sea Was Our Village*, include fascinating accounts of their pioneering life on Saltspring and their return to Canada with the yacht *Tzu Hang*. The book *Once Is Enough* is now a classic of marine literature.

Sansum Narrows

These narrows are named after Arthur Sansum, First Lieutenant aboard HMS *Thetis*, on this station from 1851 to 1853. Upon leaving British Columbia Lieutenant Sansum died suddenly of apoplexy in the Gulf of California and was buried there in 1853.

Tidal currents reach maximum rates up to three knots and there is almost always some kind of wind in Sansum Narrows, even if it is flat calm outside in Satellite or Stuart channels or in Maple or Burgoyne Bay. These winds are probably caused by a combination of "tide wind" (see 2, Chapter 8) and the funneling effect of the steep cliffs and bluffs surrounding the narrows.

There are spectacular opportunities for scuba diving here, with clear visibility and amazing fish life — an abundance of sea perch, gobies, rockfish and ling cod. Octopus can be found in small caverns about 60 feet below the northeast shore of Bold Bluff Point.

7   Burgoyne Bay

This beautiful bay is the only place in the Gulf Islands that gives the impression of being in a typical B.C. fiord. A mile to the south and north the peaks of Sullivan and Maxwell stretch almost half a mile into

138

A small government dock (lower right) provides access to country roads and fertile farmland at head of Burgoyne Bay on Saltspring Island.

the sky. The *B.C. Pilot* describes Mount Maxwell (also known as Baynes Peak) as follows: "it is the most remarkable mountain...on its southern side, near the summit, is a conspicuous perpendicular precipice" (a sheer drop of over 1,000 feet). A beautiful sand beach fronts the long, flat fertile valley which extends across the island from Fulford Harbour. Although the bay is exposed to northwesterly winds and seas and southeasterly winds, temporary anchorage is possible at the head where shallower depths and stable water provide for good warm-water swimming. A government wharf with 70 feet of moorage space provides access to roads which lead down to Fulford Harbour and up the hill to Mount Maxwell Provincial Park. This 487 acre park includes over four miles of rough hiking trails, picnic spots and spectacular views over Burgoyne Bay and the Fulford valley. Caves with limestone stalactites and stalagmites are hidden beneath the lower slopes of this mountain. A 160 acre ecological reserve adjoining the park protects an undisturbed stand of garry oak. This is an excellent place for spotting soaring birds — turkey vultures, bald eagles, peregrine falcons and hanggliders.

8   Maple Bay

Maple Bay was known to the Indians as Klup-nitz which means "deep water." The public wharf (746-7101), with over 300 feet of float space for six to eight boats, is fairly exposed to any southeasterly winds and the wash from local boats, as well as being very crowded in summer. The beach here is popular for swimming and water skiing. The community of Maple Bay stretches up the hillside above this wharf. A few hundred yards to the north are the Maple Bay Rowing Club (748-2042) and the Brigantine Inn (746-5422) — a comfortable local pub with a float for guests. The view from the inn across Sansum Narrows to Mount Maxwell is particularly inspiring.

9   Bird's Eye Cove

Good anchorage, protected from virtually all winds and seas, is available throughout Bird's Eye Cove. Paddy's Mile Stone near the entrance to this cove is located approximately one mile from the Maple Bay Inn and one mile from Octopus Point. The name Paddy's Mile Stone is possibly derived from Ailsa Cragg near Culzean in Scotland. The Maple Bay Yacht Club (746-5421) is the host for many regattas and race weekends which take advantage of the unique Sansum Narrows wind conditions, which may include the odd frustrating hour long "parking lot" calm. Care should be taken to avoid a rock just under the water at

zero tide and approximately 150 feet off the eastern entrance to the cove.

Bird's Eye Cove Marina

This marina (748-3142) provides gas, diesel, fishing supplies, gifts and charts.

10   Cove Yachts

This marina (748-8136) offers overnight moorage with power and water, haul-out facilities to 100 tons, a dockside five-ton crane for spars and small craft and a complete boat repair and maintenance service. Pressure wash, small chandlery and bareboat sailboat charters (May to September) are available.

Sheltered anchorage and several accommodating marinas can be found in Bird's Eye Cove at the southern end of Maple Bay.

Old logging trails lead up the hill behind the marina to Mount Tzuhalem and nearby are the Maple Bay Trading Post and the Quamichan Inn — phone 746-7028 for free limousine service to this delightful old Tudor House converted into a restaurant. The Jib Set (689-1477) operates bareboat, cruise 'n learn and flotilla cruises into the Gulf Islands out of Maple Bay.

Early Chief of the Chemainus Band painted by Paul Ygartua. Wallsize murals painted by some of Canada's finest artists bring colour and tourists to Chemainus — the "little town that did".

CHAPTER FOURTEEN

Stuart Channel

Chemainus & Ladysmith

The stretch of coastline between Chemainus and Boat Harbour, with the Ladysmith area in between, is one of the most protected on the B.C. coast, with minimal tidal currents, light winds, warm waters and an encircling barrier formed by several Gulf Islands.

Winds and Tide

The strongest winds generally occur in spring or fall and are generally offshore westerlies or northwesterlies. In the summer there is a marked diurnal trend with calms occurring up to 50 percent of the time during the hours of darkness, but less than 10 percent of the time from 10:00 to 17:00. Over 30 percent of the time winds are from the northeast quadrant, and over 15 percent of the time from the west. In winter calm winds are prevalent throughout the day and night (up to 40 percent of the time). Stronger winds are generally from the west (20 percent frequency) or the southeast (15 percent frequency). The tidal range for the Ladysmith area is a maximum of 13.6 feet. Tidal currents seldom exceed 1 knot, with the ebb slightly stronger than the flood.

Fishing

Salmon fishing is fair during the summer for both coho and chinook. Most fishermen troll this area, using flasher with strip or hoochy.

1   Chemainus

This is a town of superlatives. Chemainus Bay (originally Horseshoe Bay) is said to be the "first seaport in British Columbia" and has been almost exclusively used by the logging industry since 1862. The world's tallest flag pole (225 feet high) was manufactured here from a 275 foot tree and shipped to London's Kew Gardens in 1958. When MacMillan Bloedel shut down what at one time was the "largest sawmill in the British Commonwealth," the town rallied to become the "worlds largest Outdoor Art Gallery." The sides of buildings in the town are gradually being painted by some of Canada's finest artists with huge permanent murals depicting the history of the Chemainus area. You can watch these works of art being created every summer during the annual Festival of Murals, which has attracted world wide attention for "the little town that did". In 1984 a new, modernized mill was opened by MacMillan Bloedel.

The original name for this area, as well as the derivation of Chemainus, have been in dispute for a long time. Some of the possible sources include Chemainos ("a bad smelling promontory"), Tsa-mee-nis ("bitten breast" or "broken chest" from the profile of a nearby range of hills which have the appearance of a man lying prone with a deep cleft in his chest), Tsiminnis (a legendary Indian leader), and Sun-oo-

---

CHARTS
3310 — Sheet 2 — TSEHUM HARBOUR to
      SANSUM NARROWS (1:40,000)
3442 — NORTH PENDER ISLAND to THETIS
      ISLAND (1:40,000)
3443 — THETIS ISLAND to NANAIMO
      (1:40,000)
3475 — Plans of CHEMAINUS BAY and
      LADYSMITH HARBOUR (1:12,000)

The Chemainus public wharf is often packed two and three boats deep - a popular spot to visit. Chemainus' history as a logging town goes back to 1862.

etz ("a very deep bay" or "the river with two mouths").

The public wharf is located just south of the Thetis and Kuper ferry dock and has 1,000 feet of float space for about 35 boats, but it is often crammed full with many more boats moored alongside one another. It appears that Chemainus is a popular place to visit as well as to live.

An exact replica of the Cornish water wheel which provided the power for the original mill in 1862 is located in a park at the centre of town.

The old Island Wharves Marina just north of the ferry dock dispenses fuel and has facilities for complete hull and engine repairs (Chemainus Towing, 246-3216). The private floats north of here are used by the local rod-and-gun club. Although this bay is very well protected from southerly and easterly winds by Bare Point, anchorage is inhibited by active log booming and storage within the bay.

On the Chemainus side of Bare Point there is a colony of nesting seabirds, unique for the variety of species that share the same nesting sites. A recent count, made by Vancouver Island author Lyn Hancock in 1985, found 16 nests of glaucous-winged gulls, 356 nests of pelagic cormorants (on ledges in the cliff face), and 118 nests of double-crested cormorants in trees at the top of the cliffs. The colony has been protected, in part, by the nearby generating station and by log-booming activity beneath the cliffs. Observe from a distance with binoculars: observe quietly; otherwise this fascinating colony may disappear.

Wall-sized mural of the arrival of H.M.S. Reindeer in Chemainus was painted by local artist Sandy Clark.

Just north of Hospital Point is Kin Beach Park, a small community park with a good beach and a small launching ramp which is exposed to northerly winds. The coast between here and Ladysmith should not be approached too closely in deep-draught boats as there are many offshore rocks and shoals. In addition there are a great number of deadheads and sunken logs, remnants of log booms and debris from the bulk log carriers which dump their loads here.

2 Seaview Motel

Just south of Davis Lagoon is the Seaview Motel (245-3768), with a pier and float (April to September only) which dries at chart datum. Several mooring buoys, some belonging to the motel, are located to seaward of the float in deeper water. Fuel, boat rentals, restaurant, accommodation and temporary moorage are available. Owing to the exposed nature of this coast, the float is removed in the autumn and stored in Davis Lagoon over the winter.

Ladysmith Harbour

Ladysmith was originally named Oyster Harbour by Captain Richards in 1859, but it was redubbed Ladysmith in 1900, two years after James Dunsmuir established an instant town here to serve as a port for shipping coal from his nearby mines. The town was named on the date that news arrived of another Ladysmith's release from the Boers in South Africa. Many of the streets in B.C.'s Ladysmith are named after famous generals of the Boer War. The South African town, in turn, had been named after Lady Smith — "nèe Juana Maria de los Dolores de Leon, lineal descendant of Ponce de Leon, the Knight of Romance, [who] belonged to one of the oldest of the old Spanish families. Born 1798, married Sir Harry during the campaign of 1812, just before the battle of Salamanca, when she was 14 and her husband 24. Died at No. 79 Cadogan Place, London, 10 October, 1872."

John T. Walbran, in *British Columbia Coast Names*, goes on to reproduce an extract from Johnny Kincaid's diary of the meeting of Harry Smith and his future wife:

> I was conversing with a friend at the door of his tent, when we observed two ladies coming from the city, who made directly towards us. The older of the two threw back her mantilla to address us in that confident heroic manner so characteristic of the high-bred Spanish maiden, and told us who they were, the last of an ancient and honourable house. Her house she said, was a wreck, and to show the indignities to which they had been subjected she pointed to where the blood was still trickling down their necks caused by the wrenching of the ear-rings through the flesh. For herself, she said, she cared not, but for the agitated and almost unconscious maiden by her side — she saw no security for her but the seemingly indelicate one she had adopted — of coming to the camp and throwing themselves upon the protection of any British officer who could afford it, and so great, she said, was her faith in our national character, that she knew the appeal would not be made in vain nor the confidence abused. Nor was it made in vain; nor could it be abused, for she stood by the side of an angel: a being more transcendingly lovely I had never before seen, one more amiable I have never yet known.

Juana Maria ended up marrying Harry Smith, staying by his side in all his travels as a soldier. She saw the defeats of the French armies in Spain, the Americans at the burning of Washington in 1814, the Sikhs in India, and the Boers in South Africa. With her steadfast support Harry rose through the ranks to become a major general, was knighted and ended his career as Governor and Commander-in-Chief of the Cape, South Africa. She herself was much loved and respected.

Many of the beaches in the Ladysmith area glisten with the remains of discarded oyster shells. The warm waters of this area make it one of the few locations on the southern coast with optimal conditions for natural oyster breeding. The oyster industry has been somewhat hampered by pollution from log dumping, booming and sorting, and other developments in the harbour.

Tucked between log booms in Ladysmith Harbour are public floats providing moorage space for about 50 boats. There is also a launching ramp and extensive parking.

3   Transfer Beach Park

At low tide Holland Bank provides some protection from southeasterly seas to a public wharf where larger vessels sometimes moor temporarily. Temporary anchorage is possible off Transfer Beach Park in favourable conditions. There is a good beach here (reputed to have the warmest swimming waters on Vancouver Island) with a protected swimming area, playground and picnic facilities on shore.

The Crown Zellerbach Logging Museum and Arboretum is located on the north side of the highway and includes a display of old rail locomotives and logging machinery. Many different native and exotic trees are found in the gardens surrounding the museum.

4   Ladysmith Public Floats

Although the foreshore immediately in front of the town of Ladysmith may appear to be totally occupied by the logging industry, there is one small gap where you'll find a public wharf (245-7511) and three finger floats with space for about 50 boats. There is also a launching ramp with extensive parking area here. Roads and trails snake up the hillside to the town of Ladysmith. The Black Nugget Museum (245-4846) is housed in a partially restored "1881" hotel and features an interesting display of relics from the early days of coal mining.

5 Ivy Green Marina

The Ivy Green Marina (245-4521) is located at the north end of the log boom and sawmill area and provides fuel, launching ramp and a coffee shop, and is protected from any northerly seas by a floating log breakwater. A mile or so north of the marina is the former site of Ivy Green Provincial Park, at the mouth of Bush Creek. This 62 acre park has been returned to the Indians now and is accessible only by canoe or other shallow-draught small craft capable of navigating along the twisting channel through the mudflats.

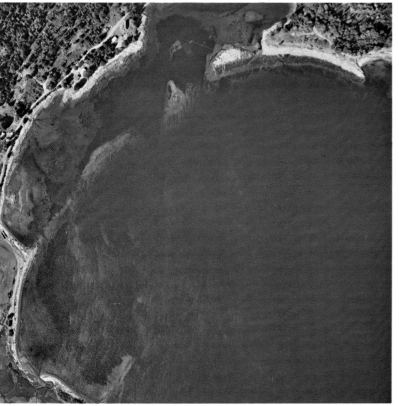

The entire shoreline of Kulleet Bay is protected as an Indian reserve and permission should be obtained before exploring ashore.

The park was designed mainly for highway access, with 51 drive-in campsites and 31 picnic sites. The many tributaries of Bush Creek provide an interesting canoeing area when the tide is high, and there is 300 feet of beach fronting onto the mudflats. Although the mud beach is not ideal for swimming, the water at this end of Ladysmith is uncommonly warm, especially after it has been warmed by flowing over the sunbaked mudflats with a rising tide.

6 Manana Lodge & Marina

Directly opposite the Ivy Green Marina is Manana Marina (245-2312). The facilities include a lodge with dining room, lounge, accommodation, showers, laundry, local craft and gift shop, groceries, fishing supplies, fuel, moorage and play area. A road and trail leading north from this marina provide access to the Woodley Range of hills with excellent views over

Ladysmith Harbour. Local boats sometimes enter Burleith Arm by way of the gap which separates Woods Islands from Page Point at high tide (the gap dries at seven feet). The log storage booms in Burleith Arm can often be used as a temporary tie-up by small craft.

7 Dunsmuir Islands

These islands, which protect the safest anchorage in the Ladysmith area, were named after the Dunsmuir family, who made their fortune in coal in the vicinity and built two castles at the south end of Vancouver Island — Craigdarroch in Victoria and Hatley above Royal Roads in Esquimalt. Hunter Point and Sibell Bay (Shell Beach) are Indian reserve and Bute and Dunsmuir Islands are privately owned. The temporary anchorage between Bute Island and the northern Dunsmuir is moderately exposed to westerly winds. The anchorage area in northern Sibell Bay offers a bit more protection and is extremely popular and often crowded.

Evening Cove

Although completely open to the southeast, Evening Cove provides good temporary anchorage in stable weather conditions or with an offshore wind (usually in the evenings). Temporary anchorage is also possible just north of Coffin Point in a tiny cove or around the corner when the tide is high. The nearby Kumalockasun Campground provides several shaded campsites by the sea, a gravel launching ramp and picnic area. Coffin Island was used as an Indian burial ground and is popular for scuba diving.

8 Kulleet Bay

The entire shoreline of beautiful Kulleet Bay is protected as an Indian reserve. The Indians have been living here for countless centuries and permission should be obtained before exploring ashore. The bay is also the location of two of the most remarkable petroglyphs on the B.C. coast — the "Shaman's Pool", described by Beth Hill in *Indian Petroglyphs of the Pacific Northwest* as "the most complex and carefully made petroglyph on Vancouver Island;" and the "Rain God," described by Ed Meade in *Indian Rockcarvings of the Pacific Northwest* as "a pure work of art, unrivalled by primitive man anywhere." It may seem strange why anyone on the west coast would want a raingod, but in autumn the salmon cannot return to spawn until after a heavy downpour has filled the spawning streams with water. The Indians were dependent on the salmon for their winter food supply and may have used the "Rain God" petroglyph to invoke supernatural powers and assure the annual return of the salmon.

The "Shaman's Pool" is a natural sandstone bowl surrounded by carvings of shrimp, frogmen, birds, fish and human heads with sunburst-hair. These carvings were probably made by young shamans — wisemen or magicians — as part of their initiation ceremony. Hill suggests that the carvings were executed while the initiate was standing waist deep in icy water (the pool dries up completely in the summer

The sun sets a brilliant orange over boats heading home in Stuart Channel.

months). According to Hill, the pool still has ritual significance for the inhabitants of the Kulleet Bay Village. Young Indian dancers are initiated into the secret societies at the winter ceremonials and are required to bathe in the "Shaman's Pool."

An interesting story about the origins of the local Indians has been related by a local historian, Harry Olsen: apparently an early shaman interpreted some of the carvings at the pool as a prophecy telling of:

> ...the coming of black-faced men [coal miners?] who will bring a new drink that drives men mad so they kill one another in their madness. These strangers will also bring new diseases that kill in many terrible ways until our village will be empty and trees will grow where our houses now stand. The villagers were very troubled until one of them had an inspiration. "Only the shaman can read the markings on the rock. If we kill him, perhaps all these terrible things won't happen." Thinking this was a good idea, the tribesmen ambushed the shaman and drove a spear through his chest.... Two months later, the man they believed was dead strode into the village and threw aside his cedar bark cloak. "Look at me" he shouted, "I have a hole in my chest and I am still alive. Spears cannot kill me and all the things I told you about will happen." They called him Tsa-meeun-iss, meaning "broken chest" and he became their chief. They were so proud of having a chief with a hole in his chest, they began to call themselves the Tsa-meeun-iss people. By the time the first white man arrived, the Tsa-meeun-iss people had spread from Kulleet Bay to beyond Chemainus and had villages on many of the nearby Gulf Islands.

9 Yellow Point

In good weather with winds from the north, temporary anchorage is possible in any of several tiny coves with white shell beaches to the west of Yellow Point. The well-known Yellow Point Lodge (245-7422) offers accommodation, canoes, sailboards, a hot tub, a saltwater pool, a sauna, and tennis. The original Lodge which burned down in 1985, was rebuilt in 1986, much of it by volunteer labour. A mooring buoy and temporary floats are located just south of the point. Several resorts are located in indentations along the shoreline north of Yellow Point.

10 Miami Islet

In 1900 the SS *Miami*, carrying a load of coal from Nanaimo struck White Rock (now Miami Islet) and sank a few hundred yards to the north. The jagged ribs of this 320 foot, 3,000-ton steel freighter uncover when the tide drops below 11 feet, and other parts of the vessel are often explored by scuba divers in depths of 25 to 60 feet. Another wreck, the wooden sailing collier *Robert Kerr*, can be found in deeper water to the south. This historic vessel took part in the incorporation festivities when Vancouver became a city, April 6, 1886, and two months later became the floating refuge for hundreds of Vancouverites who swam or rowed out to her when the city was destroyed by the Great Fire. She foundered here in 1911. The *Miami* marks the northernmost extension of a mile-long reef from Pilkey Point on Thetis Island, which also breaks the surface as the Ragged Islets. Up to 300 seals have been observed basking on the rocks in the winter.

11 Inn of the Sea

The Inn of the Sea (245-2211) offers accommodation, a gourmet restaurant, showers, a freshwater pool, a whirlpool, a sauna, tennis, and moorage. Blue Heron Park, 1.75 acres in size, is located on a triple-wide road access to the beach just south of here.

12 4 All Seasons Resort

This resort (245-4243) offers campsites, rental boats, an all-tide launching ramp, a store, a playground, a natural saltwater pool and moorage for boats up to 24 feet.

Sleek cormorants rest atop the jagged ribs of 320-ft S.S. *Miami* which struck White Rock (now Miami Islet) in 1900.

13 Mermaid Cove

Mermaid Cove Campground (245-3000) offers cottages, campsites, showers, fishing, boat rentals and moorage.

14 Roberts Memorial Park

A beautiful sandstone shore backed by a grassy meadow dotted with picnic tables marks Roberts Memorial Park, a locale offering opportunities for swimming, fishing and hiking.

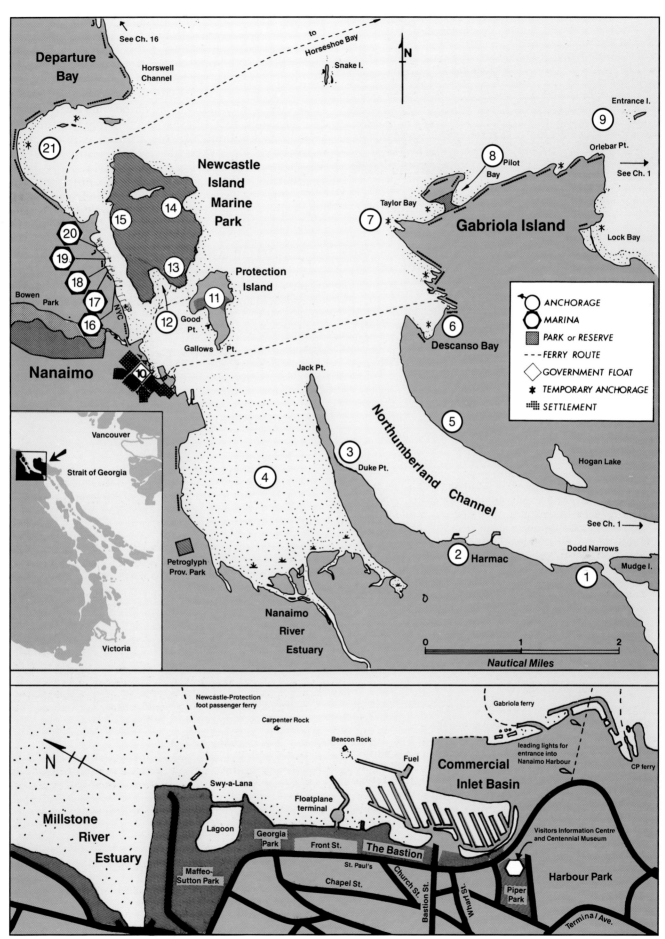

See Ch. 16

Departure
Bay

to
Horseshoe Bay

Snake I.

N

Entrance I.

Horswell
Channel

9

21

Orlebar Pt.

See Ch. 1

Newcastle
Island
Marine
Park

8 Pilot
Bay

14

Taylor Bay

Gabriola Island

15

7

Lock Bay

20

19

13

Protection
Island

18

Bowen
Park

17

12

11

Descanso Bay

6

16

NYC

Good
Pt.

Gallows   Pt.

Nanaimo

10

Jack Pt.

Hogan Lake

Northumberland

4

3
Duke Pt.

Channel

5

Petroglyph
Prov. Park

See Ch. 1

2 Harmac

Dodd Narrows

Nanaimo
River
Estuary

1

Mudge I.

Vancouver

Strait of Georgia

Victoria

0   1   2

Nautical Miles

ANCHORAGE
MARINA
PARK or RESERVE
FERRY ROUTE
GOVERNMENT FLOAT
TEMPORARY ANCHORAGE
SETTLEMENT

Newcastle-Protection
foot passenger ferry

Carpenter Rock

Gabriola ferry

Beacon Rock

N

Fuel

Commercial
Inlet Basin

leading lights for
entrance into
Nanaimo Harbour

Millstone
River
Estuary

Sway-a-Lana

Floatplane
terminal

CP ferry

Lagoon

Georgia
Park

Front St.

The Bastion

Visitors Information Centre
and Centennial Museum

St. Paul's

Maffeo-
Sutton Park

Chapel St.

Church St.

Bastion St.

Wharf St.

Piper
Park

Harbour Park

Terminal Ave.

150

Nanaimo Harbour and the Bastion circa 1860. (Watercolour on paper by E.P. Bedwell.)

CHAPTER FIFTEEN

Nanaimo

Western Gabriola and Newcastle Islands

Nanaimo, "Bathtub Capital of the World" and second largest community on Vancouver Island with an area population of over 50,000 people, enjoys a pleasant climate with warmer water temperatures than found among the more southerly Gulf Islands. Nanaimo was also known as "the Hub City", owing to its central location on the island but was redubbed "the Harbour City" by royal decree, during the visit of the Prince and Princess of Wales in May, 1986.

Winds

Winds from the west and northwest occur frequently, blowing over 50 percent of the time, and most frequently at night. The consistently strongest winds in the Strait of Georgia are the northwesterlies recorded at Entrance Island with an average wind speed for June of 15.3 mph and for January of 21.9 mph. Winds from the east and southeast are most frequent from noon to sundown (35 percent frequency). Winds from the north, northeast, south and southwest are seldom observed at the Entrance Island lightstation, as this central part of Georgia Strait is strongly influenced by the northwest to southeast pattern. Although calms are minimal at Entrance Island, they are prevalent in the more sheltered waters of Nanaimo Harbour and have a frequency of 25 percent in summer at Nanaimo Airport (Cassidy), a few miles south of the city.

Fishing

Horswell Channel, Five Fingers Island, Snake Island and around the north end of Gabriola Island are favoured angling spots, with excellent coho fishing during late September through October. Chinook are taken most of the year by mooching or trolling.

1 Dodd Narrows

The narrowest major passage into the Gulf Islands is also the swiftest, with currents of up to 10 knots possible at maximum spring tides. Even with a flood tide of two to three knots, the narrows can be dangerous to run, owing to a heavy overfall which develops as water piled up in the Gulf Islands disgorges into Northumberland Channel. Because of the hazards of meeting a tug and barge or other shipping traffic, especially close to slack water, this pass should be navigated with caution. Powerboats should *not* run the Narrows at high speed when other boats are in the vicinity. Wakes can be magnified by the current, becoming hazardous for slower boats.

2 Harmac

With a southeasterly wind, smoke from this major pulp mill dominates the whole of the Nanaimo area

CHARTS
3310 — Sheet 4 — PORLIER PASS to
     DEPARTURE BAY (1:40,000)
3475 — Plan of DODDS NARROWS (1:9,000)
3443 — THETIS ISLAND to NANAIMO
     (1:40,000)
3458 — Approaches to NANAIMO HARBOUR
     (1:20,000)
3457 — NANAIMO HARBOUR and DEPARTURE
     BAY (1:8,000)

with its acrid stench. Residents of Nanaimo have, however, become accustomed to it; some even are quite nostalgic about it when a northerly blows it away. The conspicuous 285 foot smokestacks are visible for many miles and give a convenient indication of the local wind direction as well as providing the source of many brilliant sunsets.

3   Duke (Jack) Point

The recent construction of a new deep-sea terminal has eliminated what was once Duke Point as a narrow inlet and tidal lagoon have been filled in to serve as a 345-acre industrial park for the storage and shipping

Narrowest of the major passages into the Gulf Islands is Dodd Narrows where currents sometimes reach speeds of 10 knots at maximum spring tides — caution is advised.

of forest and other products. The Jack Point peninsula was once an island at high tide, separated from Vancouver Island by a narrow cut which had been blasted through the sandstone ridge over what was once known as Bigg's Portage. The passage was only wide enough for canoes or rowboats. Early residents of South Gabriola and Mudge Island found it easier to row to Nanaimo by this route than by rounding the exposed and often wave-swept headland of Jack Point. The point is particularly difficult to round when a strong westerly is meeting a strong tide with steep seas breaking over the shallows and rocks north of the point. At the end of Jack Point there were some petroglyphs, possibly representing salmon, carved on a boulder which has since been placed in front of the

Nanaimo City Museum. According to legend, these carvings were representations of people and animals who had died on the Point and in the old days when it rained the rocks would bleed.

4   Nanaimo River Estuary

The tidal mudflats of the Nanaimo River delta are now used almost exclusively for the booming and storage of logs. Small boats of shallow draught can, however, explore behind these booms by using the channels on either side of the mudflats. A rising tide will assist navigation for a short distance up the river. Several prosperous nineteenth century farms were once located near the mouth of the river, protected by dykes from high water encroachment, but these are now abandoned and largely reclaimed by the sea. The banks of the lower Nanaimo River and upper estuary are Indian reserve, the location of Twsul'wu'lum, an early village site.

Petroglyph Provincial Park

Many petroglyphs are found in the Nanaimo area. A good place to visit some of these is at Petroglyph Provincial Park on the west side of the estuary adjacent to the Island Highway. The carvings include rare examples of the sea wolf — a mysterious creature who was half killer whale, half timber wolf. It is possible that these carvings were made by people who lived here as much as 10,000 years ago. Immediately north of here is Su'luxwum village site — "the place of many grasses."

5   Northumberland Channel

This channel was named after Algernon Percy, fourth Duke of Northumberland, a noted naval officer

Spanish explorers Galiano and Valdes named Descanso Bay in 1792. Translated, it means "small bay of rest".

and scientist. Duke Point and Percy Anchorage were named for this same man by the officers of HMS *Egeria* in 1904. Tidal currents in Northumberland Channel generally ebb and flood in the same direction — to the east at maximum rates of 1-2 knots. Cliffs up to 400 feet high line the southwest shore of Gabriola. At the base of these cliffs, concrete pilings

Intriguing rock forms and colourful arbutus are just two of the treats in store for yachtsmen cruising the Gulf Islands.

hanging lip of erosion-resistant conglomerate (see "Why Is Georgia Strait" by Colin Hempsall, Pacific Yachting, April-July, 1986 for more information on B.C. coastal geology). The galleries can be viewed conveniently by anchoring in the small bay just south of Malaspina Point. A small local park is situated on the point. Summer cottages and summer homes line the shoreline from Galiano Galleries to Orlebar Point. Almost half of the 2,000 residents of Gabriola live along this northern shoreline.

Taylor Bay

Good afternoon anchorage is available in Taylor Bay, but if you anchor here overnight be prepared for strong offshore westerlies blowing across from Vancouver Island. The Haven by the Sea (247-9211) is a waterfront lodge, conference and dining facility, located at the south end of Taylor Bay. The bay was named after an Anglican clergyman who lived here at the turn of the century and walked and rowed hundreds of miles each week to visit his parishioners and take services at the south end of Gabriola and in the Nanaimo area. He was also an avid amateur naturalist and was primarily responsible for the establishment in 1908 of the Dominion Marine Biological Station in Departure Bay, north of Nanaimo.

Gabriola Sands Provincial Park

Although only three and a half acres in size, Gabriola Sands (or Twin Beaches) Provincial Park does provide a pleasant place to stroll ashore, since it is one of the few bits of public land on this stretch of coastline. There are also opportunities for picnicking and swimming here. A foreshore reserve on both Taylor Bay and Pilot Bay across the isthmus has been added to the park in an effort to control water-skiing, which

Picturesque Hogan Lake is located on the southern side of Galiano Island, across Northumberland Channel from Dodd Narrows.

serve as moorage posts for log booms and sawdust barges entering and leaving Harmac across the channel. Near Descanso Bay a large patch of the cliff face is streaked white, indicating the presence of thousands of nesting cormorants tucked into tiny indentations which honeycomb the sandstone.

6 Descanso Bay

This bay was named by Galiano and Valdes as Cala del Descanso — "small bay of rest" — in 1792. They anchored here with the intention of asking the natives ashore if there was a nearby spring where they could replenish their water supply. The winds must have been blowing from the southeast that day for this bay might not be particularly restful with a northwest wind blowing into it. A road from the south end of the bay leads around the shore to the ferry landing from Nanaimo. A short distance up the road from the ferry landing, near the junction of North and South roads, are stores, a post office, a library and a fire hall. A golf course and an abandoned mill stone quarry are found along South Road near Hoggan Lake.

7 Galiano Galleries

The Galiano (or Malaspina) Galleries gained much publicity in Europe in the nineteenth century after publication of accounts of the voyages of Galiano and Valdes included an excellent engraving illustrating the wave-like overhangs and describing the galleries as a unique natural phenomenon. The galleries are approximately 300 feet long, 12 feet high, and between 15 to 20 feet wide. They were formed by marine erosion of sandstone that was roofed in by an over-

has proved dangerous to both swimmers and smallcraft in these often-crowded bays. Several Parks Branch buoys extend across the head of the bay and are intended to separate swimmers from boats.

8   Pilot Bay

Pilot Bay, so named for the pilot boats which would head out from here to guide ships into Nanaimo Harbour, is a fair anchorage, safe from all winds except northeasters and seas generated in the Strait of Georgia. Surf Lodge (247-9231), which provides accom-

Entrance Island is the site of one of the first three lighthouses to be erected (1870s) in the Strait of Georgia. It is often used as a turning mark in local yacht races.

modation, dining facilities and an outdoor pool, is located near Orlebar Point.

9   Entrance Island

This tiny island is the site of one of the first three lighthouses to be erected in the Strait of Georgia, in the 1870s. It is often used as a rounding mark for yacht races in the Straits. Many a person at sea has had cause to be thankful for the watchful eye of the lightkeepers, who are ready to radio for assistance should they see any vessel founder on rocks to the west of the island or on the isolated exposed coast of north Gabriola. Le Boeuf Bay and Lock Bay to the south of Entrance Island are completely exposed to Strait of Georgia easterlies, a common afternoon

wind. In calm conditions or with an offshore wind, these bays are reasonably sheltered, and offer isolated pinnacles of arbutus-topped, wave-contorted sandstone rocks and a wide sand and shingle beach backed by a tidal marsh for exploration. Four interesting petroglyphs can be seen in Lock Bay. These two round faces and two stick figure men can be found on large boulders near high tide, almost concealed by driftwood (Bentley).

Nanaimo

Prior to 1791, when Eliza named this area Bocas de Winthuysen, five native bands lived here in a confederacy known as *Sne-ny-mo*, meaning "meeting place of the tribes" or "a big strong tribe". One day in 1849 a number of Indians were digging for clams on the beach when a chief found some black rock, which he later discovered was the same type of rock used by the Hudson Bay Company in their forges at Fort Victoria. The next time he visited Victoria he brought a canoe load of the black rock which was tested and found to be excellent quality coal. In 1852, mining operations began and 480 barrels of coal were shipped out in the Hudson's Bay Company brigantine *Cadboro*, starting an industry which was to last for almost 100 years. The coal deposits here were the largest on the Pacific Coast of North or South America.

Harbour Park

The Gabriola Ferry leaves regularly from a dock in front of Harbour Park shopping centre. On the peninsula protecting Commercial Inlet basin is The Harbour Chandler (753-2425), boatbuilders and a drydock.

10   Commercial Inlet

The public floats operated by the Nanaimo Harbour Commission and located just beneath the Bastion are within a few minutes walk of the centre of the city, and several shopping centres and hotels. Over 3,000 feet of moorage space is provided in the basin and available to smallcraft, dependent on whether the fishing fleet is out or not. The wharfinger's office (754-5053) is here, with facilities for laundry and showers. Additional float space and a fuel dock are located just outside the basin. A distinctive new floatplane terminal building which includes a restaurant and pub, is located just north of here in front of the Malaspina Hotel. The Nanaimo Newstand (754-2513) on Church Street has a complete selection of coastal charts and marine books. At one time, Commercial Inlet extended further into the city, covering the present location of Terminal Avenue and almost encircling the hill where 1.3 acre Piper Park, the Visitors Information Bureau and Centennial Museum are now located. This museum features many excellent displays, including remnants of Chinatown, dioramas of mine tunnels and an Indian village, and maps of "Covilletown". McGregor Park starts at the south end of the basin and is linked to various other parks by a waterfront walkway. The first section of this is known as the Princess Royal Promenade.

The historic bastion was built in 1853 as a fort for Hudsons Bay Company employees seeking protection from expected attacks by local Indians.

Looking east over Nanaimo. The public floats (centre right) provide convenient moorage for visiting yachtsmen making shopping expeditions to nearby stores.

The Bastion

The historic Bastion, an octagonal, three-storey building, was constructed by two French Canadians in 1853. It was built as a fort for the Hudsons's Bay Company to provide protection from expected attacks by the local Indians. Sixteen cannons were mounted on the top two floors, but fortunately used only to fire ceremonial salutes. The Bastion is now a museum. Beside the Bastion is the Pioneer Rock memorial commemorating the landing of the first settlers from the sailing barque *Princess Royal* in 1854.

Queen Elizabeth II Promenade

Past the Malaspina Hotel (754-3241), with its dock for boat and floatplane moorage, the waterfront walkway becomes the Queen Elizabeth II Promenade, named in honour of Her Majesty's 1983 visit. Georgia Park features two totem poles and a Salish cedar canoe carved from a single tree in 1922. Swy-a-lana Park includes a recently constructed lagoon and tidal weir and behind this is Maffeo-Sutton Park which features tennis courts, picnic tables and a sandy playground. The Newcastle-Protection Islands passenger ferry leaves from here on a regular basis during the summer months. At high tide shallow-draught boats can navigate a short distance up the Millstone River to Bowen Park. Several small boatyards used to be located along this river. One of these — Vollmers — converted Captain Voss's dug-out canoe *Tilikum* into an ocean-going craft before he left Victoria on his voyage around the world in 1901. If you are on foot you can cross over

155

Pearson Bridge and continue along the Queen Elizabeth II Promenade up to the Nanaimo Yacht Club at the bottom of Rosehill Street.

Most yachtsmen visiting Newcastle Island Marine Park drop anchor in the accommodating waters of Mark Bay (foreground). There is also a public dock and buoys.

11 Protection Island

In the 1930s one could walk to this island from Nanaimo, under the harbour, by way of the old mine shafts which were driven to extract the rich coal seams. Miners could tell the time by the sound of the CPR steamships as they left the harbour overhead. In 1918, 16 coal miners were killed beneath Protection when an elevator cable snapped. The mine was closed in 1938 and the island is now subdivided for private homes and summer cottages. The Leeshore Resort (754-2879) is located just north of Good Point and provides moorage and rustic cottages. Access is possible by the Nanaimo foot-passenger ferry which docks here or at a public facility (drop-off or pick-up only) immediately northwest of Gallows Point. Temporary anchorage is possible between Gallows and Good Point in an area which is occasionally used for storing log booms and barges. Small community parks total-

any sound from the more than 40,000 people that live within a few miles of the island.

12   Mark Bay

The safest anchorage in the Nanaimo Harbour area is in Mark Bay (known also as Echo Bay), although it is moderately exposed to southerly winds, which are infrequent. Southeasterly seas are deflected effectively by Jack Point and Protection Island. Mooring buoys and a wharf (1,700 feet of float space) at the southern end of the island have been provided by the Parks Branch for the convenience of visitors to the park.

13   Picnic Grounds and Campsites

Large clearings carpeted with green lawns mark the former location of Saysetsen, a native winter village site. In the 1930s the CPR bought the island and developed it into a resort with playing fields, picnic shelters and a dance pavilion. The island was very popular for company picnics and excursion boats from the mainland, such as the *Charmer* or *Princess*

In earlier years cylindrical pulpstones were cut from New-castle Island stone, then shipped to coastal millsites for use in grinding wood.

Victoria, would tie up in Mark Bay to serve as floating hotels as thousands of weekending holidayers disembarked to frolic and relax. Today with no more than a few hundred visitors on a summer weekend, an atmosphere of nostalgia and peacefulness pervades the area. On summer evenings it is possible to watch the sun set over Nanaimo while a few of the 50 or so Columbian blacktail deer resident on the island emerge from the woods to graze over the abandoned playing fields. The Parks Branch has restored the dance pavillion with its unique "floating floor" and mounted an interpretive display of photographs of life here more than 50 years ago.

The "Gap" between Protection and Newcastle Islands dries four feet at low tide. Sandstone ledges on the Newcastle side are often heated by the midday sun, transferring their warmth to the incoming tide for pleasant afternoon swimming. On the Mark Bay side, near the park supervisor's residence, two large millstones over six feet in diameter can be found,

ing over 27 acres are located behind beaches east of Good Point (Pirates Park) and midway up the east coast of Protection Island (Smugglers Park).

Newcastle Island Marine Park

Newcastle Island is Nanaimo's own Stanley Park with the added advantage of no cars, since there is no bridge or car ferry access to the island. A foot-passenger ferry service provides hourly trips from Nanaimo (mid-May to October). A few hundred yards beyond the Newcastle ferry dock you can set off on a hike along the 12 miles of winding woodland trails and not see anyone for two or three hours — or hear

157

remnants of a nearby sandstone quarry where similar millstones were cut and used as grinders at early pulp mills. A small float below the quarry is used primarily by park maintenance staff. Three excellent trails lead out from this area around the shoreline of the island, up to Kanaka and Midden bays and north to Mallard (or Beaver) Lake. These are described below.

14 Kanaka Bay

This bay has an interesting history, but is not suitable as an anchorage since the shelf surrounding the tiny islets at the entrance dries 16 feet (the maximum tidal range for the Nanaimo area). Exposed temporary anchorage is possible, however, between the shelf and an offshore rock to the south which dries six feet. The bay is named after a native Hawaiian named Peter Kakua who lived in Nanaimo with his Indian wife, mother-in-law and baby son. One afternoon he returned home to find them all in bed together with another Indian. After he killed them all with his axe, he was chased up the Chase River south of Nanaimo, captured, and eventually hanged on Gallows Point at the south end of Protection Island. The judge who presided at his trial informed him that he might have been spared for chopping up the intruder, his wife and mother-in-law but that he would have to be hanged for the murder of his baby son. He was buried on Newcastle Island near Kanaka Bay. In 1913 this bay was the terminus for the "world's longest telephone cable" — it came beneath the Gulf from Point Grey. Near the head of the bay are the remains of an old ventilation shaft which provided air for the coal miners who worked 300-400 feet beneath the island from 1853 to 1883.

Kanaka Bay is fine for swimming and wading but its shallow depths discourage anchorage by craft much larger than a dinghy.

Mallard Lake

Mallard (or Beaver) Lake is so peaceful and natural it is hard to believe you are only a mile or so from downtown Nanaimo, or that the lake was created to supply water for the coal mines beneath the island. Wood ducks, great blue herons, muskrats, beavers and pumpkinseed sunfish can be found in Mallard Lake. North of here beneath the steep cliffs of Nares Point, a jumble of boulders hide caverns which were uses by early natives as burial chambers. These caverns are best seen from the water, as the cliffs here are too steep for access from the land.

15 Midden Bay

North of Shaft Point is a broad beach which fronts a large grassy open area, once the site of Q'ulutztun, a native village. From 1910 to 1941 a thriving Japanese cannery, herring saltery and boat building industry were located here. Everything but a few concrete foundations were removed after all Japanese living on the coast were forced to resettle inland during World War II. Opposite Pimbury Point is Midden Bay, where shafts for the old Newcastle coal mine were first driven in 1853. This island, and the point to the north, were named after Newcastle-on-Tyne in England, where coal has been mined for over 800 years.

Old Sandstone Quarry

Just south of Midden Bay are the remains of an old sandstone quarry, now completely enclosed by the forest. Sandstone from this quarry was of exceptional quality, increasing in strength as it was exposed to the weather, Some of it was used in a number of early Victoria and Vancouver buildings as well as the San Francisco Mint — one of the few buildings to withstand the earthquake of 1906. Sandstone quarries operated on Newcastle Island from 1869 to 1932.

Newcastle Island Passage

Newcastle Island Passage (Exit Channel) is lined with several marinas on the Vancouver Island side. The floats of the Nanaimo Yacht Club (754-7011) are at the southern entrance to the passage. Anyone who enters Exit Channel from the north (Departure Bay) should recognize that the buoy system is established for boats travelling north from Nanaimo. In particular, keep to the west of the red buoy north of Shaft Point and east of the green buoys at the mouth of the Millstone River.

16 Nanaimo Shipyard

Boat maintenance and repair are offered by this shipyard (753-1151) which is ideally situated to repair the many small craft which annually run aground on infamous "Rowan's Rock." The rock is named after Johnny Rowan, founder of the shipyard, and is located between the two beacons which mark Oregon Rock and Passage Rock. Boats should keep to the east (Newcastle Island side) when passing the beacons and not attempt to go between them.

17 Moby Dick Boatel

This boatel (753-7111) provides fuel, free canoeing and moorage for guests, and fishing supplies and charters.

Newcastle Island Passage is lined with marinas on the Vancouver Island side. Departure Bay and the western terminus of the Nanaimo-Horseshoe Bay ferry are in the background.

18   Nanaimo Marina

This marina (754-2732) provides moorage and repairs with a 30-ton capacity marine hoist.

Newcastle Marina

This marina (753-1431) offers fuel, moorage, laundry, showers and boat repairs.

19   Anchorage Marina

Here (754-5585) you can find gas, diesel, moorage, rental boats, charters, charts, a chandlery, fishing supplies, boat repairs (30-ton capacity hoist), a restaurant and groceries. Nearby are the NHL Restaurant, the Bluenose Chowder House and St. Jeans Custom Cannery.

20   Stones Marine Centre

Stones Marine Centre (753-4232) provides moorage, a cafe, Mercury products and a chandlery. A recreation park with showers and laundry is planned. Just north of here is the new Nanaimo Public Market, with fresh produce, restaurants and moorage for visiting smallcraft.

Brechin Point Marina

Brechin Point Marina (753-6122) offers aviation fuel, gas, diesel, propane, fishing supplies and guest moorage (under 18 feet). This marina could serve for embarking or disembarking passengers to or from the BC Ferry dock which connects with Horseshoe Bay on the mainland.

21   Departure Bay

Although this bay provides good protection, it is not often used as an anchorage by smallcraft, owing to wash from the ferries entering and leaving the terminal at the south end of the bay. Temporary anchorage is possible just off the popular sunbathing beach and grassy playground (Kin Park) at the west end of the bay. Restaurants, grocery stores, boat and sailboard rentals can also be found here. The water in this bay can become cold if offshore westerly and northwesterly winds are causing offshore currents and upwellings of deeper, colder water close to the shoreline. A quiet beach can be found a short distance north of Kin Park where a rocky point serves as the last visible remnant of coal-loading wharves from the last century. Sailing vessels dumped their ballast on this point and many Nanaimo fireplaces are said to have been built from pink Italian marble scavenged here. Rockhounds may still find specimens from China, Africa and Europe (Fletcher). Anchorage is prohibited within 1,000 feet of the Pacific Biological Station because of the presence of underwater instruments monitoring fish and shellfish experiments in the bay. Tours of this station, the largest of its kind in Canada, can be arranged (756-7000).

The north side of Jesse Island is a local underwater reserve, popular with scuba divers wanting a look at limestone arches, tunnels and rock falls. There are also bottles from the 1800s (discarded from waiting coal ships), steep walls covered with bright red colonial anemones and a 30-foot fishboat wreck you can enter in 90 feet of water (Pratt-Johnson).

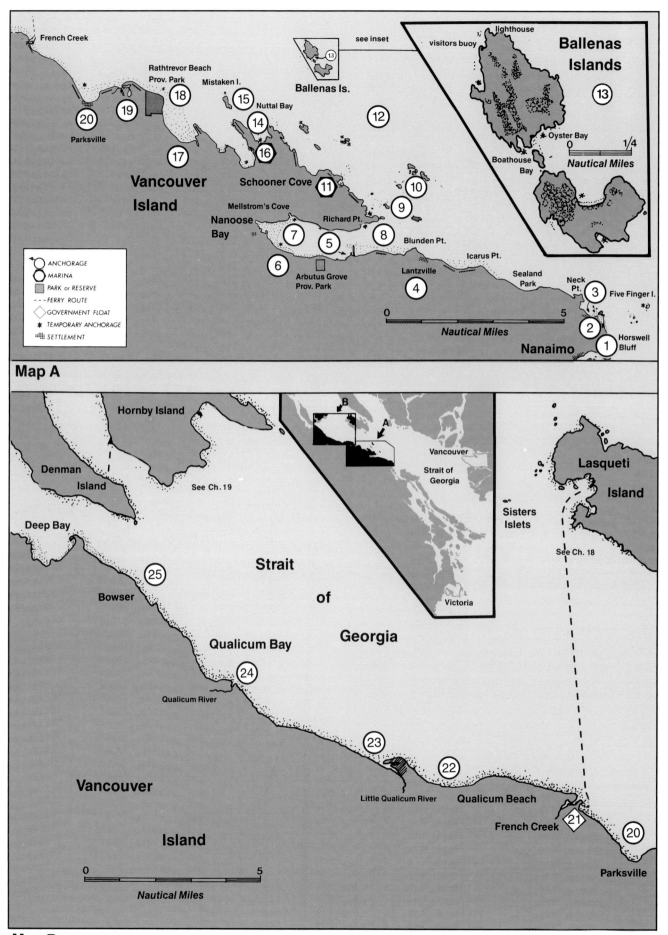

Map A

French Creek

Rathtrevor Beach
Prov. Park

Mistaken I.

⑱

⑲

⑳

Parksville

Vancouver

Island

⑰

Nuttal Bay

⑮

⑭

⑯

Schooner Cove

Mellstrom's Cove

Nanoose
Bay

Richard Pt.

⑪

⑫

⑩

⑨

⑧

⑦

⑤

⑥

Arbutus Grove
Prov. Park

Blunden Pt.

Lantzville

Icarus Pt.

④

Sealand
Park

Neck
Pt.

③

Five Finger I.

②

Horswell
Bluff

①

Nanaimo

see inset

Ballenas Is.

⑬

lighthouse

visitors buoy

**Ballenas
Islands**

⑬

Oyster Bay

Boathouse
Bay

0   1/4

Nautical Miles

○ ANCHORAGE
◎ MARINA
▨ PARK or RESERVE
--- FERRY ROUTE
◇ GOVERNMENT FLOAT
✳ TEMPORARY ANCHORAGE
▦ SETTLEMENT

0   5

Nautical Miles

Map B

Hornby Island

**Denman
Island**

Deep Bay

B

A

Vancouver

Strait of
Georgia

Victoria

**Lasqueti
Island**

Sisters
Islets

See Ch. 18

See Ch. 19

㉕

Bowser

Strait

of

Georgia

Qualicum Bay

㉔

Qualicum River

㉓

Little Qualicum River

㉒

Qualicum Beach

㉑

French Creek

Vancouver

Island

㉒₀

Parksville

0   5

Nautical Miles

The summer sun sets a brilliant orange over children enjoying the water at Qualicum Beach.

Qualicum

Nanaimo to Deep Bay

The Vancouver Island coastline north of Nanaimo is not as well known as the popular and more protected Gulf Islands area to the south. Nevertheless, this area has its own unique attractions — including long, sandy beaches, excellent fishing and several coves and bays providing safe anchorage, depending on the wind conditions.

Winds

Onshore summer winds from the north or northeast are infrequent along this stretch of coast, with westerlies being predominant, especially between sunset and noon. Onshore breezes from the east and southeast seldom blow at night, and occur most frequently in the afternoon, with maximum recorded speeds at noon. The selection of a cove in which to seek shelter should be made with an understanding of these diurnal wind patterns. For example, coves facing south or east tend to be unsafe in the afternoon and evening, but will often provide protection from the night-time westerly.

Fishing

Offshore islets and shoals north of Nanoose provide likely haunts for salmon. Blueback fishing starts in early spring and continues through summer, while chinook fishing is best during late summer and fall. Bucktailing along the eight- to 20-fathom dropoff is especially good from French Creek to Deep Bay. The Qualicum Beach area is one of the longest-established and best-known salmon grounds on the Island.

1   Horswell Bluff

Leaving Departure Bay and proceeding north from Nanaimo through Horswell Channel, you will pass Horswell Bluff and Horswell Rock (about two and a half cables — or a quarter-mile — offshore). Who was this Horswell? Another vaunted naval officer — captain or admiral? No — just an ordinary seaman from HMS *Virago* who helped row the surveying boat which sounded and charted Nanaimo Harbour in 1853. The beach below Horswell Bluff, also known as Stephenson Point, is a popular place for beachcombing, swimming, sunbathing and picnicking. Above the bluff is 12-acre Planta Park, a place for botanists and amateur naturalists, with almost every native plant and such rare species as purple sea blush and the spotted coral root represented. Five Finger Island, 1½ miles offshore, has the profile of a clenched fist when viewed from north or south. A small cove on the west side of the island could provide temporary anchorage when the weather is calm, but would not offer much protection when a southeasterly is blowing, since the island is only 40 feet high.

CHARTS
**3458 — Approaches to NANAIMO HARBOUR
        (1:20,000)**
**3459 — Approaches to NANOOSE HARBOUR
        (1:15,000)**
**3512 — Strait of Georgia, CENTRAL PORTION
        (1:80,000)**
**3513 — Strait of Georgia, NORTHERN
        PORTION (1:80,000)**

2 Pipers Lagoon Park

Also known as Page's Lagoon, this beautiful 20-acre regional park includes a diversity of landforms and habitat. Lagoon Head, a rocky outcrop heavily forested with Douglas fir, arbutus and a magnificent stand of 200-year-old Garry oak, is joined to Vancouver Island by a low sand and pebble spit built up by the crashing waves of southeasterly storms. The lagoon behind the spit is a popular place for bathing in calm weather, and once a year the capelin, a member of the smelt family, spawn by the thousands along the beach. Several kinds of ducks, mergansers and grebes use the lagoon as a feeding ground at high tide, or as a resting area when southeasterlies lash the strait. Scoters, loons, cormorants, herons, black turnstones and oystercatchers share the lagoon area, with hawks and bald eagles soaring overhead. It is possible to watch the grebes and loons following the herring and sandlance into the lagoon with a flood tide, while at low water, the scoters dive for littleneck clams.

In 1907 this lagoon was the site of a whaling station, with over 125 men employed processing whales caught right offshore. Within a few years all whales in Georgia Strait were wiped out and after a disastrous season — when the plant converted dogfish into fertilizer — it was dismantled and moved to the Queen Charlottes in 1912.

162

Hammond Bay provides reasonable shelter from southeasterly and northwesterly winds. However, seas from the north tend to curl around Neck Point.

3 Hammond Bay

This bay provides good protection from southeasterly and northwesterly winds, though seas from the north tend to curl around Neck Point and make the anchorage somewhat uncomfortable. The southern shoreline has been recently settled and there is a paved launching ramp with several private mooring buoys at the edge of the tidal flats for local residents. A recreational foreshore reserve covers the southern part of the bay and the tidal area of the lagoon. Shack Islands are also protected as Crown land and though some locals dislike the presence of the shacks erected by squatters and fishermen, they add colour to the bay and are interesting to visit. Morningside Park at the west end of the bay is grassy with a sand and gravel beach and tennis courts.

4 Lantzville

Tidal flats here extend up to one-third of a mile offshore with the edge of the flats marked in summer by a row of private moorings for local small craft. The Lantzville area has more beach access than almost any other area on Vancouver Island; Blunden Point alone has 10. These beaches are best explored at low tide. Beyond Neck Point, Fillinger Crescent gives access to a partly paved launching ramp. Sealand Park (8 acres), with a pebbly beach, is located at the bottom of Shoreline Drive; but the best beach is found off Icarus Point, accessible down Blueback Drive (254 stairs down to the beach) or Invermere Road (163 stairs). The Shoregrove Resort (390-4032) is located off Dickenson Road and offers cabins, campsites, showers, laundromat, boat rentals and ramp. At Blunden Point there is a diving platform and a lifeguard on duty most of the summer.

5   Nanoose Harbour

This harbour, named after the Nonooa Indians who were almost completely exterminated by marauding Indians in 1856, is the home base for vessels of the Royal Canadian Navy (RCN) and the United States Navy (USN) engaged in testing torpedoes off Winchelsea Islands. Guided tours of the base may occasionally be arranged by phoning 468-9922. Several Navy mooring buoys may be used by small craft in an emergency as there are no other mooring facilities within the harbour, but be prepared to move off at a moments notice should navy ships return. Shelter from southeast seas is afforded behind a sandbank and breakwater which extends out from Fleet Point on the southern shore. Log booms along this shore may also provide convenient temporary tie-ups. The Snawnaw-as Campsite (390-4363) provides ocean-front campsites, boat ramp, flush toilets and hot showers. Arbutus Grove Provincial Park, 55 acres in size, protects what is said to be the most spectacular stand of old arbutus trees known to be growing on Vancouver Island.

6   Red Gap

Pilings and bits of concrete along the shore west of here are all that remain of the Straits Mill and the community of Red Gap. Named in 1912 after the short story "Ruggles of Red Gap", this community disappeared soon after the mill burned to the ground in 1943. A wildlife sanctuary protects what is left of the estuary at the head of the bay and a pentecostal church camp is located above the south shore. Behind the estuary are a general store and a rebuilt version of the Arlington Hotel (468-7013), first established here in 1894, and now offering a pub and dining room.

7   Mellstrom's Cove

Temporary anchorage is possible near the tidal flats at the edge of the estuary or in Mellstrom's Cove, where vessels of the Hudson's Bay Company and Royal Navy were careened over 130 years ago. A stockade was erected on shore shortly after the massacre of the Nanooas to provide protection while ships were repaired. Cannon balls retrieved from a target range painted on the rock bluffs south of Nanoose Hill are now on display in Nanaimo's Bastion. Today the ex-USS *Tolman* is used instead. This hulk is occasionally towed out into the Gulf for target practice by naval ships and submarines firing blank torpedoes.

In the early 1900s Page Lagoon was the site of a prosperous whaling station. Now it's the site of an attractive 20 acre park that supports a variety of intriguing habitat and landforms.

8   Wallis Point

Temporary anchorage with good protection from westerlies is available just north of Richard Point. Although the upland behind this anchorage appears attractive, venturing ashore is prohibited as the land is used by the Department of National Defence. Brickyard Cove, just northwest of Wallis Point, would appear to provide good protection from all but easterly winds, with several reefs, drying rocks and islets hemming in the northern approach to this cove. The *B.C. Pilot*, however, does not recommend this cove, since "the bottom is rocky and a swell sets into it during onshore winds." The beach here is a popular warm water swimming nook.

9   Ballenas Channel Islands

Maude Island, one mile off Wallis Point, is popular with locals for exploring and picnicking and is protected by a provincial recreational reserve. A small cove at the south end could be used at high water, in calm weather or with winds from the northwest, but dries completely at low water. This island is virtually the only one of this group, south of Ballenas, with extensive tree cover. The others are, for the most part, barren and rocky with stunted shrub-like trees, evidence of the strong southeasterly gales which buffet this area in winter — and occasionally in summer, too. Care should be taken when navigating between these islands to avoid the many drying rocks and reefs. This area has a great deal of kelp and other warm water marine plants and the water is generally exceptionally clear making for excellent scuba diving. If the weather is stable it is a good canoeing area as speeding power boats tend to be slowed down by the many rocks in the area.

10   Winchelsea Islands

These islands serve as the torpedo tracking base for the testing range just offshore and trespassing is prohibited. Buoys in the cove west of the southernmost island may be used in an emergency, but must be

Buildings on Winchelsea Islands serve as a naval tracking base for a sophisticated torpedo testing range in adjacent waters.

vacated when needed by the navy. The northernmost island has a large conspicuous electronic surveillance building with powerful telescopes and radar domes. Safe anchorage in a protected cove just south of this island is reserved for the navy but could be used in an emergency.

11   Schooner Cove

A federal breakwater constructed in 1971 provides protection to this cove. A massive marina, resort, convention centre and "condotel" (condominium and hotel) complex has been constructed here. The Schooner Cove Resort (468-7691) also features a heated pool, jacuzzi, saunas, tennis courts, a restaurant and the Pirates Lounge. There are 450 berths for small craft, as well as fuel, a launching ramp, a small store and dive shop, and an air station. As well, Winchelsea Charters (468-9222) offers boats for sailing, fishing, windsurfing and diving.

Temporary anchorage with some protection from southeasterlies is also possible off Dolphin Beach. Camp Moorecroft, just north of here, has been used as a camping, conference or retreat centre by the United Church of Canada since 1954. Temporary anchorage in calm weather is available at either of two coves separated by a low isthmus which joins the Yeo Is-

lands, but no protection is afforded from high winds, as the islands are treeless and only 25 and 35 ft high. There is a small cove for temporary anchorage at the north end of little Gerald Island; it offers more protection from southerly seas and winds.

12   Naval Testing Range

"Whiskey Golf" is a five-mile-wide naval testing range that extends from Ballenas Islands for 14 miles in an easterly direction to north of Entrance Island. When an exercise is in progress (which may be anytime during day or night, winter or summer) and you are planning to cross the Strait to Pender Harbour or environs, it is best to pass close by Winchelsea and Ballenas islands, taking care to miss Rudder and Grey rocks just east of Winchelsea Islands. If you are sailing across the testing range, without auxiliary, you are in little danger from the acoustic torpedoes which home in on engine noise, but be prepared for submarines surfacing unexpectedly and the harassment of buzzing helicopters. To help defray expenses, the RCN operates this range jointly with the USN and naval ships and helicopters from both countries patrol the range to warn off other ships when firing is taking place. This sometimes proves embarrassing for USN vessels when the interloper happens to be a local boat. One local fisherman, shocked that a foreigner was ordering him out of his own waters, pulled out a shotgun and told the gunboat crew "where to go" in no uncertain terms.

13   Ballenas Islands

Named by the Spanish in 1791 as Islas de las Ballenas or "Islands of the Whales," these isolated, rocky, windswept islands provide spectacular viewpoints overlooking the Strait of Georgia. Unfortunately whales are seldom seen today. The lightstation at the north end of the north island is well worth visiting and if the lightkeepers are not too busy servicing their equipment, rescuing shipwrecked boaters or sending in weather reports, they will be happy to show you around. Possibly because of the excellent service lightkeepers provide, early fears that complete automation of lighthouses would force their retirement, have not yet been realized at many stations, including this one.

A buoy for visiting boats is located just west of the north tip of the island and immediately south of a dangerous rock which dries nine feet. Another dangerous rock dries eight feet and lies a few hundred yards to the south. The first lighthouse was built in 1906 on the highest point of land, in the centre of the north island, but this was later moved to the north end. Although the island is not heavily forested there are a few patches of grass on the rocky hillocks which served as greens for a seven-hole golf course constructed by a previous lightkeeper. Impenetrable scrub bush in the valleys between the hillocks serve as hazards for any one trying to cross the island. A beautiful trail from the lightstation leads underneath an overhanging canopy of bush to Boathouse Bay at the southwest end of the island. Good temporary an-

A breakwater, marina and resort provide shelter and shore-side amenities for visitors to Schooner Cove north of Nanoose Bay.

chorage, dependent on wind and sea conditions, is possible here or in a small cove on the west side of the island. Although it is possible to navigate between the two Ballenas, this should only be attempted at high water, north of the group of islets in the passage. Another good anchorage, safe in northwesterly winds but subject to swells curling around South Ballenas when a southeasterly is blowing, is located in Oyster Bay at the south end of North Ballenas Island.

South Ballenas has a beautiful cove on its northern shoreline which is protected from all dangerous winds. A large sign at the head of the cove reads "Do not anchor in this cove — submerged cables." Emergency anchorage is possible, however, at the west end of this cove, since all the cables are found under the eastern part of the cove, inshore from the orange buoy. Although this shore is uninhabited, the navy does not like to find people trespassing here. During exercises the island is under constant surveillance by helicopter, ship and telescope from Winchelsea Island.

14 Nuttal Bay

This bay, although completely open to the northwest, does provide safe temporary anchorage from southeasterly winds and seas. Unless it is high water when entering the bay, it is best to pass on the outside of Cottam Reef (marked by a green spar buoy half a mile north of Dorcas Point), since there are several rocks which dry 2-3 feet. The tidal range for this area is 16 feet for maximum tides. At the head of the bay is Sunset Cove (formerly Claytons) fishing resort (468-7111) with launching ramp, boat rentals, coin shower, laundromat and camping facilities. Fuel is also available here but there are no permanent floats. A small two-acre park just inside Cottam Point is available to patrons of the Beachcomber Marina. Small craft could anchor temporarily in a tiny nook just south of this park.

15 Mistaken Island

The status of the island north of Cottam Point can not be easily mistaken owing to the large number of "No trespassing" signs. M. Wylie Blanchet wrote about this island in *The Curve of Time*; here she sought shelter from a westerly blow and found the island was inhabited by a strange "Robinson Crusoe" with no clothes and many goats.

16 Beachcomber Marina

Located in appropriately named Northwest Bay, this marina (468-7222) caters mainly to trailer-boats and moorage space is usually reserved for the summer. Fuel, boat rentals, charters, campsites, engine parts, repairs, freshwater, coin shower, laundromat, launching ramp and groceries are available. When entering this marina be sure to pass between the green and red buoys, *not* between the end of the breakwater and the green buoy, as there is a long reef extending south of the breakwater which is hidden with tides over six feet.

There is a good temporary anchorage, protected from all winds except southwesterlies (not dangerous), immediately south of the marina. If anchoring at the head of the bay — advisable only when a southeasterly is blowing — beware of the several drying rocks which are found up to 150 yards off the eastern shore, south of the red buoy. Good protection is sometimes afforded by the log booms at the west end of the bay, but since this McMillan-Bloedel operation is fairly active, do not expect to have a peaceful night if you choose to tie to one of the booms. Anchoring in any area where extensive log booming has taken place is often futile as the anchor seldom digs in, sliding along a thick, loose carpet of bark and wood debris which has become waterlogged and sunk to the bottom of the bay. Discarded cables and logging machinery are other hazards, frequently snagging the anchor.

The first light on Ballenas Islands (1906) was built in the centre of the island, but was later moved to its present location at the north end.

17 Craig Bay

Immediately south of Madrona Point, at the mouth of Beaver (Craig) Creek, is Peace Abide Park. Log booms are occasionally stored off Madrona Point, making access into the deep water channel leading to

Qualicum Beach, three miles north of French Creek, is a popular recreational area with over 30 resorts, hotels, motels and campgrounds.

a launching ramp in the southwest corner of Craig Bay difficult. The Craig Heritage Park houses a small museum in what was once Knox United Church.

18 Rathtrevor Beach Park

One of the finest beaches on Vancouver Island has sand flats which extend out over half a mile from shore and almost completely fill Craig Bay. Anchoring over these sand flats is treacherous except with ideal conditions (calm sea and a rising tide) because of the many ridges and runnels. More than 150 species of birds have been observed in the park, including forest birds like Hammond's flycatchers, red-breasted nuthatchs, warblers and golden-crowned kinglets. Large concentrations of sea birds follow the spawning herring in February and early March of each year. Black brant are common migrants in May. This 863-acre park also includes 173 campsites, 100 picnic tables, drinking water, excellent swimming beaches and a nature program (248-8140 or 753-6300).

19 Englishman River Estuary

The Englishman River estuary is marked by a small stretch of many-hued greenery flanked by private homes to the east of the estuary mouth and a long row of trailers to the west. At high water the marshy backwaters of the still green portions of this estuary behind the beach would be interesting to explore by kayak or canoe, as this area is alive with waterfowl and other small birds and marine life.

20 Parksville

It is possible to anchor in the shallow water of Parksville Bay but beware of the afternoon onshore winds. Parksville is a fairly big resort town serving the surrounding population of over 5,000, with shopping centres, restaurants, and over 20 resorts, hotels, motels and campgrounds around the beach (phone 248-3613 for information). The Canadian Coast Guard operates a hovercraft search and rescue base (248-2724) at the east end of Parksville Bay. Immediately south of here is the Parksville Community Park, which has playing fields, a lawn bowling green, a playground and the *Queen of Parksville* — a beached fishing boat to explore. This park is also the location for Pageant Days (second week of July), which features the annual World Croquet Championship and other festivities.

21 French Creek

This breakwater-protected boat harbour offers the only small boat shelter between Northwest Bay and Deep Bay, a distance of 25 miles. The basin (248-5051) has been recently expanded and dredged, effectively doubling the public float space that is available. There is a concrete launching ramp in the west corner of the basin, and fuel, tidal grid and derrick are also available. Margetis Fish Inc. (248-5931) provides quality fresh fish direct from the commercial fisherman and nearby is a shopping complex with groceries, the Creek House Restaurant and the Boars Head Pub. Showers, laundry facilities, cottages and a campground are also available here. French Creek also serves as the terminus for the Lasqueti Island passenger ferry which makes twice-daily crossings dependent on tide and weather conditions.

Many boats avoid close exploration of the coast from French Creek north to Deep Bay because it appears to be completely open, with no protection. In addition, drying sand and boulder banks extend some distance from shore. In calm weather or with an offshore wind, this coast does have much to offer anyone

Long, sandy beaches and numerous recreational facilities make the Parksville area a popular destination for land-bound tourists. Facilities for yachtsmen, however, are minimal.

French Creek boat harbour provides the only shelter between Northwest Bay and Deep Bay, a distance of about 25 miles. Fuel, groceries, restaurant and pub are all on site or within walking distance.

travelling in a small shallow-draught boat: there are numerous tiny estuaries, broad sandy beaches and launching ramps for easy escape should the weather turn foul. Travelling by land, this stretch of coast is probably the most popular on all of Vancouver Island, judging by the number of sea-oriented resorts located here. The climate is remarkably balmy, fishing is good and the beaches are a sunbather's paradise.

22 Qualicum Beach

The village of Qualicum Beach is located three miles west of French Creek and has a population of over 2,500. There is a launching ramp close to Qualicum Beach Marina (752-6211), which supplies fuel, mooring buoys, tackle and rental boats. The sand flats extending out from shore between French Creek and Qualicum are treacherous, with several large boulders drying up to 14 feet. Between Qualicum Beach and Bowser, 10 miles to the north, there are over 30 resorts, hotels, motels or campgrounds (752-9532 for information).

23 Little Qualicum River

The Marshall-Stevenson National Waterfowl Reserve northeast of the bridge over the Little Qualicum River is a good place to watch the estuarine birdlife and other wildlife. This is an excellent place to explore by kayak or canoe.

24 Qualicum River

Over 130 years ago Adam Grant Horne, a young Hudson's Bay Company explorer, left his canoe hidden in the bush at the mouth of this river while searching for a route across Vancouver Island to Barkley Sound. A short time later several Haida war canoes swept up the river to destroy the Qualicum Indian village of Saatlem. Horne visited the site of the massacre only an hour or so after the Haidas had left finding only one old woman still alive. Horne continued up the river in search of a native who could guide his party. He found none, but continued, becoming the first European to cross Vancouver Island north of Nanaimo.

25 Bowser

Fishing resorts between Bowser and Deep Bay include Bowser Bill's (757-8363), Shady Shores (757-8595) and La Bella Vista (757-8432).

On the morning of the 23rd of June, 1946, fishermen near the shore here watched as several hundred feet of the Bowser shoreline disappeared beneath the water. In the resulting tidal wave they were hard put to keep their boat afloat while a nearby rowboat vanished beneath the waves. Nine days later a body was found (Mason). This is possibly another account of the same incident reported at Deep Bay in Chapter 19.

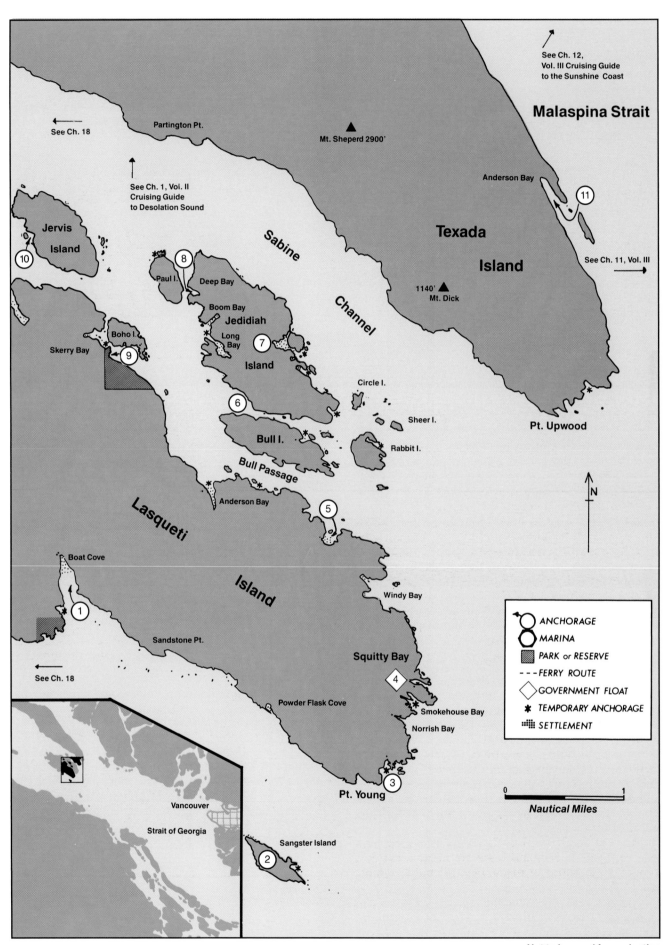

See Ch. 12,
Vol. III Cruising Guide
to the Sunshine Coast

Malaspina Strait

See Ch. 18

Partington Pt.

Mt. Sheperd 2900'

Anderson Bay

⑪

See Ch. 1, Vol. II
Cruising Guide
to Desolation Sound

Texada

Jervis

Island

⑧

Island

⑩

Paul I.

Deep Bay

1140' ▲
Mt. Dick

See Ch. 11, Vol. III

Boom Bay

Boho I.

Jedidiah

Skerry Bay

⑨

Long
Bay

⑦

Sabine

Circle I.

Island

⑥

Sheer I.

Channel

Bull I.

Rabbit I.

Pt. Upwood

Bull Passage

N

Anderson Bay

⑤

Lasqueti

Boat Cove

Island

Windy Bay

①

Squitty Bay

Sandstone Pt.

④

See Ch. 18

Smokehouse Bay

Powder Flask Cove

Norrish Bay

◇ ANCHORAGE

⬡ MARINA

▨ PARK or RESERVE

--- FERRY ROUTE

◇ GOVERNMENT FLOAT

✳ TEMPORARY ANCHORAGE

▦ SETTLEMENT

③

Pt. Young

Vancouver

0   1

Strait of Georgia

Nautical Miles

Sangster Island

②

Not to be used for navigation

168

Halyards slap a rattling chorus as a blustery southeaster pummels the entrance to Squitty Bay on southern Lasqueti Island.

Eastern Lasqueti Island

Squitty Bay, Jedidiah, Boho Bay

This relatively unknown island is avoided by many cruising yachtsmen for a number of reasons:

Isolation: Lasqueti occupies an isolated position in the centre of the Strait of Georgia just off the southwest tip of Texada Island and there are few services and amenities here. The residents have chosen not to be connected to the provincial hydroelectric transmission network and vehicle ferry system.

Winds: The eastern end of the island is exposed to the full force of southeasterly gales blowing unimpeded almost 80 miles from Saturna Island at the south end of the Gulf Islands. In summer, southeasterly winds are not uncommon (blowing over 20 percent of the time), but westerly winds predominate (blowing over 40 percent of the time). This part of the Strait is often subject to fairly strong northwesterlies which can blow for several days, inhibiting access to the mainland or Vancouver Island. These northwesterlies blow most strongly between sunset and noon.

Services: Coastal explorers in small boats travelling northward generally favour the mainland coast, which offers a more sheltered route with abundant anchorages, marinas and resorts; while the waters west of Texada offer far fewer sheltered stopping places and virtually no facilities.

Charts: The hydrographic charts for this area have been very small scale and there are many rocks and reefs close to shore to discourage all but the most careful visitor.

All these hindrances tend to make Lasqueti Island a paradise for coastal explorers seeking the solitude of quiet, uncrowded and undeveloped anchorages and shorelines. Hopefully these conditions will remain. A moderate increase in the number of people visiting an area should not necessarily mean a corresponding decrease in the attractiveness of that area. Visitors should take special care not to disturb owners of private property. If approached in the right way, most landowners or caretakers welcome the occasional visitor. This is one of the special joys of exploring out of the way parts of the Strait. Absolutely no fires should be lit ashore during the summer, for the land is tinder dry. If a small anchorage is occupied and it is obvious that another boat would create unsafe conditions with a change in tide or wind, it is best to move on and find another cove.

1 Boat Cove

Known previously as Long Bay, this cove offers good protection from westerly winds predominant in summer, but is moderately exposed to the southeast. A road from the farm at the head of the cove runs inland for a quarter-mile, where it intersects the main Lasqueti road which runs the length of the island. The shoreline south of Boat Cove is exposed, with many offshore rocks and reefs, and offers little possibility for safe anchorage. There are a few nooks such as the

CHARTS
3512 — Strait of Georgia, CENTRAL PORTION
       (1:80,000)
3312 — For LASQUETI ISLAND (1:40,000)

ones behind Sandstone Point or in Powder Flask Cove where a small boat could be beached.

2   Sangster Island

This island is unique for its spring wildflowers, which are not subject to grazing by the sheep and goats which range free over Lasqueti Island. The island is quite heavily forested, considering its exposed position.

An interesting cliff-top trail hugs the southern shoreline for a short distance north of Elephant Eye

The temporary anchorage at Sangster Island is best visited only in calm weather or in light winds from the west or northwest. The island boasts a colourful array of spring wildflowers.

Point — a unique erosional feature at the southern terminus of the island. Several rocks, marked by kelp in summer, surround this point, and one, which dries about two feet, is found near the entrance to the only safe temporary anchorage on the island. This shallow anchorage is safe only in calm weather or with light winds from the west or northwest. Large, spherical, conglomerate boulders, some almost 20 feet in diameter, are perched on the eroded sandstone ledge which protects this anchorage from the north.

3   Poor Man's Rock

This rock, which dries 12 feet at low water, gave its name to a novel written by Bertrand Sinclair in the 1920s. The story dealt with the life of local commercial salmon fishermen who fought for their living against storm, shipwreck and unscrupulous cannery owners. The coastline from Point Young to Jedidiah Island is stark and unusual for the Strait, more reminiscent of the Newfoundland coast. Barren, rocky headlands separate several deep, short inlets incised into the volcanic shoreline. Scrub grass and low,

wind-contorted bushes are the only vegetation which can survive on these headlands. Winter gales, blowing unimpeded over open sea for almost 80 miles, have tossed large chunks of driftwood up to 50 feet above the high tide line. In summer, with west and northwest winds predominating, some of these tiny inlets could be used as temporary anchorage providing you use stern lines to prevent swinging and crashing into the close cliff sides which tower overhead. At the forest's edge, in places several hundred yards back from the shoreline, there is often little underbrush, most areas being closely cropped by free-ranging sheep, goats, cattle and the odd horse.

4   Squitty Bay

The entrance to this tiny bay is very deceptive: from the east it looks much like any other of the small inlets indenting this side of the island; from the north it is sometimes only identifiable by the sight of the masts of boats tied alongside the public float. The peninsula which protects Squitty Bay from the north is low — comprising grassy knolls, rising 10 to 20 feet above sea level. Several rocks just inside the entrance dry 1-2 feet above chart datum. The safest entrance channel is along the south shore (port side, entering). Although the bay appears to be open to the southeast, it is actually quite well protected. Even in winter, with a moderate southeasterly gale sending spray and small bits of driftwood flying over the outer rocks and above the masts of boats tied to the public float, the bay is reported to be subject only to a slight swell. Residents in the area have reported, however, that the government float was once wrecked many years ago when an unusually severe gale resulted in large swells entering the bay. The public float is only 100 feet long and quite

The view north over Rouse Bay

170

From the water, Squitty Bay at the southern end of Lasqueti Island is often only identifiable by the sight of masts rising above the low peninsula that shelters public floats within.

the bay dries at low water and although the foreshore is protected by a six-acre recreation reserve, the surrounding land is private property.

The entrance to Squitty Bay as it appears at low water. Several rocks just inside the entrance dry 1-2 feet above chart datum.

often full. The bay has been dredged to eight feet for about another 100 feet beyond the float so that a few boats can anchor off.

Although there is much that is interesting to explore along this southern shore, boats do not often stay very long in Squitty Bay, as it is usually crowded, and notorious for mosquitoes. Squitty Bay marks the terminus of the main road from False Bay, 12 miles to the west, at the other end of the island. The bay is visited several times a week by the wharfinger/highway-maintenance man.

Windy Bay

A mile to the north is Windy Bay. Masses of driftwood piled above the beach at the head of the bay indicate the exposed nature of this particular area which is also said to be subject to strong winds from the west and northwest.

5   Rouse Bay

Safe anchorage is possible behind a small islet in Rouse Bay at the entrance to Bull Passage. The head of

Bull Passage

In summer the northwest wind occasionally blows quite strongly through Bull Passage, but seas are generally calm due to the protection afforded by Jervis and Boho Islands. The south end of Bull Passage sometimes has dangerously large rollers when wind and tidal stream are opposed. There are several tiny coves along the Lasqueti shore from here to Anderson Bay which could afford temporary anchorage. Anderson Bay was the location of the first store and second post office on Lasqueti Island.

Rabbit Island

The offshore islands east of Jedidiah are all stark in appearance, rising sheer from the sea and almost barren of vegetation. Cliff climbing on these islands is fascinating but treacherous — it is easy to get a fistfull of painful cactus or scotch thistle. Temporary anchorage is only possible in a small "Squitty-like" cove at the north end of Rabbit Island or just off the northwest end of this island. There is a new (1984) resort here for groups which want their own private island for seminars or other gatherings. The resort, which includes five cabins and a small lodge, also serves as the outstation for Sea Wing Sailing of Vancouver (738-8514).

6   Little Bull Passage

There are several tiny nooks suitable for temporary anchorage at the eastern end of Little Bull Passage. The narrow passage between the steep cliffs of Jedidiah and Bull islands is deep enough for small craft to navigate safely, if they stay in the middle of the channel. The only hazards are some dangerous rock pinna-

Looking north over Skerry Bay (foreground). Jervis Island is in the centre of photo and Texada Island is in the background.

cles from a recent rock-slide on the Bull Island side, halfway through the passage, and a drying rock close to Jedidiah Island at the west end.

7 Jedidiah Island

Another good temporary anchorage safe from all winds except southeasterlies is found in a small cove just around the southeast tip of Jedidiah. Here also, a spectacular 400 feet bluff of volcanic rock rises sheer from the sea. Three of the four largest bays on Jedidiah Island dry almost completely at low water, so are unsuitable as safe, all-tide anchorages unless your vessel has a flat bottom or bilge keels. One of these bays, Home Bay, on the east side of the island is where some intrepid settlers have a beautiful garden and grow their own vegetables on land originally cleared and settled in 1903. The large orchard and pasture (now grass-covered meadow) extending behind Home Bay was said to comprise almost 100 acres and to be larger than any farm on Texada or Lasqueti islands.

Sabine Channel

Sabine Channel, between Jedidiah and Texada Islands is subject to tidal streams of 1-2 knots and can get fairly rough when a strong northwester or southeaster blows over an opposing tide. On summer evenings one can watch the parade of cruise ships on their way north through the Inside Passage after leaving Vancouver. The channel is named after General

Home Bay on Jedidiah Island appears to be a safe, accommodating anchorage but take care because it dries out completely at low water.

Sir Edward Sabine who served in the Niagara campaign during the War of 1812. He was a captain of artillery at the time, but later served in the Arctic and became President of the Royal Society. He was knighted for his contributions to magnetic research in 1869.

8 Deep Bay

This bay is one of the safest anchorages this side of Lasqueti Island owing to the protection from northwesterly winds afforded by Paul Island. Because of the depth it is usually necessary to take a stern line ashore to prevent swinging. Boom Bay and Long Bay, just south of Deep Bay, both dry at low water and are therefore suitable only for temporary anchorage. Paul Island was named after Paul Lambert, an entrepreneur who made his living by selling off all the local islands to rich Americans during the first part of the century. Several years ago Paul Island was ravaged by fire — the result of an unsuccessfully doused beach fire spreading into surrounding driftwood and up into the forest three days after the boaters who had started it had departed. Although a tiny cove which could be used as a temporary anchorage exists at the north end of Paul Island (now a provincial recreation reserve), exploration ashore is difficult because of the number of downed snags.

9 Boho Bay

No one knows where this name originated, but it was pronounced "boo hoo" by early settlers. The Lasqueti side of the bay is also a provincial parks reserve which was set aside for possible future expansion as a marine park. Much of the shoreline is sheer cliff, but a small peninsula of relatively flat land jutting out towards Boho Island protects an anchorage which is moderately exposed to southeasterly winds. Better protection from southeasterlies (infrequent in summer) is found by anchoring just the other side of this peninsula in Skerry Bay. Boho Island is privately owned and known affectionately by the locals as "Keep Off" Island, owing to the large number of signs posted in the past by previous owners. As a rule, "Keep Off" signs are virtually unknown on Lasqueti. Private property owners have not been harassed as they have been in the more crowded Gulf Islands. It is imperative that visitors take pains to respect private property; otherwise the friendly atmosphere which now exists could easily disappear.

Skerry Bay is a local name, derived from the Gaelic and referring to the large number of rocks found

Looking west through Bull Passage from Rabbit Island. The narrow channel is deep enough for safe passage providing skippers stay close to the centre.

The sail-training schooner Robertson II out of Victoria cuts a handsome path through rippled waters in the Gulf Islands.

within the bay. One especially dangerous rock (which dries about five feet) is found in the middle of the northern entrance to the bay (keep to the Boho Island side). The bay offers very good protection from most winds, but a strong northwester often sends gusts over the gap at the head of the bay or through the northern passage causing anchored boats to swing through a fairly wide arc. Since 1976 an active mariculture operation, the first oyster hatchery in B.C., has been located here.

10 Jervis Island

This island is named after John Jervis Tucker, who was the son of Benjamin Tucker (Tucker Bay), secretary to Rear Admiral Sir John Jervis (Jervis Inlet) and

173

174

brother to Jedidiah Tucker (Jedidiah Island). The anchorage is partially protected from northwesterly winds by a small island known locally as Bunny Islet. Apparently the owner of Jervis Island at one time intended establishing a Playboy Club on this islet.

Texada Island

The south end of Texada Island dominates the skyline to the northeast with Mount Dick (1,130 feet) and Mount Shephard — the highest mountain on Texada, rising sharply to 2,900 feet. Some very tiny coves along this shore could offer temporary protection from the northwest but the safest anchorages (from northwesterly winds) are found at the south end of the island in tiny nooks similar to those found at the south end of Lasqueti. At the foot of Mount Dick there was a pink marble mine, with the product being shipped out of Anderson Bay on the other side of Texada. Napier Creek has a waterfall debouching into the saltchuck. However, the waterfall occasionally dries up by the end of the summer. Sea and wind conditions east of Point Upwood are often completely different

Bunny Islet (so called because of an owner's intention to establish a Playboy Club there) provides limited shelter for the anchorage on Jervis Island.

from conditions to the west. With a strong westerly or northwesterly wind, the high razor-back ridge of Texada acts as a break, and calm conditions often prevail as far north as Pender Harbour. In the mornings there is often a weak offshore or easterly wind blowing across to Point Upwood from the Welcome Pass area.

11 Anderson Bay

This bay offers good protection from all winds except strong southeasters, as can be deduced by its orientation. Several old buildings partially hidden by the forest at the head of the bay and a fairly good road are all that remains of an old logging camp. When entering the bay north of the island, keep south of the rocks in the centre of the entrance channel. The highest of the rocks, although marked on the chart as an islet, is awash at high water. The rest of Texada Island is described in *Pacific Yachting's Cruising Guide to British Columbia, Volume II: Desolation Sound and the Discovery Islands.*

175

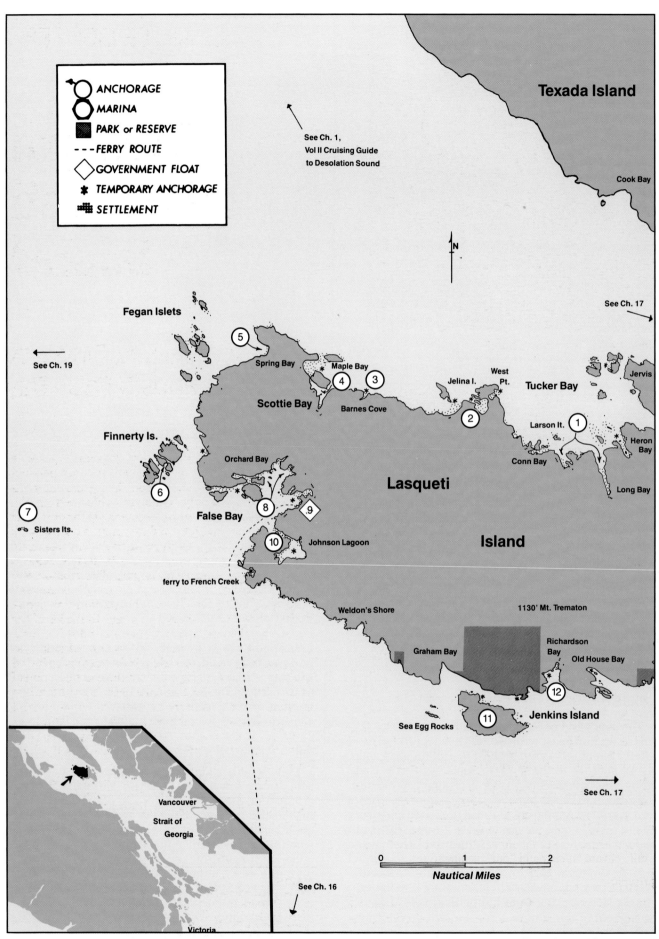

ANCHORAGE
MARINA
PARK or RESERVE
- - - FERRY ROUTE
GOVERNMENT FLOAT
TEMPORARY ANCHORAGE
SETTLEMENT

Texada Island

See Ch. 1,
Vol II Cruising Guide
to Desolation Sound

Cook Bay

N

See Ch. 17

Fegan Islets

See Ch. 19

⑤

Spring Bay Maple Bay
④ ③
Jelina I. West Pt. **Tucker Bay**
Barnes Cove ② Larson It. ①
Scottie Bay Jervis

Finnerty Is. Conn Bay Heron Bay
Orchard Bay **Lasqueti** Long Bay
⑥

⑦
Sisters Its. ⑧ ,9 **Island**
False Bay ⑩ Johnson Lagoon

ferry to French Creek

Weldon's Shore 1130' Mt. Trematon

Richardson Bay
Graham Bay Old House Bay
⑫

Sea Egg Rocks ⑪ **Jenkins Island**

See Ch. 17

Vancouver
Strait of
Georgia

0   1   2
Nautical Miles

See Ch. 16

Victoria

Not to be used for navigation

176

Tidal pool in the Finnerty Islands.

CHAPTER EIGHTEEN

Western Lasqueti Island

Scottie Bay, Finnerty Islands & False Bay

Most permanent residents on Lasqueti Island (approximately 400) live on the western half of the island, mainly around Tucker and False Bays. (This population more than doubles in the summer.) Twenty years ago Lasqueti had fewer than 50 residents. Mariculture, sheep farming, the desire to "get back to the land" or retire on a beautiful island — all have increased the population to what it was over 50 years ago, when logging and fishing were the primary industries. The local community association is very active in efforts to preserve the physical and social attributes of life here. Many summer residents have voluntarily decided to set their habitations well back from the shoreline, making them inconspicuous from the sea and preserving the natural character of the coast. This is in line with one of the stated objectives of the Lasqueti community, which could well be a model for others:

> All people who live on or have an interest in Lasqueti Island must [recognize] we are but temporary stewards of a delightful but small and fragile part of a much larger community. In this context it must be stressed that the island is part of a larger community and not just a utopian experiment for the benefit of a select few. But, being an island, having a predominantly unspoiled rural atmosphere and a small population, it is perhaps easier on Lasqueti than elsewhere for the community to develop a sense of common purpose and learn to work together for goals that transcend the usual tendency to think only of "me" and "now" and only of "our" family and "our" generation.

Winds

Much of this side of Lasqueti Island is exposed to the prevailing summer westerlies, which can increase at night to become a brisk "Qualicum".

1 Tucker Bay

Although there was once a very good large-scale chart of this bay (3508 at 1:12,000), it is not particularly favoured as an anchorage, being partially exposed to northwesterly winds and filled with reefs. The bay was surveyed in 1925, primarily for the use of coastal steamers, which used to call here once a week in the early part of the century when the bay was fairly well settled. There was once a regular ferry service to Pender Harbour on the mainland. The islands just west of Jervis Island (pronounced *Jarvis*) are interesting to explore by small boat, but there is only one moderately safe temporary anchorage in the lee of the westernmost island, subject to wind and tide conditions. Temporary anchorage safe from northwest seas but exposed to northwesterly winds can also be found in the lee of a large drying shelf in the southeast end of Tucker Bay. According to local legend this shelf was at one time much deeper in the water, but after a major earthquake in 1946 many new islets, rocks and reefs appeared in the bay as the entire area was uplifted slightly. Heron Bay was homesteaded in 1924 by a Tucker family, though no relation to the original Tucker after whom the bay was named. The bay dries out almost completely at low tide. Long Bay doesn't dry completely, however, and affords fairly good protection at its mouth.

CHARTS
3512 — Strait of Georgia, CENTRAL PORTION
    (1:80,000)
3312 — For LASQUETI ISLAND (1:40,000)
3536 — For FALSE BAY (1:12,000)

South of Lenny's Lagoon is one of the largest unbroken sand beaches on Lasqueti Island.

The remains of an old ferry dock can be seen south of Larson Islet at the terminus of a road which leads a quarter-mile south to its junction with the main island road where there is a clinic. Just south of West Point is a small bay with a delightful beach on a low isthmus which separates Lenny's Lagoon from Tucker Bay. This small bay, though protected from the northwesterly wind by West Point, is suitable only as a temporary anchorage, since it dries completely at low water.

2   Lenny's Lagoon

This lagoon is worth exploring by dinghy or shallow draught boat on a rising tide, but please avoid disturbing the oyster and clam trays on the bottom, part of a new mariculture operation here. Temporary anchorage is possible outside, in the lee of Jelina Island or off Marshall's Beach, which joins Jelina to Lasqueti at low water. Since it is one of the largest unbroken sand beaches on the island, it has become a popular spot for sunbathing.

3   Barnes Cove

Also known as Mine Bay, this cove is suitable only as a temporary anchorage because of its shallow depths. Two adits were driven at the head of this cove in the early part of the century and there are many other abandoned pits and trenches in the vicinity. Some of these can be quite dangerous so if you explore ashore be prepared for huge hollows to open suddenly at your feet. Many of the old workings were planked over and a few feet of soil and grass now cover the rotting timbers. If you feel a sinking sensation it might be wise to beat a hasty retreat or you may never be seen again. A sheerlegs on a cliff 40 feet above sea level just east of Mine Bay was used to load ore onto barges from local workings in St. Joseph's Tunnel.

4   Scottie Bay

This bay is possibly the safest anchorage on Lasqueti Island. Protected from virtually all winds and seas, depths are suitable for safe anchoring throughout the bay. Passage into the bay should be made close to the Lasqueti shore to avoid a dangerous reef which extends almost halfway across the entrance channel from the southeast corner of Lindberg Island. The private wharf and floats are used as the home base for a local fishboat construction firm. Scottie Bay is linked by road to False Bay, about a mile and a half to the south. Temporary anchorage is also possible in shallow Maple Bay, just north of Lindberg Island.

5   Spring Bay

The northern part of Lasqueti is physically similar to many parts of the Gulf Islands, with easily-eroded sandstone and hard conglomerate shorelines creating the typical honeycomb and ledge features in front of flatter, grassy backshores. "Spanish" caves, possibly formed initially by an upheaval of the land, can be found behind the bay. The interior passages are coated with lime, similar to the limestone caverns found on Vancouver Island. Spring Bay is a good anchorage when a southeaster is blowing, but the Fegan Islets offer only minimal protection from northwesterly winds and seas. The head of the bay is dotted with "No Fire" signs and there are indications that this area has been subdivided and is now being developed. Fegan Islets, previously known as Bare or Indian Islands, are interspersed with many drying reefs and rocks and offer little shelter or safe temporary anchorage.

The author's sloop Tumbo *finds shelter from a blustery southeaster in Scottie Bay on Lasqueti's northern shore.*

Scottie Bay is perhaps the safest anchorage on Lasqueti Island, protected from virtually all winds and seas and with depths suitable for safe anchorage throughout the bay.

6   Finnerty Islands

The Finnertys, previously known as the Flat Tops, are more substantial than their neighbours, the Fegans, and provide fairly good anchorage in a small cove which is subject to swells when a strong northwester is blowing. These islands were named Finnerty by mistake. They should be called the Fogartys, honouring Captain Fogarty Fegen, who died on November 5, 1940 when he attacked the German battleship *Admiral Scheer* with his scantily armed merchant ship the *Jervis Bay*. His ship was quickly sunk, but his brave action gained enough time for the bulk of the convoy he was guarding to escape. Captain Fegen was posthumously awarded the Victoria Cross. The islands are uninhabited and fascinating for exploration by dinghy along several miniature inlet-like arms, nooks and tidal pools. Passage between Finnerty and Lasqueti islands is safe though shallow, but keep clear of the drying rock east of big Finnerty

Tranquil anchorage in the Finnerty Islands provides access to countless passages, lagoons and cactus-covered islets, a pretty spot for shoreside explorations.

179

The Finnerty Islands, known previously as the Flat Tops, are uninhabited and provide numerous opportunities for exploration by dinghy or kayak.

Island. This passage can become quite rough with a strong northerly wind as the seas tend to break as they pass over the shallows.

7   Sisters Islets

The "Sisters" are well known to all who listen to summer marine weather forecasts, but since few boats cruise in this area of the Gulf, few yachtsmen actually know where they are located. Although only 13 miles northwest of Ballenas Islands, the weather here can be substantially different from that to the south, possibly due to their position further offshore. The lightkeepers work on a two-week-on two-week-off basis here as they do at Ballenas. The barren rocks do not offer much possibility for outdoor recreation.

8   False Bay

This is the most popular anchorage on Lasqueti and there is a large-scale chart which covers the bay. Many

boats spend up to a week here, exploring the many features of interest in the vicinity. There are three abandoned mine adits along the shoreline which are often only identifiable by the pile of waste at their vegetation-shrouded entrances. The adits do not penetrate for more than 20-30 feet, but because of the darkness they seem to stretch into infinity. The northern part of the bay (Orchard Bay) provides fairly safe anchorage in most winds, but because of the low nature of the surrounding topography, strong winds occasionally result in dragging anchors.

9   False Bay Village

The public wharf with a 120 foot float provides limited temporary moorage for visitors who wish to obtain water or who need supplies at the store (333-8846) — the only one on the island. The store and a licensed restaurant, the Sea View Dining Lounge, are under new (1986) ownership. The Church of the Good

Opposite: The rock-strewn entrance to False Lagoon dries at half tide and should be piloted with extreme care.

Lagoons and grassy slopes abound throughout the Finnerty Islands.

Shepherd and a post office, which opens a few hours after the Lasqueti ferry arrives, are located a short hike up the road. The Lasqueti ferry takes passengers and light freight five days a week (Thursday to Monday, dependent on tide, weather and the skipper's health) to French Creek on Vancouver Island. Although there are cars on the island, Lasqueti residents have no desire for a car ferry. They realize that this would lead to a surge in development and possible deterioration of the peaceful environment which now exists. The inside berth on the float (closest to the wharf) is reserved for the use of the ferry — a new 60-foot aluminum craft. It is unwise to hog the berthage space at this float. Not only will you arouse the ire of other

boats wishing to obtain fuel and supplies, but if you moor overnight you may be in for an uncomfortable stay. This part of the bay is subject to the night-time westerly which occasionally blows in with considerable force and subsequent high seas (there is a fetch of over 14 miles across from Vancouver Island). False Bay is also completely open to the "Qualicum" — a notorious, strong, westerly wind which blows in from the Pacific Ocean, through the Alberni Canal and across from Qualicum Beach on the east coast of Vancouver Island. This wind often arrives unexpectedly, "with sudden and terrifying fury. The first warning is a feeling of lightness in the air and a stillness filled with premonition". (Mason).

10   Johnson Lagoon

This perfectly protected lagoon is often used by wintering fishboats. The entrance channel is dry at about half tide and as there is a tidal stream of 3-4 knots when the tide is flowing, it is wise to enter only at high water. The deepest channel is close to the northern shore, but take care to avoid several shelves which protrude into the channel for short distances. There is a rock which dries 14 feet midway through the channel. The large-scale chart for this area is essential if you are entering in anything bigger than a dinghy. The enclosed nature of this lagoon has produced higher water temperatures, hundreds of jellyfish, and a new oyster farm. There are also reported to be unusually large dogfish, a unique species of coral, and other warm-water exotica.

The coastline south of False Bay is much indented with tiny nooks and bays interspersed with many rocks close offshore. One tiny cove immediately south of False Bay offers good protection from southeasterly seas, but is completely open to the west. There is one tiny sandy beach along Weldon's Shore and two small park reserves, established to protect beach access points and possible future boat launching sites.

11   Jenkins Island

A 496-acre ecological reserve has been established across from Jenkins Island to protect a portion of the unique Juniper-Cactus parkland, in this the driest of all Pacific coast ecosystems. The reserve is primarily for educational and scientific purposes and is not a park, nor is it intended for use as a recreation area. There is a tiny anchorage area just west of a small peninsula at the south end of the reserve providing fairly good protection from the southeast and west. There is also a tiny cove at the north end of Jenkins Island which provides good protection from westerlies but is open to the southeast.

12   Richardsons Cove

Richardsons Cove is overlooked by conspicuous, turret-shaped Mount Trematon (1,130 feet), the highest point on Lasqueti. The mountain was named (1860) after Trematon Castle in Cornwall. Apparently they are somewhat similar in appearance. This castle was the home of the Tucker family, whose members

With its numerous nooks and islets False Bay has become the most popular destination for yachtsmen visiting Lasqueti Island. A large-scale chart covers the area in detail.

Government floats in False Bay provide access to nearby store, restaurant and the local post office.

have other places around Lasqueti Island named after them. The summit of the mountain can be reached by a hike of an hour or two from the cove and the view is well worth the effort, with panoramas extending out over several tiny lakes and all of Lasqueti Island. Although the cove is open to the south, there is fairly good protection from westerlies. The owner of the property at the north end of the cove has constructed a private breakwater to protect a small boat harbour which dries at low water.

Old House Bay

Old House Bay provides fairly good protection behind a tiny islet found in the centre of the entrance to the bay. The bay was named sometime ago and no trace of the old house remains. Fairly safe anchorage, offering more protection from southeasterlies, is found in adjoining Graveyard Bay to the south. A group of rocky islets guard the entrance and rocks surrounding the group dry at low water. The safest entrance is close to the southern shore. Two stones mark the graves of children of early settlers who died at the end of the last century. The graves are set in a small glade at the head of the bay. The rocky peninsula which protects this bay extends seaward in two narrow arms, encompassing many tidal pools which are interesting to explore.

183

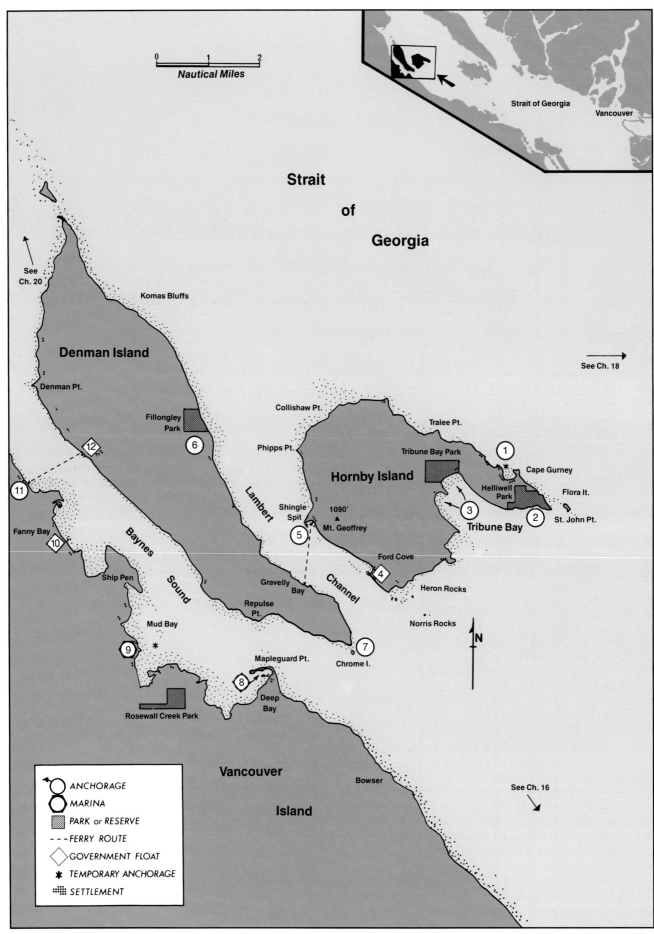

0   1   2
Nautical Miles

Strait

of

Georgia

Strait of Georgia

Vancouver

See
Ch. 20

Komas Bluffs

Denman Island

Denman Pt.

Fillongley
Park

⑥

See Ch. 18

Collishaw Pt.

Tralee Pt.

Phipps Pt.

Tribune Bay Park

①

Cape Gurney

Hornby Island

Helliwell
Park

Flora It.

⑫

⑪

Shingle
Spit

1090'
▲
Mt. Geoffrey

③

②

Tribune Bay

St. John Pt.

Fanny Bay

⑩

Baynes

⑤

Ford Cove

Heron Rocks

Ship Pen

Lambert

Gravelly
Bay

Channel

④

Sound

Repulse
Pt.

Norris Rocks

N

Mud Bay

⑨

⑦

Chrome I.

Mapleguard Pt.

⑧

Deep
Bay

Rosewall Creek Park

Vancouver

Bowser

See Ch. 16

Island

○ ANCHORAGE
○ MARINA
▨ PARK or RESERVE
- - - FERRY ROUTE
◇ GOVERNMENT FLOAT
✳ TEMPORARY ANCHORAGE
▦ SETTLEMENT

Not to be used for navigation

CHAPTER NINETEEN

Denman and Hornby Islands

Tribune Bay, Baynes Sound, Fanny Bay

Totems on Denman Island were painted by Josephine Crease circa 1883. (Watercolour on paper.)

Denman and Hornby are seldom visited by yachtsmen for the simple reason that their coastlines offer little opportunity for safe anchorage, or for beaching if the weather is foul. For the most part, the shores are exposed, and fringed with drying sand banks or rocky shelves. This fact of geography is unfortunate, for these islands are among the most beautiful in the Strait in their own unique way. The islands have long been popular with visitors crossing by car ferry from Vancouver Island and there are several resorts and campgrounds catering to tourists who arrive by car. There are, however, only two small government wharves and two bays which offer moderately safe anchorage for large boats.

Winds

In the summer months over 40 percent of the winds blow from the northwest quadrant and under 20 percent from the southeast. The northwesterly winds, which can be strong, do not kick up much of a sea because of the limited fetch between these islands and Vancouver Island. The waters here are so little disturbed by heavy seas in the summer months that, although the tidal range may be large — up to 17 feet, there is little flushing or exchange of waters. This encourages warmer water temperatures, accelerated oyster growth, and pleasant sea-bathing conditions.

Fishing

There is good chinook fishing most of the summer, from Whaling Station Bay around to Norris Rocks at the south end of Hornby and in Lambert Channel between the islands down to Chrome Island. Bluebacks appear in May and coho from June through October. Trolling, mooching and drift-fishing are the preferred methods.

Hornby Island

Hornby Island was referred to by early mariners as the "leg o' mutton" because of its distinctive shape. The present island name and that of its most prominent features are derived from its protection by the Royal Navy in 1859 and 1860, when Captains Geoffrey (the mountain), Phipps (the point), and Hornby (the island) arrived in HMS *Tribune* (the bay). John T. Walbran notes in *British Columbia Coast Names* that the island is probably named after Captain Hornby's father, Admiral Hornby, who had been one of the junior officers in HMS *Victory* under Nelson in 1803. Hornby Island was also called Ja-dai-aich ("outer island") by the Comox Indian people, and Isle de Lerena by the Spaniards who sailed by here in 1791. The resident Hornby population of 900 swells to over 3,000 in the summer.

1 Whaling Station Bay

Over 100 years ago this bay was an active centre of operations for the B.C. Whaling Company. Large

CHARTS
3513 — Strait of Georgia, NORTHERN PORTION (1:80,000)
3527 — BAYNES SOUND (1:40,000)

More than 100 years ago Whaling Station Bay was an active centre of operations for the B.C. Whaling Company. Today the main attraction is a broad white sand beach, popular with islanders who have built homes around the bay.

A three-mile circle trail winds along the grass-covered bluffs of Helliwell Park to Tribune Bay. Deep water offshore is suitable for temporary anchorage while crews watch birds nesting along the cliffs.

buildings were erected to render down the hundreds of sperm, humpback and bowhead whales caught in the northern straits. Although the bay is completely open to northerly winds and extremely shallow (drying 7 feet at the entrance at low water), historical records indicate that many boats made use of the bay and of a wharf, reputed to be the "first pile-driven wharf north of Nanaimo". No trace of the wharf or whaling station remains today. Traces of earlier Indian occupation are still visible, however, in the petroglyphs of birds, arrows and leaping whales carved in the fast eroding sandstone ledges here and further north at Tralee Point near the Sea Breeze Guest Farm

(335-2321), the first resort on the island. Temporary anchorage is possible just outside the bay in calm weather or in the lee of Cape Gurney, which offers some protection from southeasterly seas. The hard white sand beach is one of the finest in the Strait and is extremely popular with the islanders, many of whom have homes around the bay. There is public beach access located near the road to Helliwell Park.

Nearby Flora Islet is now owned by a non-conformist who, unable to get permission from the authorities to build a home on the island, has built a shipwreck instead. The island and shipwreck are fascinating to visit. In July 1972 a 14 foot, 6-gilled, 3-ton shark was photographed near here — at a depth of 110 feet — by John Hembling.

2   Helliwell Park

This scenic 160 acre provincial park is largely composed of natural meadow — the result of exposure to strong southeasterly winds — and wind-contorted oak, pine, arbutus and virgin stands of Douglas fir. The park and treeless Flora Islet just offshore are especially beautiful in the spring, when a profusion of colourful wildflowers carpets the meadowland. There is a three-mile circle trail through Helliwell Park and along the bluffs leading to Tribune Bay. Dramatic seacliffs of interbedded sandstone and conglomerate rock provide a home for nesting cormorants, murres, pigeon guillemots and gulls along the southern shore west of St. John Point. If you enjoy bird watching at close quarters, these cliffs provide a unique opportunity, for the water is deep close inshore, and it is often possible to bring your craft right up to the base of the cliffs all the way into Tribune Bay. This is virtually the only coastline on either Denman or Hornby where navigation so close to shore is possible. Hazards to watch for are the odd guano splat or park visitors and cliffside hikers peering down at you from 200 feet above. These hazards can be unnerving, especially if you enjoy sunbathing in the nude.

3   Tribune Bay Provincial Park

Tribune Beach remains the finest beach in the Strait of Georgia. Moreover, it is a reasonably safe anchorage in summer when southeasterlies are infrequent. The beach here is pure sand, almost a mile across and almost as deep at low tide. If you land by boat, your dinghy will ground about 100 feet from the waters edge, as the beach slope is so gentle. The water is crystal clear, relatively warm, and the sand is exceptionally clean. The tremendous fetch to this beach (almost 90 miles from the southeast) means that winter storms bring in waves of enormous power, pounding the beach and churning up any organic debris to deposit it above the tide line. All that remains is the finest of hard-packed sand grains. Tribune Bay is fringed with a variety of interesting rock formations including grotesque mushroom-shaped remnants and honeycomb-like caves made by waves washing over the sandstone bedrock. The land behind the beach is now a 234-acre park and is largely open field, with scattered windswept clumps of trees gradually

Above and below: Crystal clear waters and one of the finest beaches in the Gulf make Tribune Bay Provincial Park one of the most popular destinations for yachtsmen cruising this area.

thickening into a forest several hundred feet back from the shore. The remains of Hornby Island Lodge, one of the oldest and once one of the largest resorts in the Gulf Islands, is located at the northeast end of the beach and is now used by the Education Society as a children's camp. A trail leads from here up and along the cliff-top through to Helliwell Park.

On a road leading west from the junction of Spray Point Peninsula and North Tribune Beach there is a private campground with 130 campsites (335-2320). Two hundred yards inland from the sea along this road is the Co-op Store, providing groceries, post office and hardware; and the Ringside Market — a bazaar of stalls offering a unique selection of the local pottery and crafts for which Hornby Island is famous. Other items regularly include fresh local fruit, vegetables, ice cream, *precious things* and books.

Another private campground is located at Heron Rocks, south of Ford Cove. Informal camping on Hornby Island beaches is discouraged by the locals. Stunning sandstone rock formations can be seen along a beach trail from Norman Point to Ford Cove.

4 Ford Cove

A breakwater-protected public wharf with 800 feet of berthage space at three floats provides the only all-weather protected moorage on Hornby Island. A store (335-2169) at the head of the wharf is open 09:00 to 21:00 in summer and 09:30 to 18:30 in winter. Sup-

187

plies (including Pepperidge Farm products!), fuel, campsites, cottages, boat rentals, sail charters (335-0721), fishing gear and fresh water can be found here.

If you wish to visit Shingle Spit (a mile and a half to the northwest) there are five routes available to you:
• An interesting shoreline trail beneath the cliffs of the first bench of Mount Geoffrey is the easiest land route (a one-hour hike), It was once a road but has been made impassable to vehicles by rockslides, mudslides, fallen trees and marine erosion.
• Another is an old logging road atop the first bench, which can be reached by taking the road east from Ford Cove. This road angles up the southern flank of the mountain (via Strachan and Euston Roads), above the pastoral farmland behind Heron Rocks. The view from here (Cove Hill) has been described as "certainly the most beautiful scene in all of the Gulf Islands, perhaps in all of British Columbia!" (Stormwell). The way continues along the bench, and down behind Shingle Spit.
• Another route is along an old game trail which starts about one mile up Strachan Road and peters out near the summit of Mount Geoffrey. This trail hugs the rim of the top bench and provides a spectacular view over the top of Denman Island into Baynes Sound. Long distance panoramas of Vancouver Island from Comox to Qualicum are possible on a fine day. The route down the conglomerate rock cliff face from the summit to the first bench is treacherous. The only other choices are to retrace your steps or to fight your

A breakwater provides protection for boats sheltering at the public wharf in Ford Cove, the only all-weather moorage on Hornby Island. Fuel, a store, campsite and boat rentals are available nearby.

way through the bush to the main road, two miles to the north.
• There is also the main road around the island, Central Road. This road is over eight miles long and has infrequent traffic.
• By water, you can sail, paddle or motor to Shingle Spit and anchor.

5 Shingle Spit

Behind the ferry landing is the Shingle Spit Resort (335-0136), home of the Thatch Neighbourhood Pub, a restaurant, Rosemary's Corner grocery store, a gift shop and a serviced campground with showers and laundromat. Because of the spit, there is usually a leeward side offering limited protection from seas. The most commonly used anchorage is just south of the spit, protected from the prevailing summer north-westerly winds, which can blow quite fiercely down Lambert Channel. There is a small dock for shallow draught boats just north of the ferry wharf. A small, shallow basin exists between the ferry wharf and a stone breakwater to the south. Inside the basin are a wooden launching ramp and a catwalk out to some piles to which a yacht could secure alongside in an emergency. This basin dries almost completely at low water. One can occasionally see goats grazing the grass on the turf-roofed private cottages on the spit.

At Phipps Point, the old ferry landing site, there is a concrete ramp which could be used for boat launching. Bradsdadsland Campsite and Picnic Ground (335-0757/0851) is just to the south and fossils can be found along the beach to the north. Warm sandbar bathing is possible off Collishaw Point, accessible by way of Savoie Road.

Denman Island

Denman Island was first called Sla-dai-aich ("inner island") by the Indians, then New Orkney Island after the large number of early settlers who came here from the Orkney Islands. The shoreline of Denman discourages close exploration by keeled boat because of the drying sandbars and boulders extending out up to a half mile offshore. The coast is best explored by small, shallow draught vessel in calm, stable weather or by foot, along the beach.

6 Fillongley Park

Fillongley park offers a good beach with 10 campsites surrounded by 56 acres of attractive woodland and an open field. This park includes the remnants of a bowling green and an old farmstead which was the home of an early settler, George Beadnell, who loved the surrounding woodland so much that he had personal names for all the trees. When he died in 1958 he was buried within the park, which he donated to the province.

North of Fillongley Park are the Komas Sand Bluffs, towering up to almost 500 feet above high water. Huge sandstone concretions from below these bluffs are displayed in the rock gardens in front of the Provincial

Beach picnic at Tribune Bay on Hornby Island.

Museum in Victoria. These spherical concretions are formed by a process of lithifaction of sand around a hard centre such as a fossil.

Three miles south of Fillongley Park is Gravelly Bay, where hourly ferries leave for Shingle Spit. At the south end of East Road there are trails to Eagle Rock, accessible only at low tide, where one can view petroglyphs; and you can walk down to Lands End (or South End), overlooking the red-and-white clapboard lightstation buildings of Chrome Island, the Strait of Georgia and distant mountains.

Shelter from summer northwesterlies can be found in the lee of Shingle Spit off Lambert Channel. The wharf is the eastern terminus of the Denman-Hornby Island ferry.

7 Chrome Island

Chrome Island (formerly known as Yellow Rock) is distinctive, in shape and colour. It is steep-sided and flanked on its eastern shore by massive yellow sandstone pillars, streaked white with guano from the nesting cormorants and gulls. Indian petroglyphs are carved into the sandstone rock beneath the lighthouse on Chrome Island. The passage between Chrome and Denman islands dries at low water.

The easternmost lighthouse on the island was built in 1891, but this did not prevent disaster befalling the 222 foot steamer *Alpha* which foundered in a gale on December 15, 1900 while trying to make the entrance to Baynes Sound. The *Alpha*, with a cargo of canned dog-salmon for Japan, was on her way to bunker at the coal wharf in Union Bay at the end of Baynes Sound when she crashed broadside into Yellow Rock. Quartermaster Anderson took a light line to the bow and attempted to lower himself over the side. While he was perched on the flukes of the anchor a wave crashed over the ship and he disappeared from view. All hope seemed lost when a faint cry was heard above the roar of the gale. There was Anderson, high above the ship, perched precariously on the top of the cliff face. Making one end fast to a rock pinnacle, he threw the line back to the ship and one by one, 26 men hauled

themselves onto the island. Nine men left on the ship hesitated, afraid to trust themselves to the rope, now lashing with each stagger of the ship into the side of the island. The ship lurched, disappeared and the nine men, including the captain, were lost. A further casualty was recorded the next day when an islander eager for salvage (the shores of Baynes Sound were now littered with crates of canned dog-salmon) found a case of over-proof rum and drank himself to death. The anchor from the *Alpha* was recovered by divers in 1972 for a memorial on the roadside near the ferry terminal on Denman Island.

Immediately west of here, in Hermit John's Bay, is the ghost village of Princeton, occupied in the hungry thirties and now the home of one or two denizens of the island. The trail from here continues on through "magical woodland glens" back to the East Road. Brad Stormwell also notes that "Should a person do the entire walk (via South End), he or she would begin to understand the very understated magical attraction of the Gulf Islands - their true nature". Please remember, campfires on these islands are forbidden, as the fire hazard in summer is extremely high.

Baynes Sound

Baynes Sound (and Baynes Peak on Saltspring Island) are named after Rear Admiral Robert Lambert Baynes, who was Commander-in-Chief of the Pacific Station with the flagship, HMS *Ganges*, from 1857 to 1860. Walbran notes that:

> While in command of the Pacific station it was through his wise forbearance that no collision took place on San Juan Island between the British and American

Chrome Island light is perched atop a steep-sided rock at the southeastern end of Denman Island. The passage between the two islands dries at low water.

forces when General Harney was placing troops on that island, with a view of holding it for the United States, in the summer of 1859. Neither the provocation of his enemies nor the rashness of his friends would allow him to hurry into ill-considered action, though he had an ample force to have prevented them landing or to effect their capture afterwards.

Tidal streams between Repulse Point and Mapleguard Point at the south entrance to Baynes Sound run up to three knots at springs and can raise a nasty chop when flowing against an opposing wind. Baynes Sound is well known for its oysters and both the Vancouver Island and Denman Island shores are covered by commercial oyster leases. On many beaches, the brilliant white remains of shucked oyster shells stand out for miles, giving the impression of a tropical coral beach.

The Ocean Park Campground, just west of Repulse Point on Denman Island at the end of Lacon Road, offers quiet, grassy waterfront campsites, beachcombing, hiking and picnicking. Metcalf Bay offers a fine sandy beach.

Vancouver Island is very attractive along this stretch of coast, with extensive plateau-like lowlands coming down to the sea. All is forested; there is very little settlement and beyond the plateau the mountains rise steeply, deeply incised by many valleys with extensive bare patches where the valleys steepen. A few of the taller mountains still have snow in mid-summer and Mount Arrowsmith — the tallest mountain on southern Vancouver Island at 5962 feet — can be seen dominating the horizon above Deep Bay.

8   Deep Bay

This bay offers the safest natural anchorage between Nanaimo and Comox as well as abundant moorage for small craft with over 2,200 feet of space provided by five public floats (257-9331). The floats are protected from westerly seas by a floating breakwater. Fuel, store, boat rental and launching ramps are available in the bay and laundromats, showers, campsites and accommodation are available at fishing resorts in the vicinity including Ship & Shore Marine (757-8750) and Deep Bay Auto Camp (757-8424).

Deep Bay is the location of the only casualty of the 1946 earthquake: this was a man who drowned when a huge wave swamped his boat. His relatives recall seeing him swimming frantically for a shoreline that grew farther away as he swam towards it. The spit (which at that time had no houses on it) completely disappeared for several minutes under the immense wave.

9   Mud Bay

Mud Bay is fairly open and shallow and not all mud as the name implies. Shoals in the middle of the bay and to the south of Ship Peninsula include large stones and boulders which dry up to five feet above the mudflats. Temporary anchorage is possible inside the shoal area in depths averaging 18 feet. Limited moorage for shallow-draught small craft is provided in a tiny basin for patrons of the Pacific Village Resort (335-2333). The entrance channel to the basin is very narrow, shallow and flanked by drying mudflats. Facilities include launching ramp, service station, store, boats, coffee shop, restaurant and accommodation.

10   Fanny Bay

A small public float with 240 feet of berthage space is protected from seas by Base Flat and Ship Peninsula as well as by two floating log breakwaters which are arranged in a manner which may be confusing to those unfamiliar with the approach. Just south of the wharf is the old (1908) cable-laying ship *Brico*, which was towed north from Victoria, run aground here and surrounded by oyster shells to serve as an exotic restaurant and gift shop. The Fanny Bay Inn, known locally as the FBI, is located a half-mile down the highway and includes a delightful pub. Oysters and other shellfish can be bought from nearby Mac's Oysters (335-2233).

11   Buckley Bay

Fanny Bay and Buckley Bay are separated by Base Flat, the unique, almost perfectly semicircular delta of the Tsable River. The Buckley Bay Beachcomber (335-2266) provides groceries, fuel, post office, licensed restaurant and take-out a few hundred feet up from the ferry landing and launching ramp. Car ferries leave approximately every hour on the hour for the eight-minute ride to Denman Island.

12   Denman Island Public Floats

The tiny public floats (160 feet of berthage space) located just south of the ferry landing and main government wharf appear to be well protected by a log-piling breakwater, but this in fact offers only minimal protection from southeasterlies blowing up Baynes Sound. If you lie on the outside of the float you are also completely exposed to the wash of shipping traffic in the sound. However, if you have the inside berth and the weather is calm, or if you have arrived by ferry, it is well worth hiking inland to explore a bit of the island.

At the top of the hill is St. Saviour's Anglican Church and the Denman Island General Store (335-2293), built in 1910 and offering groceries, hardware, cafe and post office. Nearby are a restaurant and bed and breakfast establishments — the Denman Guesthouse (335-2688), Sea Canary (335-2949) and Taits

Weathered farm buildings typify the comfortable rural atmosphere found on both Denman and Hornby Islands.

(335-2640). There is also the craft shop and museum (Doras Kirk's collection in the Seniors Hall). Check the bulletin board for special events, such as the World Oyster Shucking Championships and the Farmer's Market, a highlight of the islands.

North of the ferry landing, the constant drone of traffic echoes across Baynes Sound from the Vancouver Island Highway, in marked contrast to the peaceful atmosphere of Denman Island. Lone Pine Farm is one of the few remaining pioneer homes on Denman, built in 1888.

A 35-acre public recreation foreshore reserve for picking oysters is located directly across from Denman Point on Vancouver Island.

191

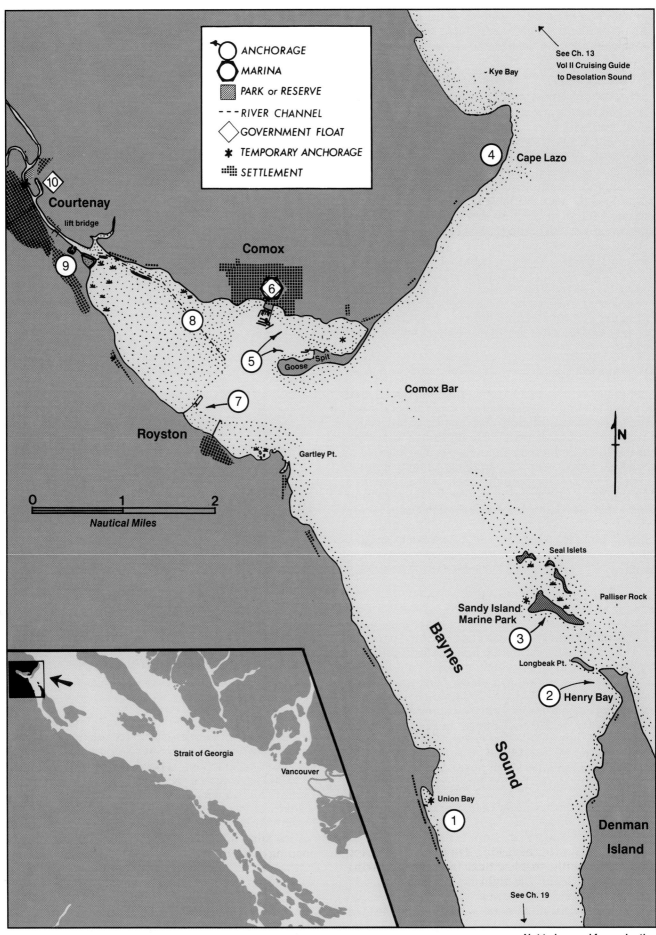

ANCHORAGE
MARINA
PARK or RESERVE
- - - RIVER CHANNEL
GOVERNMENT FLOAT
✳ TEMPORARY ANCHORAGE
SETTLEMENT

See Ch. 13
Vol II Cruising Guide
to Desolation Sound

Kye Bay

④ Cape Lazo

Courtenay
⑩
lift bridge

Comox

⑨

⑥

⑧

⑤ Goose Spit

Comox Bar

⑦

Royston

Gartley Pt.

0   1   2
Nautical Miles

N

Seal Islets

Palliser Rock

Sandy Island
Marine Park

③

Baynes

Longbeak Pt.

② Henry Bay

Strait of Georgia

Vancouver

Sound

Union Bay
①

Denman

Island

See Ch. 19

Not to be used for navigation

Courtenay slough, near the head of navigation on the Courtenay River, is similar in many ways to scenes more common along the great canals of Europe.

Comox and Courtenay

Union Bay, Sandy Island, Royston

Comox Harbour marks the northern end of Baynes Sound, a long, narrow protected waterway bounded by Denman Island, Sandy Island and Comox Bar on the east, and Vancouver Island on the west. The semi-protected nature of this sound provides ideal opportunities for calm-water boating and warm-water swimming, with water temperatures reaching 65 degrees F in the sound and up to 75 degrees F over several sand beaches which have transferred their heat to the incoming afternoon tide after being baked by the sun at midday low water.

Tides

An interesting feature of tides which is not particular to the Comox area but is unique to the mixed type of tide in the Strait of Georgia, is the present predominance of summer morning or midday lows. While many yachtsmen are aware of this situation, which is ideal for morning beachcombing, afternoon warm-water swimming and anchoring close to shore in the evening as the tide comes in, few realize that this is caused by a phase shift between the lunar and solar declinations, and is on a 900 year cycle. In other words, in about 400 years time the situation will be reversed and we will be having day-time high during the summer, with most low tides in winter occurring during the day and not at night as at present. This will result in cooler water temperatures and midnight clam digging in the summer instead of winter months.

Winds in the summer are generally light, with more calms than normal (15 percent to 20 percent). Winds with the highest frequency of occurrence come from the north or northwest (44 percent in July). There is a marked diurnal variation with the night and morning northwesterly often giving way to onshore winds during the afternoon.

Fishing

Coho and chinook fishing is good most of the summer along Comox Bar and north of Cape Lazo. Trolling is the most common method, though bucktails and cast plugs are also used.

1 Union Bay

Over 70 years ago the entire Strait of Georgia was terrorized by a gang of night marauders led by the notorious "Flying Dutchman." This gang would prey on small communities, especially those with government wharves where they could moor their getaway craft — a powerboat which developed "phenomenal speed and raced through the water in complete silence". At this time Union Bay was a bustling town with a constant stream of ships from all over the world loading coal. One night two policemen noticed a light

CHARTS
3527 — BAYNES SOUND (1:40,000) and COMOX
     HARBOUR (1:15,000)

At low water a 2¹/₂-mile long tidal flat emerges from the waters surrounding Sandy Island Marine Park south of Comox - a great place for beachcombing.

in the window of the Fraser & Bishop Store at the head of the government wharf and burst in, surprising the gang. A furious fight developed in which one of the policeman, Henry Westaway, was shot and killed. The other policeman, Gordon Ross, was reported to have had his thumb bitten off in the fight, but managed to nab the "Flying Dutchman" — who turned out not to be a Dutchman at all, but an American of German parentage called Henry Wagner. The rest of the gang escaped, but were found a week later holed up in Scottie Bay, Lasqueti Island. The government wharf and the Fraser & Bishop Store were removed a few years ago.

Safe temporary anchorage is available behind the remains of the old coal wharf and coal washings pile — an immense circular greyish brown hill which extends out from the natural shoreline about a third of a mile. Deciduous trees are beginning to grow on the periphery and at the top of the pile, providing cover and feed for grouse, pheasants and deer. Racoon and mink are also known to frequent this area close to a stream which empties north of the point. Parts of the pile are almost moon-like in their barrenness and contrast sharply with the surrounding vegetation and waters of Baynes Sound. A stone breakwater just below the Highwayman Pub (old Islander Hotel) provides a boat ramp and some protection to this anchorage. Besides the pub, Union Bay has a store, a gift shop in the old gaol which held the "Flying Dutchman," and a post office and library in the old Customs House — a unique red three-storey building built during the coal shipping days of the last century.

2 Henry Bay

Denman Island offers excellent protection to Henry Bay from southeasterlies, but the bay is moderately exposed to winds from the west and northwest. This exposure cannot be overly dangerous as there is very little driftwood above the beach (the amount of driftwood above a beach is usually a very good indication of the relative exposure of any anchorage). A beautiful sand and gravel beach surrounds this bay, which is covered by commercial oyster leases. Signs above the beach read "Warning — Keep Off," but the small print reads: "The criminal code requires that a penalty of imprisonment up to seven years with or without a fine be imposed upon every person convicted of the theft of oysters or oyster brood". In other words, the beach is owned by the Crown, guaranteeing public access, but leased for private oyster culture. You can land on it and walk along it, but do not pick the oysters or interfere with them in any way. An excellent beach walk starts from the end of Gladstone Way Road, due east across Baynes Sound from the tip of the Union Bay breakwater. Walking north from here leads you past an oyster shucking shed, a lagoon at the end of Lagoon Creek, Henry Bay, Longbeak Point and, at low tide, onto the sand flats surrounding Sandy Island Park. A midden on Longbeak Point reveals over 1,000 years of native occupation of this site. There is a colony of tree-nesting herons, and at low tide scores of herons and eagles can be seen perched on boulders or wading the shallows searching for marine goodies.

3 Sandy Island Marine Park

Sandy Island (or Tree Island) and Seal Islets to the north comprise an 82-acre park which increases ten fold at extreme low water as an extensive, two-and-a-half-mile-long tidal flat uncovers. The marine setting and landscape will seem uncannily familiar to those who have visited Sidney Spit Marine Park, 100 miles to the southeast. This is a fascinating place to roam the acres of empty foreshore. There are all types of beach, from a clam-pocked mudflat "moonscape" to white shell, sand, cobble, boulder, saltmarsh and grassy wildflower islets. At extreme low tide one can walk beyond Seal Islets halfway to Comox along White Spit. It is a strange, lonely feeling to be walking out here surrounded on all sides by miles of water with only the sea birds and clamsquirts for company.

Good temporary anchorage is available where the sand bank drops off sharply to the west of Sandy Island or south of the island, with better protection from the northwest. The boulder-studded sandbank between Sandy Island and Denman protects this anchorage from southeasterly seas, but not from southeasterly winds. Palliser Rock, east of Sandy Island, has a habit of attracting boats at high tide when the bulk of its pyramid shape is hidden beneath the water. Exploring ashore is interesting, as it is still possible to find shattered remnants of World War II fortifications and bits of barbed wire from the time when troops based at Comox stormed the beaches on training exercises. Several years ago the navy was asked to remove the pill boxes and used the request as an excuse for a major naval shelling exercise. Apparently hundreds of shells landed on the island, redistributing half the sand from one end of the island to the other; the pillboxes were obliterated.

The islands are now very popular with local Comox area boaters who use them for weekend and evening picnics. Some of the local people and cadets from the training base at Comox make valiant efforts to maintain the park and keep it tidy. But it sometimes appears to be a losing battle. It seems that once an area is known to be a park and "free" for the use of the public, it tends to be abused and converted into a garbage dump and public toilet, whether there are facilities or not. The Parks Branch takes considerable pains to maintain these parks, but is hindered by difficult access and a limited budget. The ultimate responsibility for the fate of these parks must lie with those who use them.

Native legend says that at one time (possibly when the sea was only a bit lower) Denman was permanently attached to Vancouver Island. Although only eight feet deep at low water, passage across Comox Bar is fairly straight-forward for small craft following the buoyed channel south of the rock-infested shoal which extends a mile southeast of Goose Spit. At night the leading lights on Vancouver Island are visi-

Above and below: Two views of Comox public wharf showing the stone breakwater and protected moorage within. Services nearby include fuel, repairs, showers, fishing supplies, yacht charters and a chandlery.

ble from halfway across the Strait of Georgia. Even in a southeasterly blow there is reported to be less chop here than in the Strait.

4 Cape Lazo

From the southeast, this prominent headland appears to be a separate island, and it is not until you are well north of Hornby Island that it is clearly part of Vancouver Island. The cape was named in 1791 by Jose Maria Narvaez, commanding the schooner *Saturnina* in Eliza's expedition. Lazo in Spanish means "snare," alluding possibly to the deceptive appearance or to the large extent of shoal water which surrounds the cape. Drying rocks are found up to a half-mile offshore and this part of the Strait is notorious for heavy seas, especially when a strong southeasterly blows against an opposing tide. Just south of Cape Lazo are two launching ramps, several resorts and two foreshore reserves protecting portions of the beach for recreational use.

195

5 Comox Harbour

Comox Harbour was first known as Komuckway or Komoux, meaning "place of abundance". The Spaniards named it Valdez Inlet in 1791 and the first white settlers — many from New Zealand, England and Scotland — called it Port Augusta in 1862. It later became known as The Bay, providing shelter for ships servicing the many farming communities in the Comox Valley — the largest area of arable land on Vancouver Island. Good anchorage, safe from southeasterly seas, is available anywhere within the harbour, but beware of the drying mudbanks at the northeast end.

Goose Spit has long served as a Royal Navy and Royal Canadian Navy base and is now HMCS *Quadra* Cadet Training Camp. In summer Comox Harbour echoes night and day to the crisp commands and shrill shrieks of bosun's whistles twittering across the waters, heralding the appearance of grey whalers crammed with cadets, oars flashing and white caps bobbing up and down. The end of Goose Spit is open to public recreational use as long as fires are not lit on the beach.

The Comox public wharf provides almost 2,000 feet of float space for small craft and is protected from south-westerly seas by a stone breakwater and an extension of the pier. If you want to take your boat up the Courtenay River from here and require an opening of the Highway Bridge (closed clearance is 12 ft), contact the Comox Harbour Master (339-6041), whose office is on this wharf.

Just inside the public floats is the Comox Bay Marina (339-4914) providing fuel (339-4664), moorage, showers, repairs, fishing supplies, a launching ramp, and a chandlery. This efficient operation is managed by Gordon Greer who also offers sailing courses and runs a large charter boat operation.

6 Comox

The town of Comox has a population of over 6,500 with shopping centres, hotels, restaurants and a hospital. A block up from the wharf you can find the Lorne Hotel, reputed to be the oldest licensed British Columbian hotel, in continuous operation since 1879. The walls of the pub in this hotel are lined with old photos and mementos depicting the naval history of the harbour as well as the World War II history of the Comox RCAF base. B. Hughes in his *History of the Comox Valley* notes that "it was not only the British tars who found the Lorne Hotel like home: it was a welcome haven to all those who went up and down the Straits of Georgia in ships". Across the street from here is the Comox Mall shopping complex, with supermarket, liquor store and deli. Further along Comox Avenue is Farmer Dan's for fresh produce, and the Filberg Heritage Lodge and Park on an estate of nine acres. This park contains many large, unique trees such as the rare Spanish fir, Japanese maples and an orchard with nearly 100 varieties of fruit-bearing and ornamental apple trees. Special events include the Filberg Arts and Crafts Festival (first weekend in

Looking east over the town of Courtenay and Comox Harbour in the distance. The Courtenay River is virtually the only navigable waterway for medium draft (up to 6-ft) vessels on Vancouver Island.

August) and a Children's Animal Farm. About a mile north of town, on Anderton (just far enough to work up your appetite or thirst), is the Leeward Inn, with perhaps the most attractive nautical decor of any pub on Vancouver Island. Country cooking and "real" ale brewed on the premises are featured. For those who do not care to walk this far there are several restaurants close to the harbour such as the Gaff Rig, Zorba's, Rodello's, the Bamboo Inn and The Galley.

7 Royston

Abundant anchorage is available to the south of Comox Harbour near the small community of Royston. This anchorage is partially protected from southeasterly seas by the mudflats of the Trent River off Gartley Point. A breakwater of old clipper ships, tugs and frigates provides protection for a log boom storage area at the end of the Courtenay River mudflats. The history of many of these old ships, including the *Puako, Melanope, Qualicum and Nanoose, Casco* and several others are recounted in Paterson's *Hellship!*. Several resorts, boat rentals, a launching ramp and a nice stretch of sandy beach are located along the Royston shoreline.

8 Courtenay River

The Courtenay is virtually the only navigable river for boats of medium draught (up to 6 feet) on Vancouver Island. The main channel over the mudflats at the mouth of the river is charted as drying from 1-4 feet above datum, but in fact this channel seldom, if ever, dries because of the more or less constant flow of the Courtenay River. The river is fed, in part, by glaciers and perpetual snowfields on the Forbidden Plateau via the tributary Cruikshank, Puntledge, Browns and Tsolum rivers. Even in late summer when many other island rivers are almost dry, there is usually six feet of water right up to the Courtenay Bridge south of Lewis Park. The tidal range for Comox is 17 feet, but this decreases as you go up the river. Passage up the channel over the mudflats is fairly safe, especially with calm seas, a rising tide and a pair of binoculars to aid in careful alignment of the leading daymark beacons on the north side of the river. At night these beacons exhibit a fixed yellow light, one above the other when correctly aligned. Because the channel is fairly narrow and the three-pile dolphin markers are placed up to a half-mile apart, it is not too difficult to run aground on the surrounding banks, which are charted as drying 8-9 feet. An up-to-date version of the appropriate chart (3527) is essential, as the beacons are occasionally moved to mark the best channel. Just before the first set of leading beacons on the north bank are reached, the channel narrows and veers to port. From here on up the river the channel is fairly straight-forward, favouring the north bank until the second set of leading beacons then turning to the south bank and the third set of beacons.

9   Courtenay Civic Marina

Right before the entrance to this tiny boat basin on the south side of the river is a float for temporary moorage for boats awaiting the opening of the Highway Bridge, a few hundred yards further upstream. The bridge has a closed clearance of 12 feet above high water and will open for boats requiring more clearance (334-1196). The Courtenay Civic Marina provides limited moorage for small craft (mainly local boats and trailer boats making use of the concrete launching ramp). Since this marina is located right at the end of the Courtenay Civic Airstrip, sailboat moorage is not encouraged. One block up from this basin is the Tourist Information Bureau (334-3234).

The river here is remarkably clear — it is possible to see boulders along the bottom — and the banks in

Access to the Courtenay slough can be made over a shallow bank at its entrance, shown here at low water with only a few inches of water covering it. Once inside there is a minimum depth of 6 feet.

many places are lined with alders, poplars, willows and grass-carpeted gardens coming down to the river's edge. Although there is a small sawmill operation on the north bank just below the Highway Bridge, there is surprisingly little industry considering the size of the town of Courtenay (over 9,000 population). Across from the sawmill is the Old House Restaurant (338-5406) and Dower Cottage gift shop.

A breakwater of old clipper ships, tugs and frigates provides protection for a log storage area at the end of the Courtenay River mudflats.

10   Courtenay Slough

The slough is easy to miss, as overhanging trees almost completely shroud the entrance. It is located on the north bank of the river about 150 yards below the second bridge. Just inside the slough is a bar which would dry eight feet above the local chart datum if the river ever ran dry. Passage into the slough must be timed for near the top of a high tide, when the height at Point Atkinson is more than the depth of your keel plus eight feet. Once into the slough there is always at least six feet of water and several public floats providing over 1,400 feet of moorage space. In winter the floats are jammed with fishboats taking advantage of the only freshwater, public moorage on Vancouver Island; but in summer the floats are almost deserted. This is one of the more "authentic" of the government (public) floats and attracts a unique collection of boats and people who want to relax and watch the river life. It is possible to see muskrat, beaver, racoon and river otter as well as an assortment of water birds. A row in the evening will transport you into *The Wind in the Willows* country and you can enjoy a fine meal at La Cremaillere (338-8131) or "Gourmet by the Slough" as it is affectionately known locally. The slough, although only two blocks from the centre of Courtenay (across the river), is a very quiet moorage, especially since the diversion of highway traffic by the new bridge down-river. It is possible to row further up the river, past the Native Sons Log Museum (said to be the largest log cabin in the world) to a swimming hole beside Lewis Park.

SELECTED BIBLIOGRAPHY

Akrigg, G.P.V. and Helen B. Akrigg, *1001 British Columbia Place Names*, Discovery Press, Vancouver, 1973.

Akrigg, G.P.V., *British Columbia Chronicle 1778-1846*, Discovery Press, Vancouver, 1975.

Akrigg, G.P.V., *British Columbia Chronicle 1847-1871*, Discovery Press, Vancouver, 1977.

Appleton, Thomas E., *Usque Ad Mare: A History of the Canadian Coast Guard and Marine Service*, Dept. of Transport, Ottawa, 1968.

Barrett-Lennard, Capt. C.E., *Travels in British Columbia with the Narrative of a Yacht Voyage Round Vancouver's Island*, Canadiana House, Toronto, 1969.

Bell, Betty, *The Fair Land: Saanich*, Sono Nis Press, Victoria, 1982.

Bentley, Mary and Ted, *Gabriola: Petroglyph Island*, Sono Nis Press, Victoria, 1981.

Berssen, William, *Sea Boating Almanac*, Sea Magazine, Costa Mesa, U.S.A., 1985.

Blanchet, M. Wylie, *The Curve of Time*, Gray's Publishing, Sidney, 1968.

Borradaile, John, *"Lady of Culzean" Mayne Island*, John Borradaile, Victoria, 1971.

Bultman, W., *Journal of the West*, Vol. 20, #3, 1981.

Calhoun, Bruce, *Northwest Passages: A Collection of Pacific Northwest Cruising Stories*, Vol. I, Miller Freeman Publications, San Francisco, 1969.

Calhoun, Bruce, *Northwest Passages: A Collection of Northwest Cruising Stories*, Vol. II, Miller Freeman Publications, San Francisco, 1972.

Calhoun, Bruce, *Cruising the San Juan Islands*, Miller Freeman Publications, San Francisco, 1973.

Canada, Department of the Environment, *British Columbia Small Craft Guide*, Vol. I, *Vancouver Island, Port Alberni to Campbell River, Including the Gulf Islands*, Marine Sciences Directorate, Ottawa, 1984.

Canada, Department of the Environment, *British Columbia Pilot, V. 1 (Southern Portion of the Coast of British Columbia)*, Marine Services Branch, Ottawa, 7th Edition, 1969.

Canada, Department of Fisheries and Oceans, *Current Atlas: Juan de Fuca Strait to Strait of Georgia*, Ottawa, 1983.

Capt. Lillie's British Columbia, Puget Sound & S.E. Alaska Coast Guide and Radiotelephone Directory, Progress Publishing, Vancouver, 1972.

Carl, G.C., *Guide to Marine Life of British Columbia*, Handbook #21, B.C. Provincial Museum, Victoria, 1971.

Chettleburgh, Peter, *An Explorers Guide: Marine Parks of British Columbia*, Special Interest Publications, Vancouver, 1985.

Clapp, C.H., *Geology of the Victoria, Saanich and Nanaimo Map Areas*, Memoirs #36, 51, Geological Survey of Canada, Ottawa, 1914.

Clark, Lewis J., *Wild Flowers of British Columbia*, Gray's Publishing, 1973.

Cole, Douglas, *Captured Heritage: The Scramble for Northwest Coast Artefacts*, Douglas & McIntyre, Vancouver, 1985.

Conover, David, *Once Upon An Island*, General Publishing, Toronto, 1968.

Conover, David, *One Man's Island*, General Publishing, Toronto, 1971.

Corrigal, Margery, *The History of Hornby Island*, Revised Edition, 1978.

The Craigflower Women's Institute, *The Craigflower Story*, The Craigflower Women's Institute, Victoria, 1967.

Cramond, Mike, *Vancouver Island Fishing Holes*, Pattison Ventures, Victoria, 1981.

Cuddy, Marylou and James J. Scott, *British Columbia in Books*, J.J. Douglas, Vancouver, 1974.

Cummings, Al and Jo Bailey-Cummings, *Gunkholing in the Gulf Islands*, Nor'westing Inc., Edmonds Inc., Edmonds, Washington, 1986.

Dawson, Will, *Coastal Cruising: An Authoritative Guide to British Columbia, Puget Sound-San Juan Islands waters and the Waterways of Southeast Alaska*, Mitchell Press, Vancouver, 1973.

Edwards, R. Yorke, ed., *Naturalist's Guide to the Victoria Region*, Nature Council through Victoria Natural History Society, Victoria, 1967.

Elliott, David R., *Adventures in Arrowsmith Country*, District 69 Community Arts Council, Parksville, 1983.

Elliott, Marie, *Mayne Island & the Outer Gulf Islands: A History*, Gulf Islands Press, 1984.

Fletcher, Anne, et al, *Tides & Trees: A Guide to Nanaimo's Beaches and Parks*, SPEC, Nanaimo, 1983.

Forward, Charles N., Ed., *Vancouver Island: Land of Contrasts*, Western Geographical Series, Vol. 17, University of Victoria, 1979.

Freeman, Beatrice, J. Spalding, comp., *A Gulf Island Patchwork: Some Early Events on the Islands of Galiano, Mayne, Saturna, North and South Pender*, Gulf Islands Branch, B.C. Historial Association, Sidney, 1969.

Garner, Joe, *Never Fly Over An Eagles Nest*, Oolichan Books, Lantzville, 1980.

Gibbs, James A., *Sentinels of the North Pacific, the Story of Pacific Coast Lighthouses and Lightships*, Binford and Mort, Portland, Oregon, 1955.

Gough, Barry M., *The Royal Navy and the Northwest Coast of North America, 1810-1914: A Study of British Maritime Ascendancy*, University of British Columbia Press, Vancouver, 1971.

Gould, Ed., *Bridging the Gulf*, Review Publishing, Sidney, 1970.

Graham, Donald, *Keepers of the Light*, Harbour Publishing, Madeira Park, 1985.

Griffiths, Garth, *Boating in Canada: Practical Piloting and Seamanship*, Univertisy of Toronto Press, Toronto, 1969.

Gustafson, Lillian, *Memories of the Chemainus Valley*, Chemainus Valley Historical Society, 1978.

Hamilton, Bea, *Saltspring Island*, Mitchell Press, Vancouver, 1969.

Hamilton, James H. (Capt. Kettle), *Western Shores: Narratives of the Pacific Coast*, Progress Publishing, Vancouver, 1933.

Hancock, David, *Hancock's Ferry Guide to Vancouver Island*, Hancock House, Saanichton, 1973.

Hancock, David and David Stirling, *Birds of British Columbia*, Hancock House, Saanichton, 1973.

Henderson, Lydia and Phil Capes, eds., *A Naturalist Guide to the Comox Valley and Adjacent Areas including Campbell River*, Comox-Strathcona Natural History Society, Courtenay, 1973.

Henderson, Vi, *Pipers Lagoon*, Quadra Graphics, Nanaimo, 1984.

Hill, Beth, et al, *Times Past: Salt Spring Island Houses and History before the turn of the Century*, Ganges, 1983.

Hill, Beth, *Upcoast Summers*, Horsdal & Schubart, Ganges, 1985.

Hill, Beth and Ray, *Indian Petroglyphs of the Pacific Northwest*, Hancock House, Saanichton, 1974.

Holland, Stuart S., *Land Forms of British Columbia*, Bulletin #48, B.C. Dept. Of Mines, Victoria, 1964.

Holloway, Godfrey, *The Empress of Victoria*, Pacifica Productions, Victoria, 1968.

Hughes, Ben, *History of the Comox Valley*, 1962.

Hutchinson, Bill and Julie, *Rockhounding and Beachcombing on Vancouver Island*, Tom and Georgie Vaulkhard, The Rock-Hound Shop, Victoria, 1971.

Ince, John and Hedi Kottner, *Sea Kayaking Canada's West Coast*, Raxas Books, Orca Sound Publishers, Vancouver, 1982.

Isbister, Winnifred A., *My Ain Folk: Denman Island 1875-1975*, E.W. Bickle Ltd., Comox Valley, 1976.

Jackman, S.W., *Vancouver Island*, Griffin House, Toronto, 1972.

Johnson-Cull, Viola, *Chronicles of Ladysmith and District*, Ladysmith New Horizons Historical Society, 1980.

Johnson, Patricia M., John G. Parker and Gino A. Desola, eds., *Nanaimo Scenes from the Past*, Nanaimo and District Museum Society, Nanaimo, 1966.

Jupp, Ursula, ed., *Home Port: Victoria*, Ursula Jupp, Victoria, 1967.

Kozloff, Eugene, N. *Seashore Life of Puget Sound, the Strait of Georgia and the San Juan Archipelago*, J.J. Douglas, Vancouver, 1973.

Lewis-Harrison, June, *The People of Gabriola*, 1982.

Luxton, Eleanor Georgina, ed., *Tilikum: Luxton's Pacific Crossing*, by Norman Kenny Luxton, Gray's Publishing, Sidney, 1971.

Lyons, C.P., *Milestones on Vancouver Island*, Evergreen Press, Vancouver, 1958.

Mason, Elda, Copley, *Lasqueti Island: History and Memory*, South Wellington, 1976.

Meade, Edward, *Indian Rock Carvings of the Pacific Northwest*, Gray's Publishing, Sidney, 1971.

Middleton, Lyn, *Place Names of the Pacific Northwest: Origins, Histories and Anecdotes in Bibliographic Form about the Coast of British Columbia, Washington and Oregon*, Eldee Publishing, Victoria, 1969.

Molar Enterprises, *A Guide to Galiano Island*, 1985.

Morris, Frank L. and W.R. Heath, *Marine Atlas*, P.B.I. Co., Seattle, 1968.

New, Donald A., *A voyage of discovery: Gulf Island Names and Their Origins*, Donald New, Sidney, 1966.

Norcross, E. Blanche, *The Warm Land: A History of Cowichan*, 1975.

Norcross, E. Blanche and Doris Farmer Tonkin, *Frontiers of Vancouver Island*, Courtenay: Island Books, 1969.

Obee, Bruce, *The Gulf Islands Explorer*, Grays Publishing, Sidney, 1981.

Olsen, W.H., *Water Over The Wheel*, Chemainus, Crofton and District, 1981

Ormsby, Margaret A., *British Columbia: A History*, Macmillan, Toronto, 1958.

Ovanin, Thomas K., *Island Heritage Buildings*, Islands Trust, Queens Printer, Victoria, 1985.

Paterson, T.W., *Shipwreck! Piracy and Terror in the Northwest*, Solitaire Publications, Victoria, 1972.

Paterson, T.W., *Hellship!*, Stagecoach Publishing Co., Langley, 1974.

Pearson, Anne, *Sea-Lake: Recollections and History of Cordova Bay*, Victoria, 1981.

Pethick, Derek, *Victoria: The Fort*, Mitchell Press, Vancouver, 1968.

Pethick, Derek, *James Douglas: Servant of Two Empires*, Mitchell Press, Vancouver, 1969.

Pethick, Derek, *S.S. Beaver: The Ship that Saved the West*, Mitchell Press, Vancouver, 1970.

Polovic, Marina, *Boat Charters in B.C.*, Rhapsody Productions, Vancouver 1983.

Rankin, Laird, *The Nonwuch*, Clarke Irwin and Company, Vancouver, 1974.

Reimer, Derek, Ed. *The Gulf Islanders*, Sound Heritage, Volume V, #4, Provincial Archives of British Columbia.

Rogers, Fred, *Shipwrecks of British Columbia*, J.J. Douglas, Vancouver, 1973.

Shortt, Marjorie, *Westerly Wanderings: Metchosin Area*, Word Magic Publications, Victoria, 1985.

Sierra Club, *Victoria in a Knapsack: A Guide to the Natural Areas of Southern Vancouver Island*, 1985.

Smeeton, Miles, *A Change of Jungles*, Hart-Davis, London, 1962.

Smeeton, Miles, *The Sea Was Our Village*, Gray's Publishing, Sidney, 1973.

Smith, Ian, *The Unknown Island*, J.J. Douglas, Vancouver, 1973.

The Sooke and North Sooke Women's Institute, *Sooke: Past and Present*, edited by Derek Pethick, The Sooke and North Sooke Women's Institute, Sooke, 1971.

Stewart, Dave, ed., *Salt Water: Fishing Guide to B.C.*, BC Outdoors, 1984/85

Stirling, David, *Birds of Vancouver Island for Birdwatchers*, Hancock House, Saanichton, 1972.

Stormwell, Brad, *The Undiscovered Islands: Denman and Hornby Isle*, 1984.

Thomson, Richard E., *Oceanography of the British Columbia Coast*, Department of Fisheries and Oceans, Ottawa, 1981.

Van der Ree, Frieda, *Exploring The Coast by Boat*, Gordon Soules, Vancouver, 1979.

Waddell, Jane, ed., *Hiking Trails: Victoria and Southern Vancouver Island*, The Outdoor Club of Victoria, Trails Information Society, Victoria, 1972.

Waddell, Jane, ed., *Hiking Trails: Southeastern Vancouver Island*, The Outdoor Club of Victoria, Trails Information Society, Victoria, 1973.

Walbran, John T., *British Columbia Coast Names*, The Library's Press, Vancouver, 1971.

Walton, Avis, *About Victoria and Vancouver Island*, Felindical Publications, Victoria, 1969.

White, Charles and Nelson Dewey, *How To Catch Bottomfish!*, Saltaire Publishing, Sidney, 1971.

White, Charles R. and Bruce Colegrave, *Where To Find Salmon! Sooke to Cowichan Bay*, Saltaire Publishing, Sidney, 1972.

Wilson, Herbert Emmerson, *Canada's False Prophet: The Notorious Brother XII*, Simon and Schuster, Richmond Hill, Ontario, 1967.

Wolferstan, Bill, *Pacific Yachting's Cruising Guides to British Columbia*, **Vol. 1 - Gulf Islands, 1976; Vol. II Desolation Sound, 1980; Vol. III - Sunshine Coast, 1982;** Special Interest Publications, Maclean Hunter Ltd., Vancouver, B.C.

INDEX

ILLUSTRATION CREDITS

All photographs except those listed below were taken by the author. Aerial photographs were taken from planes piloted by Mark Adams, Doug Chickhak, George McNutt, Al Nairne, Chris Sprague and Irv Young. Pages 32, 36, Al Fairhurst; pages 20, 21, 37, 95, 49, 105, 115, 151, 155, 161, 177, 185, B.C. Government; pages 65, 69, 157, 158, Peter Chettleburgh; page 59, Jack Borradaile; page 71, Gar Lunney; page 116, Federal Government; page 129, S.V. Wright; page 169, Hubert Havelaar; front cover photo, Rick Marotz, Photo/ Graphics.

METRIC CONVERSION

Because of the conversion to metric, charts may be in feet, fathoms or meters, temperatures given in celcius and wind speed in kilometers. For those unfamiliar with this system, the following conversion tables are provided.

C°	F°		Meters	Feet
− 15	5		1 m	3.28
− 10	14		2 m	6.56
− 5	23		3 m	9.84
0	32		4 m	13.12
5	41		5 m	16.40
10	50		10 m	32.80
15	59		50 m	164.00
20	68		100 m	328.00
25	77		1000 m	3280.00
30	86			
35	95			
40	104			
45	113			
50	122			

TO CONVERT

meters to feet	multiply by 3.28
fathoms to feet	multiply by 6.0
kilometers to miles	multiply by 0.62
kilometers to nautical miles	multiply by 0.5399
litres to gallons	multiply by 0.22
celcius to Fahrenheit	multiply C by 9/5 add 32
feet to meters	multiply by 0.305
miles to kilometers	multiply by 1.61
nautical miles to meters	multiply by 1,852.0
nautical miles to kilometers	multiply by 1.852
fathoms to meters	multiply by 1.828
gallons to litres	multiply by 4.55
Fahrenheit to celcius	subtract 32, then multiply by 5/9

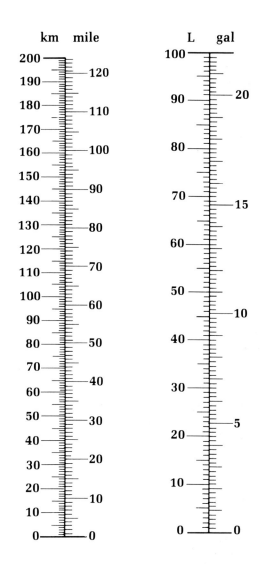

BEAUFORT SCALE

Force on Beaufort Scale	Nautical miles per hr.	Description	Height of sea in ft.	Deep sea criteria
0	0-1	Calm	—	Flat calm, mirror smooth
1	1-3	Light Airs	1/4	Small wavelets, no crests
2	4-6	Light Breeze	1/2	Small wavelets, crests glassy but do not break
3	7-10	Light Breeze	2	Large wavelets, crests begin to break
4	11-16	Moderate Breeze	3 1/2	Small waves, becoming longer, crests break frequently
5	17-21	Fresh Breeze	6	Moderate waves, longer, breaking crests
6	22-27	Strong Breeze	9 1/2	Large waves forming, crests break more frequently
7	28-33	Strong Wind	13 1/2	Large waves, streaky foam
8	34-40	Near Gale	18	High waves of increasing length, crests form spindrift
9	41-47	Strong Gale	23	High waves, dense streaks of foam, crests roll over
10	48-55	Storm	29	Very high waves, long overhanging crests. Surface of sea white with foam
11	56-65	Violent Storm	37	Exceptionally high waves, sea completely covered with foam
12	above 65	Hurricane	—	The air filled with spray and visibility seriously affected

CHART INDEX

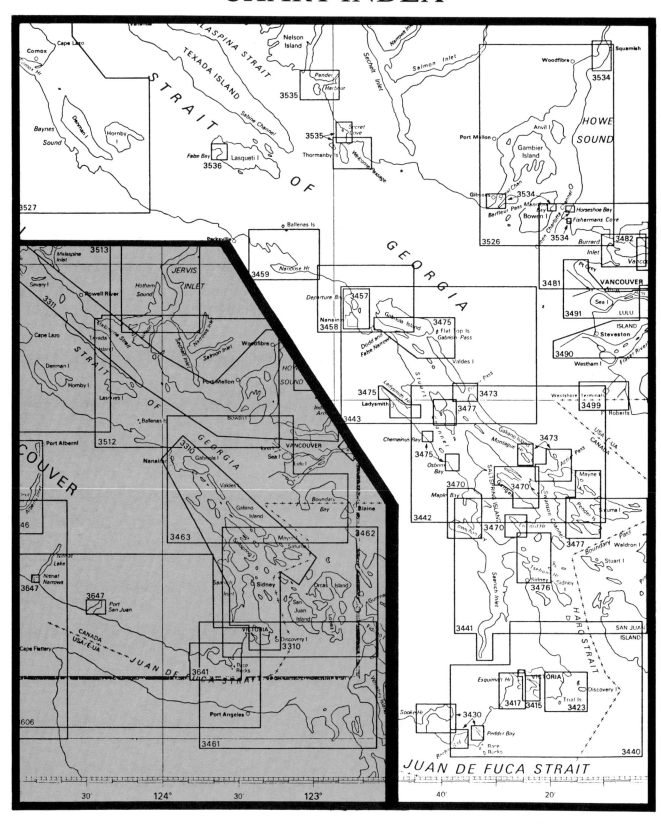

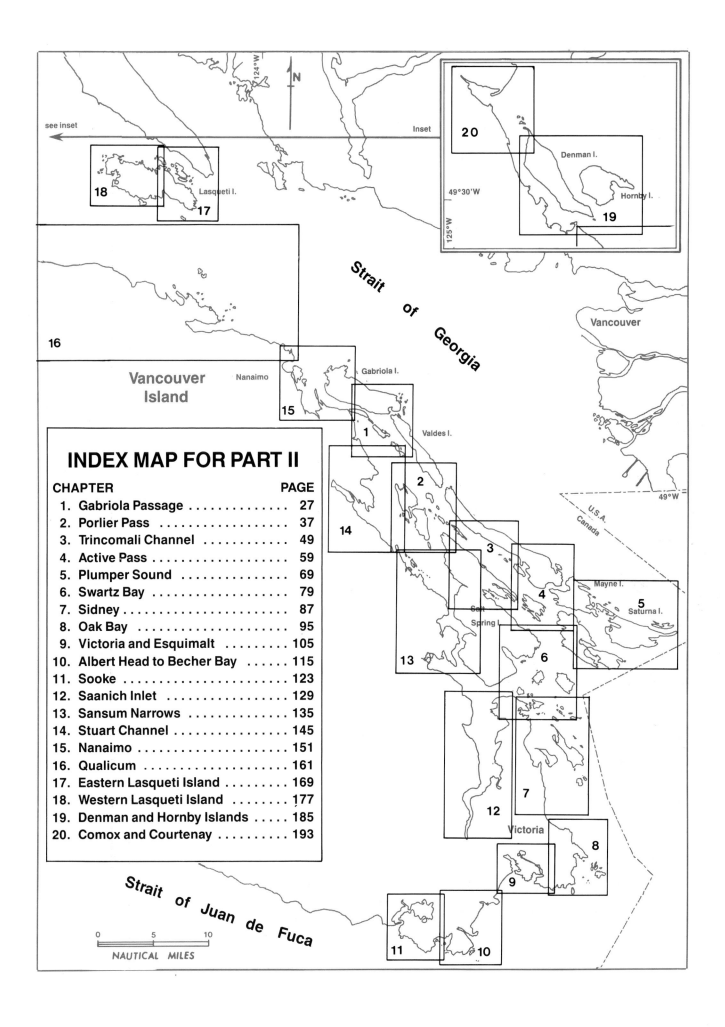

INDEX MAP FOR PART II

see inset

Inset

N

20

Denman I.

49°30'W

Hornby I.

19

125°W

124°W

Strait of Georgia

Vancouver

Lasqueti I.

18

17

16

Vancouver
Island

Nanaimo

Gabriola I.

15

1

Valdes I.

2

U.S.A.

Canada

49°W

14

3

4

Mayne I.

5

Saturna I.

Salt
Spring I.

6

13

7

12

Victoria

8

9

11

10

Strait of Juan de Fuca

0   5   10
NAUTICAL MILES

Canadian Cataloguing in Publication Data

Wolferstan, Bill, 1942-
Cruising Guide to British Columbia
   Includes bibliographies and indexes.
   Contents: v.1. Gulf Islands and Vancouver Island from Sooke to
Courtenay. (Rev. ed).

   ISBN 0-921061-10-2 (v.1) — ISBN 0-921061-11-0 (set)
   1. Yachts and yachting – British Columbia – Guide-books. 2.
British Columbia – Description and travel – 1981 – Guide-books.*
I.Title. II. Title: Cruising guide to British Columbia.
FC3817.4.W642   917.11'34   C87-091022-1
F1087.W642

Second paperback printing, 1989.
Third paperback printing, 1991.

Typesetting and assembly by
Vancouver Typesetting Co. Ltd., Vancouver
Printed in Canada by D.W. Friesen & Sons,
Altona, Manitoba